THE AUTOBIOGRAPHY OF
PHILOSOPHY

THE AUTOBIOGRAPHY OF PHILOSOPHY

Rousseau's *The Reveries of the Solitary Walker*

MICHAEL DAVIS

ROWMAN & LITTLEFIELD PUBLISHERS, INC.
Lanham • Boulder • New York • Toronto • Plymouth, UK

ROWMAN & LITTLEFIELD PUBLISHERS, INC.

Published in the United States of America
by Rowman & Littlefield Publishers, Inc.
A wholly owned subsidary of The Rowman & Littlefield Publishing Group, Inc.
4501 Forbes Boulevard, Suite 200, Lanham, Maryland 20706
www.rowmanlittlefield.com

Estover Road
Plymouth PL6 7PY
United Kingdom

British Library Cataloguing in Publication Information Available

Library of Congress Cataloging-in-Publication Data

Davis, Michael, 1947–
    The autobiography of philosophy : Rousseau's The reveries of the
solitary walker / Michael Davis.
        p.   cm.
    Includes bibliographical references and index.
    ISBN 0-8476-9226-4 (alk. paper).—ISBN 0-8476-9227-2 (pbk. :
alk. paper)
    1. Rousseau, Jean-Jacques, 1712–1778. Rêveries du promeneur
solitaire.   2. Philosophy.   I. Title.
PQ2040.R5   1998
848'.509—dc21
[B]   98-38402
                                                                        CIP

Printed in the United States of America

♾ ™ The paper used in this publication meets the minimum requirements of
American National Standard for Information Sciences—Permanence of Paper
for Printed Library Materials, ANSI Z39.48–1984.

For my children, Jessica and Sarah

to gar auto noein estin te kai einai

Contents

PREFACE

I first read *The Reveries of the Solitary Walker* more than fifteen years ago in a summer reading group with four students—Diana Finnegan, Lorraine Klagsbrun, Ellen Schattschneider, and Peter Vedder. I have since taught the book often and learned much more than I knew then, but the direction that the following interpretation takes was already implicit in what we saw that summer. Of the five of us, I was the only one at the time who had a professional interest in Rousseau. The others were still amateurs in the etymological sense—lovers. I am grateful to them not only for helping me to understand the *Reveries* but also because we are forever in need of good students to remind us that philosophy is not really a profession. Others have helped me to think through the issues presented in this book, whether in conversation or by reading earlier versions of all or part of the manuscript. I want especially to thank Seth Benardete, Robert Berman, Ronna Burger, Michael Golluber, Pamela Jensen, Angela Moger, Mary Nichols, Denise Schaeffer, Richard Velkley, and my wife, Susan Davis. The Earhart Foundation has once again been very generous in its support of my work.

PHILOSOPHY AS AUTOBIOGRAPHY

Philosophy is, on the one hand, a body of writings—something to be shelved systematically in libraries. Whether we organize it historically or thematically, we think of it as a product. As a body of knowledge, matter to be learned, philosophy is appropriately housed in a department of the university, where courses in it might induce some familiarity with Aristotle and Descartes, metaphysics and epistemology. In this sense, it is solidly a noun. At the same time, philosophy is an activity in principle having nothing at all to do with the Plato to whom its whole history is nothing more than "a series of footnotes" or with the division of itself "into three sciences: physics, ethics and logic."[1] Indeed, there is a long tradition for which philosophy was understood to be the highest human possibility. To ask "What is philosophy?" was to ask both the theoretical question "What is human nature?"—philosophy is concerned with the true—and the practical question "What is the best way to live?"—it is at the same time concerned with the good. Philosophy in this sense never wanders far from the verb *to philosophize*. But we perennially run the risk of losing the verb in the noun, the body of philosophy being the most visible manifestation of its soul.

Our age has given birth to the expression "professional philosopher." When philosophy becomes a career choice—one of a variety of possible jobs—philosophizing comes to be understood as what philosophers do during working hours. It is a job in principle like all others with a wage. A temporary and accidental modification of our humanity (like being a florist or a lawyer), it is no longer paradigmatic of that humanity, for during off hours it no longer characterizes us. The noun deriving from a verb is now reverbalized, but this movement is no straightforward return to its original meaning. A world more comfortable institutionalizing things than instituting them and in which we call psychic phenomena psychological can scarcely be expected to resist the professionalization of philosophy. Rather than the naïve sense of loving wisdom, philosophizing now means what professors do. Something important is threatened with this loss of amateur status. While philosophy does not—indeed, cannot—vanish as a phenomenon, as its significance becomes more difficult to discern, so too does the nature of the human soul become more difficult to discern.

This is a book about the connection between the nature of philosophy and the nature of the human soul. Its title, *The Autobiography of Philosophy*, is meant to indicate that in some sense all philosophy is autobiographical. I do not mean that every philosopher is, perhaps without realizing it, simply rendering his idiosyncratic view of the world in a universal form, as though those most irascible will place anger at the center of their world. I mean rather that it is not really possible to philosophize without making the conditions for the possibility of one's own activity the deepest concern of this activity.

The connection between philosophy and human nature is most obviously the theme of Greek philosophy. Platonic dialogues celebrate the philosophic life in their content and exemplify it in their form. It is not always clear that Plato's Socrates lives the life he celebrates.[2] Still, even if there is a tension between what Socrates does and what in a particular context he says one ought to do, however equivocally, philosophy is always the theme. By rendering into writing the life of a "Socrates having become beautiful and young,"[3] Plato makes the question of the life of philosophy prominent to an extent far exceeding any who came before him. Accordingly, a Platonic dialogue is always something like the writing (*graphein*) of its own (*auto*) life (*bios*) by the one loving (*philein*) wisdom (*sophia*). And while it would be foolish to deny that the *Phaedo* is about death as that the *Philebus*, *Symposium*, and *Republic* are about pleasure, love, and justice, beginning with everyday concerns need not rule out concluding that the ultimate truth of death, pleasure, love, and justice is philosophy. For Plato, at least, philosophy is the autobiography of philosophy.

That the activity of philosophy has a special status in Aristotle also is clear in both the theoretical works, where "first philosophy" is the godlike activity emerging from the structure of wonder and the fact that "all human beings by nature desire to know,"[4] and the practical works, where philosophy is the most choice-worthy life because most self-sufficient and is more important even than friends—without which "no one would choose to live even having all the remaining goods."[5] While it seems less obvious that Aristotle's writings point to the importance of philosophy in their form, as we shall see, it is no less true. The *Nicomachean Ethics* explicitly places the contemplative life, and so philosophy, at the peak of human activity. Yet the life it so describes—the genuinely good life—is at best a caricature of any possible human life. The reality of contemplation is rather manifested in the action of the argument of the ten books of the *Nicomachean Ethics* than in the content of Book 10. Similarly, the movements of thought of both the *Politics* and the *Poetics* reveal the underlying dependence of politics and poetry on philosophy.[6] In Aristotle too, then, philosophy seems to be autobiographical; whatever it first appears to be about, in the end it is about itself. And, once again, this underlying saturation of everything else by philosophy shows itself in the form of its presentation.

Let us jump ahead some twenty-four centuries.[7] For Nietzsche the question of philosophy is clearly central. From his earliest writings he is at once a severe critic of the philosophic impulse and full of praise for philosophers.[8] This ambiguity is significant; for Nietzsche, the status of philosophy is perhaps the single most important sign of the health or sickness of an age. Accordingly, the history of the West—of "how the 'true world' finally became a fable"—is really a history of philosophy, and the hope for the world is "a philosophy of the future."[9] Philosophy, for Nietzsche, is "the most spiritual will to power."[10] Yet,

> suppose that one could trace all organic functions back to this will to power and in it could find the solution to the problem of generation and nourishment—it is *one* problem—therewith one would have thus obtained the right to determine *all* efficient force univocally as: *will to power*. The world seen from within, the world determined and characterized with respect to its "intelligible character,"—this would plainly be "will to power" and nothing else.[11]

Philosophy is then the most spiritual form of that efficient force characterizing everything. Philosophy's perennial attempt to understand the whole is thus a form of self-determination—whether self-consciously or not. Accordingly, for Nietzsche, too, it is autobiographical.

As with Plato and Aristotle, with Nietzsche the importance of the activity of philosophy brings with it an emphasis on the mode of philosophy's presentation. The notorious difficulty of Nietzsche's writing has something to do with his understanding of the problem of writing, which is, in turn, a version of the problem of thinking.

> Alas, what are you indeed, you my written and painted thoughts! It is not long since you were still so brightly colored, young and malicious, full of thorns and secret spices so that you made me sneeze and laugh—and now? You have already taken off your newness, and some of you are, I fear, ready to become truths: so deathless they look already, so heartbreakingly righteous, so boring! And was it ever different? What matters do we copy—writing and painting—we mandarins with Chinese brush, we immortalizers of matters which let themselves be written, of which alone we are able to paint copies? Alas, always only what plainly wants to become faded and begins to lose its scent! Alas, always only thunderstorms moving on and exhausted and yellow late feelings! Alas, always only birds that tire themselves flying and fly away and now let themselves be caught by hand—by *our* hand! We immortalize what cannot live and fly much longer, only tired and mellow things! And it is only your *afternoon*, you my written and painted thoughts, for whom alone I have colors, many colors perhaps, many brightly colored caresses and fifty yellows and browns and greens and reds:—but no one will guess for me from that how you looked in your morning, you sudden sparks and wonders of my solitude, you my old, beloved— —wicked thoughts![12]

Given this understanding of the problem inherent in any attempt to articulate the essence of things (to make nouns of them), it is not surprising that Nietzsche should write as he does—in aphorisms, for example— even though

> the aphoristic form makes for difficulties: they consist in this—that today one does not take this form gravely [*schwer*] enough. An aphorism thoroughly stamped and poured out is not thereby, because it has been read through, yet "deciphered"; rather, now its *interpretation* must first begin, for which an art of interpretation is required. . . . Admittedly, in order to practice reading as an *art* in such a manner, one thing is necessary above all, what nowadays has come to be so well unlearned—and for that reason there is still time until my writ-

ings are "readable"—for which one must be nearly a cow and in any
case *not* a "modern human being": *chewing the cud*.[13]

Learning how to interpret requires learning how to chew; disclosing this
activity is in some way the intent of each of Nietzsche's writings.

In our time, Heidegger provides perhaps the most striking example
of the autobiographical character of philosophy. For Heidegger, philosophy is above all concerned with the question of being. This question in
turn points to that being able to raise the question of being. By characterizing human beings by the expression *Dasein* (literally, being there),
Heidegger calls attention to the fundamental feature of human nature—
that for us to be at all means for us to be in a world. We are, in fact,
unintelligible apart from the world we project and into which we are
thrown. And there is no possibility of a world that is not a world for
such a being. Since our situatedness in the world is at the same time
what it means for there to be a world, any question about the being of
the world must be a question about the being of *Dasein*. Philosophy is
autobiographical, for it consists in the attempt to give an account of the
conditions of its own possibility. We begin with the question of being
because, even in a decayed form, the question itself is evidence of the
presence of a certain kind of being without which no such question
could emerge.

It is not so clear that Heidegger wishes to identify what is distinc-
tively human with philosophy—indeed, he does not even wish to identify it with the human. At the same time, it is hard to see *Dasein* as
belonging to beings other than human. *Dasein* cannot be in the world
without already bringing a tacit understanding to the world—an understanding that necessarily involves a relatedness to things and to others.
Our concern for the elements of our world is rooted in care (*Sorge*) as
the being of *Dasein*. This in turn is what it means for us to be temporal
beings. This brief and admittedly inadequate summary of a complex
argument is still enough to suggest that the elements of older understandings of human nature are taken up in Heidegger's account, even if
they are interpreted in a radically different way. To say that with *Dasein*
an understanding of the world is always present is something like saying
that for human beings the world is first, and perhaps in some sense always, *doxa*—seeming or opinion.[14] Beings (*onta*) are encountered by us
as always already having some meaning for us; they are always *pragmata*.

That the world has meaning (*Meinung*) is connected to the fact that it is always mine (*mein*). Furthermore, to say that this being in the world is of necessity a being with others—a shared being—is something like saying that human beings are political by nature because they are rational by nature.[15] And to characterize our being in the world by care is not so different from saying that things are for us only in the light of the good.[16] Finally, that *Dasein* cannot be in a world except concernfully, but nevertheless that it has a tendency to lose awareness of its own being—to fall—and so be inauthentically in the world, means that *Dasein*'s revealing to itself of its own being is in some sense the truth of its own being. To praise the recovery from this fallenness amounts to something very like a praise of the philosophic life—the life devoted to the pursuit of self-knowledge.[17] Now, if to be authentically in the world means to be autobiographically in the world, Heidegger stands with Nietzsche, Aristotle, and Plato. There would seem to be a core of philosophy as activity—as verb—that must be common to philosophers however different the philosophies they produce. To articulate this core without becoming a partisan of a certain philosophy would be a task of great difficulty, for it would be to articulate the nature of the human soul for which this activity is the defining possibility.

In the conventional sense of autobiography, the most famous autobiographer among the philosophers is clearly Jean-Jacques Rousseau. But Rousseau's writings about himself—*The Confessions, Rousseau Judge of Jean-Jacques*, and *The Reveries of the Solitary Walker* are the most prominent—are not usually understood philosophically. More often the tantalizing idiosyncrasies of his rather eccentric life obscure Rousseau's deeper purposes. But if thinkers as different as Plato, Aristotle, Nietzsche, and Heidegger display the implicitly autobiographical quality of philosophy, might not Rousseau's explicit autobiography be meant to make this issue thematic? While his other autobiographical works are no doubt philosophic, in *The Reveries of the Solitary Walker*, by giving an account of the uniqueness of his present condition—"the strangest position in which a mortal could ever find himself"—Rousseau speaks of his life for the purpose of reflecting on life as a whole. It is selective in its use of details not because it is a collection of random memories but because it means to be a reflection on what it means that we are able to have such memories. And the details, on closer inspection, only seem random. Rousseau treats himself much as Plato treated Socrates; the overall story seems more or less historically accurate, but by manipulating the details, Rousseau presents his own condition as an exaggerated version of the human condition generally. When he urges us "to give ourselves up entirely to the sweetness of conversing with [his] soul," Rousseau invites us to use his soul as a paradigm of the human soul simply. More than a charming, if slightly paranoid, autobiographical fragment, then, *The Reveries of the Solitary Walker* amounts to a philosophical account of the human soul and of philosophy that places Rousseau firmly in a tradition beginning at least with Plato and Aristotle and still present in Nietzsche and Heidegger. For Heidegger, to understand being we must begin with *Dasein*, which leads us to an awareness that the beings of our world are known to us insofar as they are *zuhandene*—objects of which we make use. Objects are thus generally not *vorhandene*—objective—even though we have a natural tendency to so understand them. Furthermore, we cannot understand our own being in the world apart from *Mitdasein*—being with others. The being of *Dasein* is care—*Sorge*. These terms have their analogues in Plato. We experience things not as beings (*onta*), but only insofar as they are matters of concern for us (*pragmata*).[18] These *pragmata* are the beings insofar as they appear (*dokein*) to us in opinion (*doxa*), and opinion is what constitutes our lives together in the *polis*. Socratic philosophy involves turning away from the heavens toward the city because it is in the city that we come to see that things come to be things for us only in light of their being good. For Aristotle, man is both a political and rational animal, and the two are somehow the same. Our ability to question the world is inseparable from its being good for us. Nietzsche seems at first to call into question the truth of our claims about the goodness of the world but ends by elaborating a way of understanding—genealogy—that grounds truth in goodness.

These questions are obviously present in Rousseau's *Reveries*. The Fourth Walk is quite explicit about the relation of the true to the good, and in the very first paragraph of the book, Rousseau makes it clear that in order to understand himself, he will have to go "from them to me." We are beings fundamentally constituted by being able to question our world. This means that we encounter it as it seems to us and not unproblematically as it is—its being is to seem for us. It seems to *us* by virtue of seeming good. This fact connects us—we are beings who are essentially with others (*Mitdasein*) or political animals—and yet at the same time also fundamentally alienates us from one another and from the world. In the discussion of these issues that follows, I will seek to show first what it means that for Heidegger and Aristotle, Plato, and Nietzsche philosophy is essentially autobiographical and second how, in what amounts to a philosophical psychology, Rousseau makes the autobiographical character of philosophy thematic.

The first part of the following study will turn briefly to the introduction of Heidegger's *Being and Time*, the preface of Nietzsche's *On the Genealogy of Morals*, the first book of Aristotle's *Metaphysics*, and Plato's *Lysis* as particularly revealing instances of philosophy as autobiographical. The second part is an extended interpretation of *The Reveries of the Solitary Walker* as perhaps Rousseau's deepest understanding of the "resolution" of the tension that constitutes the human soul. By following the action of Rousseau's argument in the *Reveries*, it is my hope to make visible his understanding of the nature of the human soul and the ground for all philosophy.

NOTES

1. See Alfred North Whitehead, *Process and Reality* (New York: Free Press, 1969), 53; and Immanuel Kant, *Grundlegung zur Metaphysic der Sitten* (Hamburg: Felix Meiner, 1965), 3 (translation is my own).

2. See, for example, *Republic*, 472c–506a, and *Theaetetus*, 172a–177c.

3. See Plato, *Second Letter*, 314c.

4. See, for example, *Metaphysics*, 980a22–23, 982b11–983a23, and 1026a18–32.

5. See, for example, *Nicomachean Ethics*, 1096a11–18, 1155a5–6, 1164b2–5, 1177a12–1179a32, and *Politics*, 1323a14–1325b33.

6. I have argued this at length elsewhere in *Aristotle's* Poetics: *The Poetry of Philosophy* (Lanham, Md.: Rowman & Littlefield, 1992) and in *The Politics of Philosophy: A Commentary on Aristotle's* Politics (Lanham, Md.: Rowman & Littlefield, 1996).

7. Had we paused along the way, Descartes would have proved a particularly interesting case of philosophy as autobiographical. See, for example, *Discourse on Method* with my *Ancient Tragedy and the Origins of Modern Science* (Carbondale: Southern Illinois University Press, 1988), chapters 2 and 3 as well as *Les Passions de l'âme, Troisième partie*, Articles 149–56.

8. For the criticism see *The Birth of Tragedy*, sections 11–15, and for the

praise, see the whole of *Philosophy in the Tragic Age of the Greeks*. These works were written at more or less the same time of Nietzsche's life.

9. See *Twilight of the Idols*, "How the 'True World' Finally Became a Fable" as well as "The Problem of Socrates" and " 'Reason' in Philosophy," and *Beyond Good and Evil*, parts 1 and 2.

10. *Beyond Good and Evil*, section 10.

11. *Beyond Good and Evil*, section 36.

12. *Beyond Good and Evil*, section 296.

13. *On the Genealogy of Morals*, preface, section 8.

14. Consider, for example, Plato, *Republic*, 514a1.

15. Compare Aristotle, *Politics*, 1253a.

16. Compare *Republic*, 505d-506a.

17. Compare Plato, *Phaedrus*, 229c-230a.

18. See Plato, *Phaedo*, 99d-100a.

Part One

THE QUESTION OF PHILOSOPHY

1

PHENOMENOLOGY AND PHILOSOPHY: THE GOOD OF BEING

If philosophy is a longing for comprehensive knowledge of the way things are, it is fair to say that in some sense it must always have as its primordial question the question of being. According to Martin Heidegger, our age is particularly blind to the importance of the question of being and so, we would imagine, to the nature and importance of philosophy. As a question, the question of being no longer perplexes us. Ironically, this is due in large measure to those who, owing to their own perplexity, generated a series of answers to it. We have inherited their answers but have lost sight of their questions. If, for example, we say that being is the most universal concept, then, since definition proceeds by way of specifying what differentiates one class from another, being will be undifferentiable and so indefinable. If it is indefinable, then, if it is known at all, it will have to be self-evident. But if we know it to be self-evident, we will not be moved to call it into question.[1] This is our position, says Heidegger, and the consequences are dire, for an age may be measured by its authentic awareness of the question of being. We are beings whose peculiar nature shows itself only in the fact that a world unfolds for it. The relation between us and our world is rather like the relation between the eye and its visual field.[2] The eye is not outside its visual field—it is nothing apart from its visual field—and yet it is not and cannot come to sight as an object within its visual field. Just as to raise the question of the meaning of the visual field as a whole would mean necessarily to raise the question of the eye, to raise the question of the meaning of being is to raise the question of being there, of *Dasein*, of human being. Thus, to be unaware that the question of being is a question is to be radically unaware of what one is authentically or in one's own right (*eigentlich*). It is to be radically unself-aware. We are all, by virtue of what we are, in the world—we cannot be eyes without visual fields. But we are not authentically so without being aware that we are so. To raise the question of being is thus to raise the question of our own being, and this is authentically to be.

On the one hand, Heidegger clearly means us to understand this laxity with regard to the question of being as a new problem. On the other hand, he begins *Being and Time* with a quotation from Plato's *Sophist* that calls attention to the fact that we tend to take for granted that we know what we mean when we utter the word "being," and that a certain turnaround occurs when we discover that we do not know.[3] If more than two millennia ago the question of being was known to have been forgotten and was then recovered, what is so unique about our present situation? In fact, Heidegger will argue that *Dasein* always has a tendency to fall into its world—to treat itself as an object alongside other objects. When we understand soul as "immaterial substance," do not our souls fall into the trap of thinking of themselves merely as modified versions of the material substances of our daily experience—that is, as things one can come across in the world like rocks and houses and books? For *Dasein* to lose sight of its own uniqueness in this way is for it to be inauthentically in the world. Yet this, too, is complicated; even to be inauthentically in the world is authentically to be in the world, just as it is certainly possible to raise the question of being only nominally, and so inauthentically. Contrary to contemporary usage, not all professors of philosophy are philosophers.

> And because *Dasein* essentially is its possibility, this being [*Seiende*] can in its being [*Sein*] itself "choose," itself, win and can lose itself, or else never and only "seemingly" win. It can have lost itself and not yet won itself only insofar as it is in conformity with its essence as the possibly *authentic* [*eigentliches*] , i.e. itself belonging to itself. The modes of being of both *authenticity* [*Eigentlichkeit*] and *inauthenticity* [*Uneigentlichkeit*] (these expressions were chosen in the strict terminological sense of the words) are grounded in this—that *Dasein* is determined altogether through mineness [*Jemeinigkeit*]. The inauthenticity of *Dasein* means, however, not something like a lesser being or a lower degree of being. Inauthenticity can rather determine *Dasein* in conformity with its fullest concretion—in its states of being busy, excited, interested or ready for enjoyment.[4]

This double possibility—which is at the same time one—for being in the world is not so very different from the doubleness of philosophy, which is simultaneously the nature of all men and the practice of very few men (it is what will enable Rousseau to announce that his own position is unique and at the same time to use it as a paradigm for the human condition generally[5]). *Dasein* may vary as the manner in which the question of being is raised varies from age to age, but it seems at its core to be invariable. The differences are important (especially so to Heidegger), but the underlying sameness that permits *Being and Time* to begin with the suggestion that Plato, too, knew of the primacy of the question of being is no less important. Accordingly, much of the existential analytic of *Being and Time* prior to the introduction of the historicity of being in division 2 allows itself to be understood ahistorically. As Heidegger indicates by his beginning, with regard to the tendency to forget the question of being, his view has in many ways been anticipated by Plato. This core understanding of human nature has as its analogue a core understanding of philosophy that comes into view in Heidegger's brief treatment of his own procedure in *Being and Time*, his account of phenomenology in the introduction.[6]

The introduction divides into two chapters. The first begins with an account of the necessity to reraise the question of being. Heidegger then moves to the structure of a question generally, a structure that seems to highlight the temporality of questioning; a question always emerges out of a background of what is being asked about (*das Gefragtes*), is stimulated by a present occasion (*das Befragtes*), and anticipates an answer (*das Erfragtes*). It is thus constituted by past, present, and future. This structure is present as well in the question of being, where an understanding of being (*Sein*) is always presupposed, a particular being (*Seiende*)—*Dasein*—is the occasion for raising the question, and the sense or meaning (*Sinn*) of being (*Sein*) is what is sought.

Yet the question of being is not altogether like other questions. As what all other questions somehow presuppose, it is ontological. As characterizing a particular being—*Dasein*, it is ontic. It thus calls our attention to that being whose being ontically is to be ontological. Like all questions, the question of being presupposes that we somehow know what we are asking. So, for example, in the question "What is being?" the "is" must be meaningful. But this "average" and "everyday" understanding of being is vague and not at all transparent. The question of being thus seems to presuppose that we at first mistake being. It is therefore not accidental that Heidegger proceeds as he does. The first division of the first part of *Being and Time* is a "*preparatory* [my emphasis] fundamental analysis of *Dasein*." It is an account of *Dasein* apart from its temporality that is at once necessary for the subsequent temporal account of division 2 and, strictly speaking, not correct.

> This understanding of being may indeed so greatly fluctuate, grow hazy and border perilously on pure word recognition—this indeterminateness of an already available understanding of being is itself a positive phenomenon that requires clearing up. An investigation into the meaning of being will not want to give this [clarification] at the beginning. The interpretation of the average understanding of being will be guided first by the already developed concept of being. In the light of the concept and of the ways of explicit understanding belonging to it, it will be possible to make out what the darkened, or not yet lit up understanding of being means, what kinds of darkening or hindrance of an explicit lighting up of the meaning of being are possible and necessary.[7]

Since what we are asking about—being (*Sein*)—is what determines beings (*Seiende*) as beings, it is not itself to be understood as *a* being—it cannot be part of the story it makes possible. Stephen Hawking makes a similar point in a slightly different context by way of an anecdote:

> A well-known scientist (some say it was Bertrand Russell) once gave a public lecture on astronomy. He described how the earth orbits around the sun and how the sun, in turn, orbits around the center of a vast collection of stars called our galaxy. At the end of the lecture, a little old lady at the back of the room got up and said: "What you have told us is rubbish. The world is really a flat plate supported on the back of a giant tortoise." The scientist gave a superior smile before replying, "What is the tortoise standing on?" "You're very clever young man, very clever," said the old lady. "But it's turtles all the way down!"[8]

Of course, it cannot be "turtles all the way down." At some stage—the ultimate stage—the "support" for beings must "be" in a way other than the being of the beings it supports. Accordingly, it must have a way of showing itself unlike the way ordinary beings show themselves.

The *Erfragte*—the meaning of being at which the question aims—thus requires its own mode of conception. Still, that to which we address our question—the *Befragte*—must in some sense be available to us in the ordinary way; there is really nowhere else to start. The ordinary beings with which we begin must be gotten at as they are in themselves if we are to get at them in their being. This is easier to say than to do, for

> we name "being" [*seiend*] in many ways and in a variety of senses. Everything we talk about, which we opine, toward which we comport ourselves in this or in that way is being [*seiend*]; also what and how we ourselves are is being [*seiend*]. Being (*Sein*) lies in being that and being so, in reality, in being present at hand, enduring, validity, *Dasein*, in "there is." In *which* beings [*Seienden*] should the meaning of being [*Sein*] come to be read off; from which beings [*Seienden*] should the unlocking of being [*Sein*] take its beginning?[9]

How then can we begin to get at beings as they are in their being? With what being are we to begin in our attempt to raise the question of the meaning of being, and how are we to begin without already presupposing what we mean by being?

> Looking at, understanding, conceiving of, choosing, access to these are constitutive approaches to the question and so are themselves modes of being [*Sein*] of a determinate being [*Seiende*], of a being that we, those questioning, are, in fact, ourselves. Working out the question of being [*Sein*], therefore, means making a being [*Seiende*], the one questioning, transparent in its being [*Sein*]. The raising of this question is, as a mode of *being* [*Sein*] of a being [*eines Seinden*] itself essentially determined from that which is questioned in it, from being [*Sein*]. This being [*Seiende*], that we are in fact ourselves and that has, among others, questioning as a possibility of being [*Sein*], we shall fix terminologically as *Dasein*. The expressed and transparent posing of the question of the meaning of being [*Sein*] requires a preparatory proper explication of a being [*Seiende*] (*Dasein*) with regard to its [*Seines*] being [*Seins*].[10]

The being with which we must begin is *Dasein*, for it is *the* being [*Seiende*] for which its being [*Sein*] is already necessarily an issue. Ontically, *Dasein* is already in some sense ontological. This does not mean that every human being has developed an explicit ontology; it does mean that all of us have necessarily a tacit understanding of being. Accordingly, being will begin to show itself, however obscurely, in an analysis of *Dasein*.

Does this mean that what is required is a science of *Dasein*—a *Daseinology*? Heidegger makes it very clear that *Dasein* cannot be approached in this way. Being is always the being of *a* being, and beings always come to be known within certain boundaries or areas. These areas are, in turn, defined by fundamental concepts or principles (*Grundbegriffe*), and these concepts mark the limits of the several sciences. So, for example, biology is an account (*logos*) of life (*bios*); minerals stand outside its boundaries. Now, authentic (*eigentlich*) movement in the various sciences occurs not by piling up data within the specified boundaries—for example, by simply adding an additional species of animal to the biological ledger. Movement, rather, occurs by using what information is accumulated to turn back to interrogate the founding principles of the science—to ask, for example, what life is. Accordingly, a science progresses only to the extent that it is capable of fundamental crisis—that is, to the extent that its area of rule can become a question for it (this may well be why Heidegger insists on identifying the object of his inquiry as *Dasein* rather than man—to put the "science" of man in crisis). Thus, while these fundamental concepts determine what counts as a being for their respective sciences, the particular beings they circumscribe can somehow call into question the validity of the fundamental concepts themselves. Grounding these concepts, then, requires an inquiry into the area they circumscribe—namely, into the beings in the area. This seems circular—the sciences of particular kinds of beings are the means whereby we know these beings, but the sciences themselves are known to be sciences only by knowing the beings of which they are supposed to make knowledge possible. This can only mean that there is a manner of "knowing" the beings in their being prior to the "knowledge" proper to the particular sciences. This "knowledge" or understanding is necessary to the sciences and lays the foundation for them. It amounts to "jumping ahead" into a partial disclosure of the beings it knows. As a disclosure of part of a being—biology is concerned with living body only as living—this understanding will itself be partial. Unless it understands itself as partial, as treating one area of beings among others, it will be an account of the principles of a class of beings (an ontology), but it will not be a fundamental ontology. Unless the being in the area of a particular science comes to sight as a type of being distinguishable from other types of being, it will not be fully understood. Accordingly, all science or knowledge is dependent on an awareness of the partiality of the part of being it singles out. But awareness of the partiality of the part is not possible without some awareness of the larger whole of which it is a part—finally, being as being and not, for example, living being. How will this "science" be possible? What will provide the ground for that "jumping ahead" so necessary to the particular sciences? The boundaries of biology are both determined and stretched by those beings that do not belong within them. Is anything comparable possible for an ontology—a science of being?

The "what" of the question of being has proved provisionally to be *Dasein*. The "how" of the question of being is more difficult to pin down, especially given the peculiar character of the "what."

> If the interpretation of the meaning of being becomes our task, *Dasein* is not only the primary being to be questioned; it is, all in all, the being that in its being already relates itself to *that toward which* the question is directed. The question of being is then, however, nothing other than a radicalizing of a tendency of being belonging to *Dasein* itself, of a pre-ontological understanding of being.[11]

Fundamental ontology names a problem as much as it does a mode of science. The science of being cannot be like the sciences of the various kinds of beings. The difficulty is compounded by the peculiarities of *Dasein*'s being.

> *Dasein* is, to be sure, not only ontically near, or, indeed, the nearest—we *are* it, yes even ourselves. In spite of this, or precisely because of it, it is ontologically the farthest.[12]

This ontological farness from itself has to do with *Dasein*'s tendency to understand itself as though it were a being in its world and so miss the most important thing about its being (it is the same condition of our being that Rousseau calls *amour-propre*; we are most severed from ourselves when we see ourselves as other). This is not a simple mistake; the difficulties it causes belong peculiarly (*eigentumlich*) to *Dasein*. Interpretations of *Dasein*'s being spring naturally out of its nature, but something about that nature hinders them. Accordingly, while we need an analysis of *Dasein*, it is not at all clear how we are to approach it. We cannot assume an idea of being and apply it to *Dasein*; rather, we need a way to let *Dasein* show itself from itself and as it is in its average everydayness prior to being "known" as a kind of being. *Dasein* always has an understanding of being and therefore of beings in the world—this is what makes its world a world and it what it is. It, therefore, naturally tends to understand itself as it understands these beings even though this is an inauthentic understanding of itself. To make visible to *Dasein* what it has done would require making its tacit, and partial, understanding of being explicit and, by so doing, destroying its illusion as a complete understanding of being. In this respect Heidegger's analysis is a destruction of a tradition. At the same time, disclosing to *Dasein* its tacit understanding of being means disclosing *Dasein* to itself in its relation to being. The destruction of the tradition is accordingly a preliminary disclosure of being.

In reraising the question of being, *Dasein* is the being that must first be questioned, but it must not be brought to light as it has been constituted by the tradition. How, then, are we to get at it without presupposing a concept of what it is? The way is what Heidegger calls phenomenology.

> With the provisional characteristic of the thematic object of the investigation (being [*Sein*] of being [*des Seienden*], or meaning of being altogether) its method already seems [*scheint*] to be prescribed.[13]

We need to see what it means that the method, the how, shows itself (*scheint*) with the characterizing of the object, the what. In part, it simply indicates that there can be no possible appeal to anything apart from being to explicate being. Accordingly, being will have to be made clear in terms of itself.

> With the guiding question of the meaning of being the investigation stands in the presence of the fundamental question of philosophy altogether. The manner of managing this question is the *phenomenological* one. Therewith this treatise pledges itself neither to a "standpoint" nor to a "direction," because phenomenology is nothing of either and can never come to be so as long as it itself understands itself. The expression "phenomenology" signifies primarily a *methodological concept*. It does not characterize the what of the subject matter of the

object of philosophical inquiry, but the *how* of it. The more genuinely a methodological concept works itself out, and the more comprehensively it determines the fundamental principles for conducting a science, the more primordially is it itself rooted in the discussion with the things [*Sachen*] themselves. . . .[14]

So phenomenology has no particular point of view, no direction, and no preconceptions about what the object of inquiry is. Instead, it characterizes only "the *how* of this/of these [*dieser*]." Still, this *dieser* is ambiguous; it could refer to "objects" or to "inquiry." The ambiguity is suggestive and will have something to do with what it means for Heidegger to go *zu den Sachen selbst*—to the things themselves.

To make the meaning of phenomenology clearer, Heidegger divides the word into its elements—the Greek words *phainomenon* and *logos*—and points out that it does not mean what it would mean, if it worked as words like *biology* do. Phenomenology does not mean "science of phenomena." We may wonder at what Heidegger is doing here. He means to tell us what the significance is of coupling two Greek words that were never coupled in Greek. The word *phenomenology* seems to have been invented in the eighteenth century and to have had related but not identical meanings in Wolff, Kant, Hegel, and Husserl, but Heidegger is quite explicit in rejecting the need for any actual history of how it came to be coined.[15] Is he then explaining why he has coupled them and why they allow themselves to be coupled in this way? Is this perhaps, without their realizing it, why such a word could originate in the school of Wolff?

Phainomenon is the neuter, nominative, middle/passive, present, progressive participle of the verb *phainô*. In the active voice the verb means "to cause to appear or bring into the light"; in the middle voice, Heidegger translates its meaning as "to show itself." He then traces the verb stem, *pha*, to the Greek word for light, *phôs*—that which is light or bright and in which something can therefore become manifest and visible in itself.

> We must therefore hold onto this as the meaning of the expression "phenomenon": *that-which-shows itself-in-itself*, the manifest. The *phainomena*, phenomena, are, then, the totality of what lies in the day or can come to be brought to light—what the Greeks sometimes simply identified with *ta onta* (being [*Siende*]).[16]

Still, beings show themselves in various ways, even as what they are not. Showing, as looking like, is seeming—*scheinen*. *Phainomenon* accordingly comes to have a second meaning—seeming or semblance, what looks like something. So, for example, when we say that something seems good, we mean that it is not really good but only presents itself as such. Now, this does not mean that there is no showing in this second sense of phenomenon, for

> only insofar as something altogether makes a pretense of showing itself in its meaning, i.e., to be a phenomenon, *can* it show itself *as* something that it is *not, can* it "only look like. . . ." Within this meaning of *phainomenon* (seeming [*Schein*]) the primordial meaning (phenomenon as the manifest) already lies included as founding the second one.[17]

We now have two versions of phenomenon, one dependent upon the other, but neither is what Heidegger here calls appearance—*Erscheinung* (although *phainomenon* can have this meaning in Greek). Appearances are like symptoms of an illness. As indicating something that they are not themselves, they point to what does *not* show itself. This is at odds not only with the first sense of *phainomenon* but also with the second, for in the second sense something does show itself even if it does so only insofar as it is like something else. Still, for an appearance to be, *something* must show itself.

> If one then says that with the word "appearance" we point out something there in which something appears without itself being an appearance, the concept of phenomenon is not thereby circumscribed but rather *presupposed*, which presupposition, however, remains concealed because in this determination of "appearance" the expression "to appear" is used equivocally. That wherein something appears means wherein something announces itself, i.e. does not show itself; and in the locution [*Rede*] "without itself being 'appearance'," appearance means *showing itself*.[18]

There is understandably some confusion over the meaning of *phainomenon*. We have already discovered three versions, to which Heidegger now adds a fourth. The primary meaning is that which shows itself. This supports a secondary meaning—that which seems, or shows itself as being like. The third is the appearance of what "shows itself" only through something else; this is phenomenon as symptom of what does not itself appear. Of course, a phenomenon in this third sense may later show itself. The fourth sense differs from the third in that it is the appearance of that which never shows itself as itself and is thus merely a symptom of an authentic (*eigentlich*), but ever hidden, being.

What unites this multiplicity of meanings of *phainomenon* is the first and primordial meaning—phenomenon as that which itself shows itself. Every subsequent version of phenomenon depends on the fact that *something* comes to light. Even an illusion must be manifest as something for it to work its wiles.[19] Heidegger further shows us how the subsequent versions of *phainomenon* develop rather naturally each out of its predecessor. He provides us a history of the transformation of the primordial meaning into later meanings that makes apparent both the dependence of the later meanings on the primordial meaning and the way the later meanings, given what they are, tend to obscure the primordial meaning.

If *phainomenon* means primarily that which itself shows itself, what does *logos* mean?

> In Plato and Aristotle the concept of *logos* has multiple significations, and indeed in a way that the meanings compete with one another without positively being led through one fundamental meaning. In fact, this is only semblance [*Schein*], which will maintain itself so long as the interpretation is not able to grasp suitably the fundamental meaning in its primary content.[20]

That the variety of meanings of *logos* is only a *Schein*, or *phainomenon* the unity of which Heidegger will disclose, suggests that his account of *logos* is a phenomenology of *logos*. In retrospect, this also seems true of his treatment of *phainomenon*. Phenomenology seems to have something to do with examining how the way something has of concealing itself, on inspection, reveals its way of showing itself. This seems the movement underlying the treatment of phenomenology as a whole, which Heidegger began by saying that the method of the investigation shows itself (*scheint*) along with the object of the investigation.[21]

The primary meaning of *logos* is *Rede*—talk or discourse. But

> the later history of the meaning of the word *logos* and, above all, the various and arbitrary interpretations of subsequent philosophy con-

stantly conceal the authentic [*eigentlich*] meaning of talk, which lies
sufficiently open in the daylight. *Logos* comes to be "translated," i.e.,
always interpreted, as reason, judgment, concept, definition, ground,
relation. But how can "talk" be able to be so modified that *logos*
means all the things listed, and indeed within the scientific use of
speech?[22]

Once again, Heidegger suggests that to see how *logos* comes to be covered up, or perhaps covers itself up, is to understand what it is. What,
then, does *Rede* mean?

> *Logos*, as talk [*Rede*], rather says much the same as *dêloun*—to make
> manifest that in the talk about which "the talk" is. Aristotle has more
> sharply explicated this function of talk as *apophainesthai*. The *logos* lets
> something be seen (*phainesthai*), namely, that about which the talk is,
> and indeed, either *for* the one talking (the medium) or for those talking
> with one another.[23]

So *logos* as talk is the same as making manifest, which is, in turn, the
same as *apophainesthai*—to show forth from. What comes to light from
the *logos* is what the *logos* is about. *Logos* may be deceptive, but even
deception cannot avoid being a revelation. *Logos*, in its being, discloses;
were it not to do so it would simply be noise or scratches on a page.

There is, however, a long tradition that identifies *logos* with that
which joins in thought two beings not previously together. As predicat-
ing one thing of another, *logos* has the form S is P. When *logos* announces
this *sunthesis* of one thing with another, it brings to light their togetherness; by way of *logos* we see something as something else. Yet for this to
be possible *logos* must already be present in its primary meaning. It is
apophantic insofar as it lets two things *be seen* or come to light together.
When *logos* has the form S is P, as when we say "the dog is black," it
shows off the dog *as* black.

This second meaning of *logos* makes possible a third—that which
can be true or false. At the very end of the first division of *Being and
Time* (section 44), Heidegger discusses truth. His beginning point both
there and in the part of the introduction we have been discussing is the
Greek word *alêtheia*. The verb *alêtheuein* is formed from *lanthanein*, "to
escape notice," and a privative alpha. Heidegger, accordingly, interprets
alêtheia as un-covering or dis-closure. Truth is the uncovering of the

being about which the *Rede* is. At the very beginning of philosophy thinking and being are identified in the famous claim of Parmenides that "it is the same thing to think and to be."[24] Despite this fact, a long philosophical tradition separates truth from being by locating it in assertion or judgment. Truth is thought to be the agreement of a judgment with its object so that the validity of an assertion is assessed by comparing it with its object. But what exactly do we mean by this agreement? With respect to what are judgment and object said to agree? Clearly the image of a dog in my mind and the dog of which it is the image cannot be identical. And yet, if an assertion about the dog is to be true on the basis of a comparison with the dog, it should make the dog manifest exactly as it is. This version of truth, not sufficiently representing what it means to have an idea of or to see something as, errs by treating the idea of a thing and the thing as beings of the same order and, hence, as comparable.

In addition, is it not the case that if I want to claim that two things agree, to compare them I must first grasp them independently? And does this not mean that the being of each must be truly disclosed to me prior to any comparison? The primary meaning of truth, then, cannot be agreement. Something like *aisthesis* (sensory perception) or *noein* (perceptual understanding) is required. Thus, while it might be true to say that truth is a feature of *logos*, it cannot be true to say that *logos* understood as a judgment or assertion having the form S is P is the home of truth. Just as truth as agreement presupposes a more primordial truth, so too *logos* as judgment presupposes a more primordial *logos*.

This primordial meaning is *logos* as *apophainesthai*—showing forth from. All the subsequent meanings of *logos* are dependent on it.

> And because the function of *logos* lies in merely letting something be seen, in *letting beings be perceived*, *logos* can mean *reason*. And because, moreover, *logos* is used not only in the meaning of *legein* but at the same time in that of *legomenon* (that which is exhibited as such), and because this is nothing other than the *hupokeimenon*, what lies already on hand [*vorhanden*] at the foundation [*Grunde*] for each ongoing addressing or discussing, *logos* qua *legomenon* means foundation [*Grund*], *ratio*. And finally, because *logos* qua *legomenon* also can mean that which, as something addressed, comes to be visible in its being related to something, in its "having been related" *logos* maintains the meaning of being related and relationship.[25]

As with *phainomenon*, Heidegger identifies a primary meaning and shows how the secondary meanings that arise out of it also tend to obscure it.

Heidegger appeared to set out to articulate the meaning of phenomenology by analyzing it into its constituent parts: *phainomenon* and *logos*. All that should now be necessary is to put the pieces together. This seems not very complicated; *logos* points to the method or procedure of phenomenology—its *how*, and *phainomenon* points to its object—its *what*. In the end, however, it is not so easy.

> The expression, phenomenology, can be formulated in Greek as *legein ta phainomena*; however, *legein* means *apophainesthai*. Phenomenology, then, means *apophainesthai ta phainomena*—to let that which shows itself be seen from itself just as it shows itself from itself.[26]

In the deepest sense, the object of inquiry is the same as the manner of inquiry—*phainomenon* and *logos* are one. What is more, this is also true on the level of Heidegger's presentation, in which his account of phenomenology has been throughout an example of phenomenology. Heidegger began with the claim that the object of his inquiry (the meaning of being) shows itself (*scheint*) with its method and began his account of *logos* with the semblance (*Schein*) of multiplicity in its meaning. Phenomenology, which is concerned with *scheinen*, can have as its motto "to the things themselves" because the process of laying bare how something shows itself is at the same time a showing of the being of a thing—*to gar auto noein estin te kai einai*. This "laying bare" proves to involve uncovering how it has progressively covered itself up. Phenomenology is something like the truth of a history of error. Its ultimate object is the ultimate object of philosophy simply—being.

> What is in terms of its essence *necessarily* the theme of an *explicit* exhibition? Manifestly, something of the sort that proximally and for the most part precisely does *not* show itself, something which, in contrast with what proximally and for the most part does show itself, is *hidden*, but at the same time something which is essential to what proximally and for the most part shows itself, belonging to it so that it constitutes its meaning and ground.
>
> But what in an exceptional sense remains *hidden* or falls back into being *covered up* or shows itself only *in place of another* is not this or that

being [*Seiende*] but is rather, as the foregoing observations have shown, the being [*Sein*] of the beings.[27]

Our only access to being is through the beings in which it shows itself. At the same time, what makes all of these beings beings is *that* they show themselves. Ontology, then, in its attempt to understand being as being can only be phenomenology for, if what being does is show itself as something else, then to understand what it means for something to show itself as anything at all is to understand what it means for it to be. This, of course, is not possible without understanding at the same time that being to whom beings show themselves.

> Ontology and phenomenology are not two different disciplines among others belonging to philosophy. Both terms characterize philosophy itself with respect to its object and its way of handling it. Philosophy is universal phenomenological ontology proceeding from the hermeneutic of *Dasein*, which as an analytic of existence, has made fast the end of the guiding line of all philosophical questioning from the point from which it springs and to which it falls back.[28]

Heidegger first divided philosophy into ontology and phenomenology, the one characterizing the object of inquiry, the other the way of inquiry. He then turned to phenomenology and divided it into its elements, *phainomenon* and *logos*, in a way that seemed to repeat the initial distinction between object and way. In the end, however, *phainomenon* and *logos* seem to collapse back into each other, and in their wake so also do ontology and phenomenology. Heidegger's admittedly provisional account of his own procedure in *Being and Time* thus points to and exemplifies that combination of distinctness and identity that will later characterize *Dasein* in its relation to its world.

Heidegger is, of course, not Plato, and any account of his philosophy that ignores the difference does so at great risk. Nevertheless, the two (and not just they) share an understanding of the problem at the core of philosophy. This brief account of a part of the introduction to *Being and Time* is certainly not exhaustive. It does, however, indicate the extent to which the philosopher arguably the most influential of our century embraces an understanding of philosophy as autobiographical. For Heidegger, philosophy is ultimately concerned with being. But the only way to being is *Dasein*, and the nature of *Dasein* is philosophy.

NOTES

1. See Martin Heidegger, *Sein und Zeit* (Tübingen: Niemeyer, 1993), 3–4.
2. See Ludwig Wittgenstein, *Tractatus Logico Philosophicus*, 5.63–5.641 and *Philosophical Investigations*, I.398–99.
3. See *Sein und Zeit*, 1. The Greek is as follows:

delon gar hôs humeis men tauta (ti pote boulesthe sêmainein hopotan on phtheggês-the) palai gignôskete, hêmeis de pro tou men ôiometha, nun d'êporêkamen . . .

For it is clear, on the one hand, that you have been familiar with these things for a long time—whatever you wish to signify when you utter "being"—and, before this we used to believe it, but now we have been perplexed.

Heidegger translates this as follows:

Denn offenbar seid ihr doch schon lange mit dem vertraut, was ihr eigentlich meint, wenn ihr den Ausdruck "seiend" gebraucht, wir jedoch glaubten es einst zwar zu verstehen, jetzt aber sind wir in Verlegenheit gekommen.

For manifestly you have indeed been comfortable with this for a long time already, what you really [*eigentlich*] mean when you use the expression "being"; once indeed we believed ourselves to understand it to be sure, but now we have come into embarrassment.

4. *Sein und Zeit*, 42–43. This and all subsequent translations from the German in this chapter are my own although I have consulted the translation of John Macquarrie and Edward Robinson (*Being and Time* [New York: Harper & Row, 1962]) throughout.
5. See especially *The Reveries of the Solitary Walker*, First Walk, paragraph 12, and Second Walk, paragraph 1. All references to Rousseau are to *Oeuvres complètes*, edited by Michel Launay, 3 vols. (Paris: Editions du Seuil, 1967).
6. If the introduction is "The Exposition of the Question of the Meaning of Being," then it is an inquiry or a questioning of that question. As such, according to Heidegger, it must be constituted by that which is asked about (*das Gefragtes*), that which is questioned (*das Befragtes*), and that which is found out by asking (*das Erfragtes*) (*Sein und Zeit*, 5). The question of being is what is asked about, and presumably what we are aiming at is the meaning of the question of being. But what is it to which we address our questions about the question of being?

If the interpretation of the meaning of being [*Sein*] is the task, *Dasein* is not only the primary being [*Seiende*] to be questioned, it is besides the being [*Seiende*] that is itself already related in its being [*Sein*] to *what* comes to be asked after in this question. The question of being is then, however, nothing other than the radicalizing of an essential tendency of being belonging to *Dasein* itself, the preontological understanding of being. (*Sein und Zeit,* 14–15)

7. *Sein und Zeit,* 5–6.

8. Stephen Hawking, *A Brief History of Time* (New York: Bantam Books, 1990), 1.

9. *Sein und Zeit,* 6–7.

10. *Sein und Zeit,* 7.

11. *Sein und Zeit,* 14–15.

12. *Sein und Zeit,* 15.

13. *Sein und Zeit,* 27.

14. *Sein und Zeit,* 27.

15. See *Sein und Zeit,* 28.

16. *Sein und Zeit,* 28.

17. *Sein und Zeit,* 29.

18. *Sein und Zeit,* 29–30.

19. Heidegger seems to have reproduced something like Descartes's *cogito ergo sum*—an argument that spells out the consequences of the fact that anything at all appears to us in thought regardless of whether the appearance reveals the truth of what it is.

20. *Sein und Zeit,* 32.

21. *Sein und Zeit,* 27.

22. *Sein und Zeit,* 32.

23. *Sein und Zeit,* 32.

24. *to gar auto noein estin te kai einai.* See also *Sein und Zeit,* 221–23.

25. *Sein und Zeit,* 34.

26. *Sein und Zeit,* 34.

27. *Sein und Zeit,* 35.

28. *Sein und Zeit,* 38.

2

NIETZSCHE'S GENEALOGY
AND PHILOSOPHY:
THE BEING OF THE GOOD

I n *Beyond Good and Evil*, Nietzsche is explicit about the autobiographical character of philosophy.

> Gradually it has become clear to me what each great philosophy up to
> now was: namely, the self-knowledge of its author and a kind of un-
> willed and unnoticed *mémoires*; similarly, that the moral (or immoral)
> intentions in each philosophy made up the real germ of life out of
> which the whole plant always grew. In fact, one does well (and
> wisely), by way of explanation of how the most remote metaphysical
> assertions of a philosophy really came to exist, first always to ask one-
> self this: At what morality does it (does *he*) aim?[1]

On their face, these remarks suggest that philosophy is simply the unself-
conscious and willful imposition of an idiosyncratic order on the world.

> "My judgment is *my* judgment; no other easily also has the right to
> it"—such will a philosopher of the future perhaps say.[2]

And yet, if philosophy is not to be distinguished from "the prejudices of
philosophers," what are we to make of the unrelenting demand for honesty that characterizes Nietzsche's "free spirits"?[3] Moreover, how are we
to understand Nietzsche's own intent? What is it that he wishes to teach
us?

For Heidegger, being is the first question, although he is led to
understand it in terms of something like the good—*Sorge*. For Nietzsche,

31

as we shall see, the good grounds all questioning. This leads him to an implicit understanding of being. Accordingly, Nietzsche's inquiry into wisdom concerning the good, *On the Genealogy of Morals*, must become an inquiry into the goodness of wisdom concerning the good (the value of value judgments), which amounts to an inquiry into the goodness of wisdom simply. This, in turn, has certain implications for the way things are—for being. Nietzsche's *Genealogy* moves toward the conclusion in the last of its three essays that the will to truth is simply the most spiritualized form of that will to power standing at the heart of all human action and especially standing at the heart of morality. At the same time, in writing a book about the truth of morality, Nietzsche does make certain claims about the truth of the product of his own will to truth. The problematic status of his own inquiry will become the deepest concern of that inquiry.

From the very first, it is clear that, for Nietzsche, the human soul is at odds with itself. "We knowing ones" do not and cannot know our own knowing—we cannot know ourselves as we are engaged in the activity that most characterizes us. This is just a version of the problem of ascetic idealism in the third essay. If to know means to know in terms of something fixed and unmoving, then what is essentially moving must perforce remain unknown. In the past this has meant the disparaging of what we initially seek to know, the world in which things come to be and pass away, in the name of an eternal and unchanging world— perhaps heaven, perhaps the world of Platonic ideas. Along with this contempt for the world comes self-contempt since, in seeking to come to know, we ourselves, most of all, must change. To know ourselves would mean to know the being of our own coming to be. For this to be possible, there would have to be a form of knowing not requiring the fixity of the object of knowledge. This, in turn, would be supported only if the world were of a certain sort. Nietzsche calls this mode of knowing genealogy. Its importance is clear from the title: its nature is harder to unearth. Still, whatever its nature, should genealogy prove impossible, human life would always be at odds with itself, and Nietzsche's account of the meaning of morality is simply unintelligible. Although he never makes genealogy explicitly an issue, in the preface Nietzsche does give a brief account of how his own book came to be—a genealogy of *On the Genealogy of Morals*.

Unlike "phenomenology" or "ontology," "genealogy" is authentically Greek.[4] It is the *logos*, or account, of the *genea*, the family, race, or offspring and means the tracing of a pedigree. *Genea* ultimately derives from *gignesthai*—to come to be. As an account of a coming to be, a genealogy stands on a different plane from what it accounts for—the atemporal stability of *logos* providing the way to comprehend a movement in time.[5] Its goal would seem to be the truth of the pedigree of morality. The subtitle of *On the Genealogy of Morals* is *A Polemic, eine Streitschrift*—it is compounded of two parts, one meaning strife or conflict and the other, writing. Now, if the purpose of a polemic is victory, the measure of the *Genealogy* would be practical rather than theoretical—not the true but the good—and it would owe its success to the will. The subtitle thus characterizes the book in a way that seems at odds with the title. If, however, we understand the *Genealogy* to be a writing (*Schrift*) about conflict (*Streit*), the book would somehow freeze and make permanent the conflict about which it writes. This ambiguity in the subtitle reproduces the earlier tension within the title between *logos* and *gignesthai*, which, in turn, is reproduced in the relation between the two titles. It is at once a tension between the activity of inquiry and the object of inquiry (between philosophy as verb and philosophy as noun) and between the true and the good.

Nietzsche provides yet a third characterization of the *Genealogy* as a whole: "Added to the lately published *Beyond Good and Evil* for Completing and Clarifying." Of *Beyond Good and Evil* Nietzsche remarks in a letter to Jacob Burckhardt that "it says the same things as my *Zarathustra*, but different, very different."[6] The *Genealogy* is a gloss on *Beyond Good and Evil*, which, in turn, is a gloss on *Thus Spoke Zarathustra*, the book about which Nietzsche says that "perhaps never at all had anything come to be done out of a similar overflow of strength."[7] *On the Genealogy of Morals* is, accordingly, part of a developing story; its "truths" need a context and cannot be understood as timeless. Still, Nietzsche's account of its structure in *Ecce Homo* does suggest that he intends the book to point to the truth of what it means for a story to develop. The context of the truths of the *Genealogy* is not accidental.

> Every time a beginning that *should* mislead—cool, scientific, even ironic, intentionally foreground, intentionally holding back. Gradually more unrest; scattered lightning; very unpleasant truths in the distance becoming audible with muffled grumbling—until finally a *tempo*

feroce is reached where everything is impelled forward with a monstrous tension. At the conclusion, each time under altogether ghastly detonations, a *new* truth visible between thick clouds.[8]

The very beginning of the preface calls attention to the problem of self-knowledge.

> We are unknown to ourselves, we knowing ones, we ourselves to ourselves; this has its good ground. We have never sought after ourselves—how should it happen that we one day *find* ourselves? With right has it been said "Where your treasure is there also is your heart"; *our* treasure is where the beehives of our knowledge stand. We are always on the way to it, born winged beasts and honey gatherers of spirit, we trouble ourselves authentically (*eigentlich*) from the heart with only one thing—"bringing something home."[9]

If knowledge is the sort of thing one can bring home—an object or noun—those who seek knowledge can never know themselves, for to do so they would have to cease being "always on the way." The seeker cannot become what is sought without staying put, and that would mean not being a seeker. On the other hand, if knowledge is what we treasure and is laid up "in heaven" and is where our hearts are, then our natures place us in permanent exile from heaven.[10] What we most want is to cease to be what we are—we are filled with self-contempt.

The problem is that we are temporal creatures.

> Whatever else there is of life concerns so-called "experiences"—who among us has sufficient earnestness for it? Or time enough? With such matters (*Sachen*), I fear, we would never be directly "with the things (*Sache*)": even our heart is not there—and not once our ear. Rather, as one divinely dispersed and immersed in himself, to whom the bell, with all its power, its twelve strokes of noon has just resounded in his ear, suddenly awakens and asks himself, "What was it that actually struck?", so also do we sometimes rub our ears *afterward* and ask, completely astounded, completely startled, "What did we actually (*eigentlich*) experience there?", moreover "Who are we really (*eigentlich*)?" and re-count afterward, as was said, all the twelve trembling bell strokes of our experience, of our life, of our *being* (*Seins*)—alas, and thereby miscount. . . . We remain even to ourselves necessarily strange, we do not understand ourselves, we *must* mistake ourselves,

for us the principle (*Satz*) holds through all eternity "Each is himself furthest from himself"—for ourselves we are not "knowers". . . . (preface 1)

We cannot know ourselves because in attempting to do so we are always necessarily one step behind ourselves. Time, as the condition of our experience, disperses us and immerses us in ourselves so that it is not a possibility for us to collect ourselves. Yet, we can apparently know this about ourselves—that we are essentially alienated.[11] We know it as the result of recounting to ourselves what we have undergone. Noon comes with the twelfth bell, but it is known as twelfth only because we have counted the first eleven. At the end of the day, knowledge of ourselves is available only as genealogy.

If how we view the world depends on who we are, "knowing" the world will depend on self-knowledge. Nietzsche therefore prefaces his genealogy of morals with an account of the origin of his thoughts on the origin of moral prejudices—a genealogy of the *Genealogy*. He first expressed these ideas in *Human All Too Human*, a book he began after stopping (*haltmachen*) for the winter in Sorrento to look back over the wandering of his spirit. The vantage point of this beginning at first seems arbitrary. Why Sorrento? Why at this time? This arbitrariness is highlighted by the fact that the account of *Human All Too Human* was "frugal and preliminary"[12] and that Nietzsche followed it with other accounts. So there is more than one place and time to stop to survey one's thoughts. Yet, while Nietzsche's thoughts on the development of morality develop, they do not simply change.

> *That*, however, I still hold fast to them today, that in the interim they themselves have always held more fast to each other, have even grown into and grown over one another, strengthens in me the joyful confidence that they might have arisen in me from the beginning not single, not arbitrary, not sporadic, but out of a common root, out of a *fundamental will* of knowledge bidding into the depths, always speaking more determinately, always demanding the more determinate. This way alone is fitting for a philosopher. We have no right to be in any way *single* about it. Much more do our thoughts, our values, our yes's and no's and if's and whether's grow from us with the necessity with which a tree bears its fruit—related and altogether connected to one another and evidence of *one* will, *one* health, *one* realm of earth, *one*

sun—Whether they are to *your* taste, these our fruits?—But how does that concern trees! How does that concern us, us philosophers![13]

Yes, we come to understand the world only by understanding ourselves, but it is equally true that we come to understand ourselves only by way of our attempt to understand the world. In this activity a certain wholeness and uniformity of nature shows itself. Philosophy involves the attempt to put things together into a coherent whole. As philosophers do not choose this activity, they cannot choose to stop it. Neither their truths nor their errors stand apart, single and isolated; they are rather connected as parts of an overall approach to the world. Fitting the world together is the project of a will to wholeness the other side of which is the pain of being at odds with oneself. The pain of contradiction is a moral phenomenon.

In Nietzsche's case the initial moral spur to his will to truth was the problem of evil, a question that brought his curiosity and suspicion to a stop (*haltmachen*). Why are things not perfect, or why is the whole not a perfect whole? He first blamed God but then realized that in looking for an origin of evil beyond the world, he was not doing justice to his initial question, for the world clearly made it possible for men to make the distinction between good and evil.[14] Since men do what they do for some end or good (they act out their a priori), the true question was deeper.

> Under what conditions did the human being invent or discover [*er-finden* can mean either] for himself that value judgment good and evil? *And what value does it itself have?*[15]

All questioning has its purpose and so is an implicit affirmation of value. To ask after the origin of a question is to ask after the judgment of value that lies beneath it and makes it possible. However, as the products of the will are "not single, not arbitrary, not sporadic but out of a common root," so long as one has the patience, progressively deepening one's questions so as to disclose their presuppositions, this will amount to an articulation of a whole world.

> Thereupon I found and dared various answers, I distinguished times, peoples, degrees of rank of individuals, I specified my problem, from the answers new came new questions, inquiries, suppositions, proba-

bilities—until finally I had a country of my own, a ground of my own,
a complete, discrete, growing, blooming world, like a secret garden
of which no one might have suspected. . . . Oh, how happy we are,
we knowing ones, presuming that we only know how to keep quiet
long enough.[16]

If questioning leads to the disclosure of a value, then genuinely to question the value of values would mean to disclose the ground of all questioning. Nietzsche cautions us, however. One does not jump immediately to the question of questions, for only when taken seriously as a
question does each question disclose its part of the world to us. If we are
not silent long enough, if we ask further questions too soon, this process
is short-circuited. The question of the value of values is only genuinely
asked when we have moved through the series of questions that precedes
it. This process is what Nietzsche means by genealogy—thinking
through a question so as to lay bare the assumptions underlying it,
which, in turn, are seen to be based on further assumptions so that gradually the true implications of our initial question are revealed to us.[17] In
coming to know what we were really asking, we come to understand
the "secret garden of which no one might have suspected." Because he
understands inquiry to be of this sort, Nietzsche can be deeply interested
in the mistakes of men like Paul Rée. Even though Nietzsche can say
that

> I have perhaps never read anything [Rée's *The Origin of the Moral
> Sentiments*] to which, sentence by sentence, conclusion by conclusion,
> I would have said no to myself to such an extent as to this book,[18]

he can nevertheless find satisfaction in "setting down the more probable
in the place of the improbable, under some circumstances one error in
the place of another."[19]

While Rée's book is not finally interesting, Rée himself is interesting, for understanding why he makes the mistakes he makes forces one
to articulate a deeper level of his question. So, for example, Nietzsche
also finds the "English psychologists" interesting (first essay, sections
1–3). He wonders what moves them to embrace psychological reduc-
tionism and so drag into the open our *partie honteuse* with such relish.
Yet by bringing our shameful parts into the open, they attempt to give a

shameless account of us. They undermine human freedom but do so for the sake of freeing human beings from guilt. Therefore, however much the English seem to belittle men with their doctrines, underneath, all the belittling is for the sake of saving men by releasing them from weight of the slave morality of Christianity. Nietzsche thus understands the importance of a question by way of how it is of value to someone.

> At bottom, for me at that time lay something much more important at heart than a fuss about hypotheses (*Hypothesewesen*), my own or strangers', over the origin of morality. . . . It was for me much more about the *value* of morality.[20]

The particular value Nietzsche has in mind is pity.

> It concerned itself especially with the value of the "unegoistic," of instincts of compassion, of self-denial, of self-sacrifice, precisely those which Schopenhauer had so long gilded, deified, and furthered until finally they were left over for him as "value in itself," on which ground he *said no* to life, and also to himself.[21]

If morality is meant to be life affirming (and so to identify what is of value) and yet has come to be life denying (nihilistic), of what value is it? Why does the ground of all questioning lead to the undermining of all questioning? This is the question with which Nietzsche begins. Were he to answer too quickly, he would say questioning was of no value and be done with it. Instead, Nietzsche begins a genealogy of morals and so attempts to see what previous questions are implied by this final most destructive question.

> This problem of value and of compassion and of compassion-morality (I am an opponent of the disgraceful modern weakening of feeling) appears first of all only something isolated—a question mark by itself; but whoever only hangs tough here, learns to question here, for him will it go as it has gone for me—an enormous new prospect opens itself up for him, a possibility grabs him like a vertigo, every kind of mistrust, suspicion, fear springs to the fore, belief in morality, in all morality, wavers—finally, a new demand comes to be audible. Let us utter it, this *new demand*: we have need of a *critique* of moral value, *for the first time to put into question the value itself of these values*—and that

makes necessary an awareness of the conditions and circumstances out of which they grew, under which they have developed and been displaced (morality as consequence, as symptom, as mask, as tartufferie, as illness, as misunderstanding; but also morality as cause, as remedy, as stimulant, as restraint, as poison), an awareness such as this never existed until now nor was it ever even longed for.[22]

Until now the value of values has been taken for granted—the good praised at the expense of the evil. And yet if the good, as what is of value, shows itself most deeply as a ground for questioning, once taken for granted, it will cease to spur questioning and so cease to be good. That in the name of which the future is lived will in fact undermine the future, and morality will turn out to be the greatest enemy of morality. Then only by going beyond the established good would it be possible to reestablish the good.

> So that precisely morality would be guilty if a *highest power and splendor* possible in itself of the type human being were never reached? So that precisely morality would be the danger of dangers? . . .[23]

Nietzsche ends the preface by indicating how strange his work may seem to some. Like *Thus Spoke Zarathustra*, it will simultaneously wound and delight its readers. *On the Genealogy of Morals* will be playful and at the same time in deadly earnest. Its aphoristic form will be especially open to misunderstanding, for

> today one does not take this form gravely [*schwer*] enough. An aphorism thoroughly stamped and poured out is not thereby, because it has been read through, yet "deciphered"; rather, now its *interpretation* must first begin, for which an art of interpretation is required. In the third essay of this book, I have presented a paradigm of what in such a case I take to be an "interpretation"—an aphorism has been placed before this essay, of which it itself is commentary. Admittedly, in order to practice reading as an *art* in such a manner, one thing is necessary above all, what nowadays has come to be so well unlearned—and for that reason there is still time until my writings are "readable"—for which one must be nearly a cow and in any case *not* a "modern human being": *chewing the cud.*[24]

Apparently Nietzsche thinks that there is an insufficient "spirit of gravity" among his contemporaries. Is this the same spirit about which he

speaks in *Thus Spoke Zarathustra*? "Almost from the cradle are we given
grave words and values: 'good' and 'evil'—thus is this dowry called."[25]
His aphorisms must be interpreted morally even as they claim to undermine morality. This is perhaps why the title of the third essay is so seemingly inapt. In asking what ascetic ideals mean (*Was bedeuten asketische
Ideale?*), Nietzsche appears guilty of the same sin he is exposing in the
essay. He seems to be demanding their essence, but in doing so is he not
enacting the will to truth as the most spiritualized form of the will to
power? This irony is not lost on Nietzsche; in the third essay he numbers
himself among the philosophers (*wir Philosophen*) and reminds us that he
is one of the knowing ones (*Seien wir zuletzt, gerade als Erkennende*).[26] So,
in some sense, to interpret Nietzsche requires the same earnestness that,
according to *On the Genealogy of Morals*, is so hostile to life.

It is, of course, ultimately important what the paradigm is that
Nietzsche claims to place at the beginning of the third essay. It may be
the quotation from "On Reading and Writing," the seventh section of
the First Part of *Thus Spoke Zarathustra*, where Nietzsche says of reading
aphorisms that

> he who writes in blood and aphorisms does not want to be read but
> to be learned by heart.
>
> In the mountains the nearest way is from peak to peak: but for
> that you must have long legs. Aphorisms should be peaks: and those
> who are spoken to, great and tall-growing.[27]

These long strides are not so easy to square with reading understood as
the grave project of cud chewing, especially given Zarathustra's remarks
shortly thereafter on the spirit of gravity: "I no longer feel with you:
these clouds that I see under me, this blackness and gravity (*Schwere*), I
laugh over it—precisely this is your thundercloud."[28] So, to interpret
the aphorism at the beginning of the third essay properly would seem to
require understanding how cud chewing, the spirit of gravity, and the
ascetic idealism involved in asking after the meaning of something are,
and yet are not, to be left behind.

On the other hand, the paradigmatic aphorism may not be the quotation but rather the first numbered section of the third essay. The way
the section ends surely suggests that the whole of the essay is an interpretation of what is already to be found in an admittedly dark form in the
first aphorism.

Am I understood? . . . Have I been understood? . . . *"Absolutely not, sir [mein Herr]!"*—Let us, then, start again from the beginning.[29]

To start from the beginning is, of course, to give a genealogy. But here we cannot be sure what the beginning is. Is it the first section or the quotation? This process of getting underneath what seems to be the beginning in order to arrive at a more appropriate first beginning is the true structure of *On the Genealogy of Morals*. At first, we expect the book to provide us with a linear history of morality beginning from its origin and tracing its transformations through time in ways that define it but are rather accidental than essential. The *Genealogy*, however, does not move in this way at all. Instead, its three essays each trace morality to a somewhat different origin. We are naturally puzzled about the relation of these three genealogies.

What is perhaps most frequently "brought home" from the *Genealogy* is the distinction between master morality and slave morality— Rome versus Judea. The one is based on the distinction "good and bad," the other on the distinction "good and evil." At first Nietzsche seems to have unalloyed praise for "Rome" and contempt for "Judea," but his teaching is considerably more complicated. Masters are said to be like birds of prey. They do not resent their prey, the lambs. They do not really think much about them at all, except to enjoy the thought of eating them. Masters simply take what their very natures—their superior strength—make it impossible for them not to take. They are simple, unself-reflective innocents. Slaves, on the other hand, are constituted by their resentment of the masters. Their own will to power is less innocent, more subtle. As weaker, they are unable to dominate the masters individually, and so they band together. Each member of the group must therefore subordinate his individual will to power. This means celebrating those traits that make it possible to do so: meekness and selflessness. These "goods" are placed in opposition to whatever tends to undermine them. Accordingly the virtue of the masters, their unself-conscious courage and self-affirmation, is understood by the slaves to be evil. The victory of the slave morality of the herd—of democratic values—over the aristocratic morality of the splendidly solitary "blond beast" is the history of the development of morality in the West. This is the genealogy of contemporary morals.

Now, while all of this is not exactly wrong, neither is it exactly right. The problems begin with the title of the first essay—"Good and Evil," "Good and Bad." We expect four terms but get only three. Slave morality and master morality surely differ in understanding what is *not* good, yet, although Nietzsche chooses not to make it explicit, the difference is grounded in a more fundamental agreement about what is really valued as "good." Both masters and slaves wish to master the other. It is simply that the slaves, being weaker, must exercise duplicity to do so. They are cleverer in the pursuit of their not so very different goal. That both master and slave are motivated by will to power of course means there is something of the master in the slave.

> The slave uprising in morality begins at that point where *ressentiment* itself becomes creative and gives birth to values: the ressentiment of such beings [*Wesen*] as those for which the authentic [*eigentliche*] reaction, that of deed, is denied, those who compensate themselves only through an imaginary revenge. While every noble morality grows from a triumphant yes-saying to itself, slave morality from the beginning says no to an "outside," to an "other," to a "not-itself": and *this* no is its creative deed.[30]

This is rather like Heidegger's understanding of the authentically inauthentic.[31] If will to power is behind everything, then, of course, it must also be behind the slave. Accordingly, Nietzsche is not simply critical of the turning inward of the slave, for

> in fairness thereto may also in any case be added that first on the soil of this *essentially dangerous* form of human existence, the priestly, did the human being become at all *an interesting beast*, that first here did the human soul in a higher sense acquire *depth* and become *evil*—and these are the two fundamental forms of superiority until now of human being over beasts.[32]

Furthermore, the slave does not become interesting by turning inward so much as by refusing to do so. The slave objectifies a hatred that is really internal. His self-contempt is objectified in his hatred of the master and his demand that the master, a bird of prey, be what he cannot possibly be, a lamb. This is in its way a textbook case of imposing one's will upon the world. It is like the naming that Nietzsche attributes to the aristocratic master morality.

Now, Nietzsche has done something very similar in this essay. He portrays what goes on within human beings as a contest between types, objectifying, purifying, and giving independent existence to what is in reality subjective, mixed, and dependent. In this he seems, on the one hand, close to slave morality—he objectifies an internal resentment—and on the other hand close to master morality—he *names* and so takes possession of what he names. Left at this, we have simply the standard contemporary interpretation of Nietzsche as advocating will to power as the fundamental principle of all interpretation, the radical subjectivity that tells us that there are no texts but only interpretations of texts. Nietzsche, however, does not leave it at this. Having objectified an internal resentment in the form of a somewhat willful interpretation, he proceeds to let the objectification run its course and generate questions that finally undermine it. Nietzsche shows us the fragility of his distinction by attacking the priests of the morality of "good and evil" as evil ("the priests, as is known, are the *most evil enemies*").[33] And in the midst of addressing his contemporaries about contemporary morality—the slave morality of the Jews and Christians—he uses the familiar *ihr*, as though to say "I, too, am of this type."[34] Yet he is not simply admitting to slavishness, for not only are his slaves duplicitous masters; his masters are secretly slaves. They are metaphorically solitary beasts of prey but, in fact, social beings who must regularly suppress their naked will to power and so are regularly themselves duplicitous. Contrary to what one expects, the "master morality" must lead by itself without any intervention of the slave morality to an internalizing of the noble. This is perhaps why Nietzsche commits what otherwise seems simply an error and introduces the priests before he provides any account of the origin of the morality of which they are said to be the priests.[35] The priests—the pure ones—are outgrowths of the master morality. The contempt for the lower conquered class that is the sign of master morality in its most extreme form becomes utter detachment from the world. When Nietzsche says that there is something from the very beginning unhealthy about the priestly morality, he seems to imply that there must also be something unhealthy from the beginning about master morality. Why else do these masters name themselves? Since naming is an act of taking possession, they would have no need to do so if they were already in possession of themselves. Or, more simply, why would perfectly unselfconscious beings boast?

If the masters cannot be as innocent as they at first seem, neither can they be as strong as they at first seem. That there is a master morality at all—a public teaching—means that we are dealing with a people. Masters are not isolated birds of prey but Romans or Vikings. As peoples, though, they are socialized.

> [H]e who comes to know those "good ones" only as enemies comes to know also nothing but *evil enemies*, and the same human beings who are so strictly held within bounds *inter pares* through custom, respect, usage, gratitude, even more through watching each other, through jealousy and who, on the other hand, in relation to each other prove themselves so inventive in consideration, self-mastery, delicacy, loyalty, pride, and friendship—on the outside where the strange, the *strangers* begin, they are not much better than beasts of prey let loose. There they enjoy freedom from all social constraint, they compensate themselves in the wilderness for all the stress, which comes from a long inclusion and enclosure within the peace of society, they step *back* into the innocence of the conscience of the beast of prey. . . .[36]

Masters, thus, let themselves go as compensation for controlling themselves in the group. But this means that while they restrain themselves within the group, they reproduce the conditions of slave morality. If they need others, why should this not be born of the resentment of those who do not need others? So the masters are only innocent with regard to their prey, the other by whom they are called "barbarian."[37] Here Nietzsche quotes Pericles' praise of Athens. He knows, of course, that the Athenians called non-Greeks barbarians. Whether you are a barbarian and a master appears to depend on where you are. In your own city—in the case of Athens, a *democracy*—you are a lamb; outside you are a bird of prey. There are no pure masters. The simple, innocent, autonomous, and independent could not live together. Pure masters could not hunt in packs. That they do hunt in packs means that they need each other. Nietzsche knows that he has yet to explain the nature of this need.

Because it cannot account for how the master race lives as a group, master morality is problematic. To live together human beings must repress their desires, and this repression is a symptom of servility. Thus, the masters must either be part slavish, and so there are no pure masters, or there is no master race, and so there are no pure masters. Yet slave morality is equally problematic. When it considers itself the true morality (i.e., when it becomes priestly morality), it condemns noble men for being what they have to be. This condemnation involves a desire to master the masters, and while this might be condemned as "evil," it is hard to see why it should be "bad."

Initially we "bring home" from the first essay of *On the Genealogy of Morals* the view that the will of the master with regard to good and bad is the origin of a morality that then decays into slave morality—good and evil. At the heart of this account is the metaphor of the bird of prey and the lamb. The image powerfully reflects what moves us to proclaim the nobility of master morality and yet seduces us into thinking that master and slave are of radically different types—different species. But the lambs can expect the birds of prey to act like lambs only if they appear to be of the same species. This first account of the origin of morality exaggerates human inequality, but not accidentally. Morality means ranking and so will always involve the assertion of an inequality, but aristocratic morality does not go deep enough. Still, only its powerful expression in the first essay enables a new question to come to the fore. We discover through the first essay that we need to ask how it is that human beings *come to be unequal*.[38] Accordingly, Nietzsche begins the second essay with a new account of the origin of morality—this time in the act of exchange, and especially in the act of incurring a debt (*Schuld* also means guilt). Exchange requires a certain recognition of equality. There is, for example, an assumption of autonomy on both sides when a contract is signed. To promise to fulfill certain conditions is to assert that one is able to fulfill one's promises. The second essay of the *Genealogy* is entitled " 'Guilt [or Debt],' 'Bad Conscience,' and Related Things." It is on the one hand a new genealogy of morals that begins with the equality implied by exchange and attempts to give an account of how inequality is generated from it. On the other hand, it is a continuation of the argument insofar as it begins with a question that emerges from the first essay if only one knows how to remain silent long enough.

Only a full analysis of the *Genealogy* could do justice to the subtlety of Nietzsche's argument. Given what we have seen thus far, however, one would expect the beginning point of the second essay—its will to correct the first essay—also to prove insufficient and to lead to the problem explicitly addressed in the third essay. This does seem to be the case. The principle of equality assumed by the act of exchange is autonomy. At first this seems to mean that, in making his word his bond, the debtor assumes the ability to do what he says he will do, and the creditor, by having a surplus, demonstrates that he has risen above questions of immediate need. But in the course of the analysis it turns out that debtor and creditor are really equal in sharing the sense, and the resentment, of the other as autonomous. This points to the third essay and its emphasis on our sense of our lack of autonomy.[39] One might say that by beginning with the act of exchange, the second essay tacitly introduces the question of why we need to exchange goods. Plumbing the depths of this sense of incompleteness is the task of the third essay. As we have seen, in its form the essay is meant to make us aware of the structure of the *Genealogy* as a whole and therewith to make us aware of a mode of thought that does not lead to the self-contempt of ascetic idealism. Nietzsche's paradigm for understanding involves no ascetic ideal or essence so pure that what it is the essence of necessarily suffers by comparison. It does not mean being faithless to the earth or forsaking the world of coming to be in favor of an unchanging world of being. Instead, understanding the world is like interpreting an aphorism. What is already there simply needs to be spelled out, and spelling it out changes what is there. This is how things come to be what they are, and it is how genealogy as *rechewing* does in a way get at the essence of things, albeit nonascetically.

There is one model for the two things—understanding and willing—that characterize human beings—pregnancy. Understanding is like interpreting an aphorism. Since the meaning we seek is already embedded in what we have, we do not have to interpret what is in terms of what it is not. Metaphysics, Platonic ideas, and heaven are all unnecessary. Similarly, when we will, we need not reject what is in favor of what is not, since what is not yet is embedded within what is. Because the future is already implicit within the past, longing for the future need not mean rejecting the past, and embracing one's own future need not mean holding one's present in contempt. One becomes what one is.

Still, one cannot help asking why this is not simply a form of resignation—what Nietzsche elsewhere contemptuously calls "oriental Buddhism." Why is it not a form of determinism according to which the future does not really differ from the past? Perhaps we have vanquished self-contempt, but have we not merely replaced it with complacency?

Elsewhere in Nietzsche this problem takes the form of a contest between two fundamental principles: the will to power and the eternal return of the same.[40] The greatest problem for the free will, for genuine autonomy, is the past. Human beings always harbor a spirit of revenge against the past because it limits them. Accordingly, their actions are always reactions against the past. Since the will cannot be free without overcoming this greatest of burdens, it must devise a way to gain control of the past—it must will its own past. And since willing always has the form of willing the future, the only way to come to be responsible for our own pasts is for willing the future to simultaneously involve willing the past. Nietzsche calls this the eternal return of the same. In willing anything, I am to understand myself as willing it to recur for all eternity. This teaching appears unintelligible on its face—at best a clever solution to a logical puzzle about which it would be hard to be in earnest. It looks less lunatic, however, if we glance back at the structure of the third essay (and so of the *Genealogy* as a whole). The first section is admittedly unintelligible,

> Am I understood? . . . Have I been understood? . . . *"Absolutely not, sir* [mein Herr]*!"*—Let us, then, start again from the beginning.

So Nietzsche presents himself as a master (*Herr*) who provides a beginning, but one that needs to be interpreted if anything is to follow from it. This interpretation or laying out (*Auslegung*) does not simply say what is already there. It is rather the interpretation that retrospectively gives the aphorism its meaning. This is like willing something in the future that *determines* the past. Think, for example, of a formative childhood experience. The range of consequences of the "same" cause—say, child beating—vary enormously. Some abused children grow up to live rather conventional lives; others become famous artists, or unknown suicides, or famous artists and known suicides, or. . . . While in all of these cases it might be said that childhood experiences were decisive, they lead in quite different directions. So, what Nietzsche means to show is that one cannot treat the "facts" of the past as causes of the future (this is why he finds the English psychologists naive). That we cannot predict the future is not simply the result of incomplete data. Rather, it is in principle not possible to see in advance what people will make of their pasts and so what they will in some sense make their pasts be. This is only another instance of the sort of analysis that Nietzsche provides of punishment in the second essay. The brute fact of what was done remains the same, and so there is a certain reality that remains beyond the sway of interpretation. What that reality really *is*, however, changes depending on its meaning—on the interpretation that either invents meaning or discovers it or in some sense does both. It is in this way that Nietzsche understands willing and understanding to be like pregnancy. The question of the eternal return of the same and the will, of willing what is given, is the same as the relation of "facts" to their interpretations, the question with which the Third Part of the *Genealogy* is so concerned.

Nietzsche writes a book about the origin of morality in which he shows that morality is much more than a code of conduct governing our behavior in well-defined situations. In fact, it defines the situations in which we identify certain things as "behavior"; it is even that according to which we determine certain things to be things. Yet this radical "subjectivity" is itself subject to an analysis that reveals its nature. The true being of the world shows itself by way of our being. By articulating the deep connection between ascetic idealism and science, the third essay stands as a paradigm for how thoroughly our notion of the good forms our questions and predisposes us toward certain answers. At the same time, as itself the result of a question, it is subject to the very process it articulates. In being about morality, *On the Genealogy of Morals* is about the being of interpretation—of thinking—and, accordingly, about the nature of the reality that supports thinking. For Nietzsche, philosophy is surely to some extent autobiographical in a rather ordinary sense. It does amount to articulating a world born of an at least partly idiosyncratic "a priori." But it has also proven autobiographical in a deeper sense. The *Genealogy* is not meant, and is not intended, merely to record the consequences of growing up in a Lutheran home. Rather, it is meant to articulate a truth about the soul that is at the same time the soul of philosophy.

NOTES

1. Friedrich Nietzsche, *Werke in drei Bänden*, edited by Karl Schlechta (Munich: Hanser, 1966), II, 571. This and subsequent translations from the German are my own.

2. Nietzsche, *Werke*, II, 605.

3. An interesting account of the tension between the "free spirit" and the "philosopher of the future" may be found in Paul Kirkland, *Nietzsche's Masks: The Preparation of Philosophy*, master's thesis, Fordham University, Department of Political Science, May 1997.

4. It appears in Plato's *Cratylus* as a reference to Hesiod's *Theogony*. This is of some interest since the gods, as immortal beings who come to be, contain the implicit difficulty of all genealogy—the combination of the changing and the unchanging, of motion and rest.

5. In the first essay Nietzsche, himself a classicist, calls attention to the importance of naming. See especially section 10 and the note at the end of the essay suggesting that a prize be established on the question of the relation between etymology and morality. It therefore seems appropriate to pay some attention to the Greek origin of the word he chooses to describe what he is doing in the *Genealogy*. At the same time, not long after linking masters to various etymologies for words having to do with goodness, Nietzsche says, "The 'redemption' of the human race (namely from the masters) is well on its way; everything is visibly judaized or christianized or rabble-ized (Of what concern are words!)" (Nietzsche, *Werke*, II, 780).

6. Nietzsche, *Werke*, III, 1243.

7. Nietzsche, *Werke*, II, 1134.

8. Nietzsche, *Werke*, II, 1143.

9. Nietzsche, *Werke*, II, 763.

10. See Gospel According to Matthew 6:19–21.

11. Compare this with Heidegger: "*Dasein* is, to be sure, not only ontically near, or, indeed, the nearest—we *are* it, yes even ourselves. In spite of this, or precisely because of it, it is ontologically the farthest" (*Sein und Zeit*, 15). See also chapter 1, page 19 for the connection to Rousseau's understanding of *amour-propre*.

12. Nietzsche, *Werke*, II, 763.

13. Nietzsche, *Werke*, II, 764.

14. Nietzsche uses the expression *hinter der Welt* (*Werke*, II, 765). It comes very close to the Greek *meta ta physika*—beyond the natural things. Nietzsche's first exercise in philosophical writing was thus metaphysical. See as well *Also Sprach Zarathustra*, in *Werke*, II, 297–300.

15. Nietzsche, *Werke*, II, 765.

16. Nietzsche, *Werke*, II, 765.

17. This sense of genealogy is the manner in which one must read philosophic texts generally. Compare with Plato, *Philebus* 14c–17c.

18. Nietzsche, *Werke*, II, 766.

19. Nietzsche, *Werke*, II, 766.

20. Nietzsche, *Werke*, II, 766–67.

21. Nietzsche, *Werke*, II, 767.
22. Nietzsche, *Werke*, II, 767–78.
23. Nietzsche, *Werke*, II, 768.
24. Nietzsche, *Werke*, II, 770.
25. Nietzsche, *Werke*, II, 440–41.
26. Nietzsche, *Werke*, II, 851, 860.
27. Nietzsche, *Werke*, II, 306.
28. Nietzsche, *Werke*, II, 306.
29. Nietzsche, *Werke*, II, 839.
30. Nietzsche, *Werke*, II, 782.

31. On the surface it looks very different indeed from what seems to be Rousseau's account of authentic existence—the life of *amour de soi-même* characteristic of man in the state of nature. Yet further inspection makes clear that the sentiment of one's own existence is also a feature of political and theoretical man. See chapter 5.

32. Nietzsche, *Werke*, II, 778.
33. Nietzsche, *Werke*, II, 779.
34. Nietzsche, *Werke*, II, 780.
35. Nietzsche, *Werke*, II, 778–79.
36. Nietzsche, *Werke*, II, 785–86.
37. Nietzsche, *Werke*, II, 786.

38. This is, of course, the theme of Rousseau's *Discours sur l'origine et les fondemens de l'inégalité parmi les hommes*.

39. Both in the quotation from *Zarathustra* and in the first section, Nietzsche goes out of his way to make woman a central issue of the third essay. On the one hand, this points to the spuriousness of the equality of the species that provided the beginning of the second essay. We are none of us "human being" and so never truly embody the species as a whole. Just as for Adam and Eve, who cover themselves in shame when they discover their partiality, for us sex is a sign of incompleteness, of lack of autonomy. Our genitals are our "shameful parts." So, while any member of the species is by the fact of being a member equal to any other, this equality consists not in anything positive but in realizing that one is not and cannot be a true member of the species. As a member of a class, one is a defective member. Is this connected to the ascetic ideal; is it perhaps the root of ascetic thinking and willing?

On the other hand making woman an issue means making pregnancy an issue. It is a nonartificial form of making that does not require a blueprint—an ascetic ideal. That one is never temporally whole would then also be connected to a form of creativity that does not involve denying what is; instead, what comes to be would grow from what is and in some sense be indistinguishable from it.

40. Compare, for example, "On Self Overcoming" in the second part of *Thus Spoke Zarathustra* with "The Convalescent" in the third part.

3

PHILOSOPHY AND WISDOM:
THE QUESTION OF BEING IN
ARISTOTLE'S *METAPHYSICS* A

A ristotle's *Metaphysics* more than perhaps any book is supposed to provide an account of being as that which stands on its own in no need of anything else.[1] Being is substance or *ousia*; it is what "first philosophy" or "theology"—the highest kind of wisdom—is about. Yet if this is its subject matter, the *Metaphysics* certainly begins curiously.[2] The book that is supposed to be about being begins with a discussion of a universal trait of human beings—that all of us desire to know (980a20–27). The first section of Book A is followed by a discussion of the nature of wisdom understood as knowing the causes and principles of things (980a27–982b10), which, after what seems to be a digression on the origin of philosophy in wonder (982b11–983a23), leads to an account of the various ways in which things are said to be caused (983a24-b6). In the remainder of the first book (983b6–993a27), Aristotle turns to a brief history of philosophy as it pertains to causality in which he shows that, while unaware of what moved them, previous philosophers were in reality groping toward his understanding of the four kinds of causality: material, efficient, formal, and final.

In general, then, the *Metaphysics* may be said to begin with an account of the origin of philosophy and its rootedness in human nature. When Aristotle turns to the history of philosophy prior to himself in terms of its various accounts of causality, he certainly means to set the stage for the problems he outlines in *Metaphysics* B, but he also provides a glimpse of what he understands philosophy to be. This might seem merely an accidental by-product of presenting the views of a series of philosophers, but we shall see that the question of philosophy lies much closer to the heart of the first book and, indeed, the *Metaphysics* as a whole. Aristotle, too, understands that the question of being is inseparable from the question of philosophy.

Aristotle's general account of the four causes in *Metaphysics* A is very brief.

> Next it is apparent that we should grasp a knowledge of causes from the origin [*archê*], for we claim to know each thing when we recognize its first cause, and causes are spoken of in a fourfold way. We say one cause to be the *ousia* [substance, beingness] and the "what it was to be" [*to ti ên einai*] (for the "why" leads to the ultimate account [*logos*], and the first "why" is a cause and principle [*archê*]). We say another to be the matter and what is underlying, and a third to be that from which motion originates, and a fourth, the cause opposite this one—that for the sake of which and the good (for this is the end of every coming to be and motion). While we have contemplated these things sufficiently in the *Physics*, let us nevertheless take account of those before us who wished to make an inquiry into beings and to philosophize about the truth. (983a24-b3)

While similar to the account in the second book of the *Physics* (to which Aristotle seems to allude here), it is in one crucial respect different. The argument of the *Physics* takes for granted the fact of motion or change.[3] Matter, for example, is "that, being present at the outset, out of which something comes to be,"[4] while in the *Metaphysics* it is described as "the underlying" (*to hupokeimenon*). This is not surprising; in his account of the origin of philosophy, Aristotle makes it clear that it is a change from the ordinary that arouses wonder.[5] Yet, while we begin by wondering what causes an eclipse, we end by realizing that the cause of this apparent departure from the ordinary is, when properly understood, the same as the cause of the ordinary state of affairs. Metaphysics differs from physics in concentrating on the cause of the permanent even though it must proceed by way of an examination of what appears first to us—change.

Given this difference, to understand Aristotle on causality, one cannot simply turn to the *Physics*. Yet, to figure out what he means by the four causes in the *Metaphysics*, we are left to work through the series of examples he gives of philosophers who anticipated his teaching. Their imperfect and provisional understanding of what they were doing must serve as our guide to his final understanding.

Aristotle begins his history of philosophy with "those first philosophizing" (983b6–7) who thought matter was the permanently existing substrate of everything. Of this group, some thought this substrate was one—whether water (Thales, Homer, Hippo), air (Anaximines, Diogenes), or fire (Hippasus, Heracleitus)—and some thought it was various (Empedocles and Anaxagoras). Of those who sensed the need for a cause of motion, some claimed it was one—whether mind (Anaxagoras and Hermotimus) or love/desire (Hesiod and Parmenides)—and some claimed it was various (Empedocles posited both love and strife). Aristotle then seems to backtrack. He considers earlier thinkers—the material atomists (Leucippus and Democritus) and then those who consider numbers as elements (the Pythagoreans and Alcmaeon). This leads him to give an account of those who understood being to be one—whether in speech *logos* (Parmenides), materially (Melissus), or in some indeterminate sense (Xenophanes). He concludes with Plato, for whom he says there are two principles, the one and the indeterminate dyad. What links the members of this last group (beginning with the material atomists) seems to be the imperceptible character of the first principles. And beginning with the Pythagorean turn to number, there is a preoccupation with the way in which these imperceptible principles are the cause of the oneness of things. This last group, then, seems to be concerned with the way in which philosophy first approximated an understanding of what Aristotle calls formal cause.

In what remains of the first book Aristotle first turns to a summary of the history of philosophy he has just given (chapter 7) and then to a discussion of the problems with this history now understood as having four moments: the view that everything is some one material nature, that it is more than one, that the fundamental principles are imperceptible and the world unchanging, and that the principles are imperceptible but that the world is changing (chapters 8–9). He concludes that the history of philosophy from the outset hinted at the four kinds of causes that he has articulated (chapter 10).

Now, this "history" has a number of perplexing features. While in general Aristotle's list of predecessors is organized chronologically, as there are several exceptions, the account is not simply historical and so must have some other principle of order.[6] Second, since Aristotle has already indicated that to know something is to know its cause (982a2–3), it would seem that the knowledge of causality that we are seeking (983a24–25) would require that we know the cause of causality. Does this not put us in the position of giving a causal account of causes prior to knowing what causes are? Would not such an account necessarily be more like what Aristotle has called experience than knowledge, for "experience seems to be very like knowledge and art, and knowledge and art come to men through experience"?[7] Finally, Aristotle mentions several times how his predecessors saw something but could only speak of it dimly (*amudrôs*) and unclearly (985a13), or more obscurely (*moruchôteron*, 987a10), or were groping dimly (*amudrôs . . . thigganontes*, 988a23). He refers to what their accounts "wish to say" (989b5). So, for example, Anaxagoras "speaks neither correctly nor clearly; however, he wants something closer to what is said later and more in keeping to the way things appear now" (989b19–21). And in the last chapter of the first book Aristotle concludes that

> it is clear that all are likely to seek the causes spoken of in the *Physics* and that apart from these we couldn't speak of any; but all those before spoke of these dimly (*amudrôs*) and in a way but in a way not at all. For the first philosophy (*hê prôtê philosophia*) is like one mumbling (*psellizomenê*) about everything inasmuch as it is new and in accordance with origins (*archas*). (993a11–16)

On the one hand, these early philosophers mumbled; on the other hand, at certain stages "the very matter (*pragma*) itself made a way for them and compelled them to seek" (984a18–19). And "again, just as we said, being compelled by the truth itself, they sought the next principle (*archên*)" (984b9–11). So, Aristotle's account of his predecessors is not simply historical; it has an uncertain epistemic status, and it chronicles a series of dim and unclear gropings and mumblings the movement of which nevertheless seems to be compelled by the truth itself. Are these peculiarities connected?

The first philosophers thought that there must be some permanence persisting through change for some*thing* to change and, extending this legitimate observation to the whole, claimed that what persists is what truly is. The first discovery of philosophy is that what abides is the cause of things. The first first philosopher seems to have been Thales, for whom this abiding stuff was water. Now, it is interesting that Thales' view is more interesting than it at first seems. His impulse to reduce the various things in the world to one underlying abiding thing is really an impulse to make things intelligible. Thales' "water" is not really water; it is a thought thing, not a perceived thing. In a way it is not really material at all. Still, Thales somehow knows that the stuff that is to make everything else knowable to us must itself be known. So, although he cannot explain why the hidden true nature of things should sometimes be visible in things (and so unhidden), he does sense that unless this is the case he will not have succeeded in making the world knowable. In addition, Aristotle adds that perhaps Thales assumed water to be the first principle because of its connection to growth. After all, if there is only one cause of the being of things, one would be led to wonder why everything was not the same. If everything is water, why is not everything wet? But if water as a first principle has within it growth—a hidden cause of change or motion—then Thales' material cause is, without his realizing it, also an efficient cause. Furthermore, if the fundamental stuff of the world is water, and if water is a principle of growth, then there is some sense in which everything can be said to be alive. Thales' account of matter not only leaks into an account of motion; it also suggests goal directed motion.[8]

Empedocles, the first of those who are not monists, introduces four kinds of material cause: earth, water, air, and fire. This seems necessary because something must account for the variety to which we are accustomed in the world. A multiplicity of kinds of matter, depending on how they combine, seems to account for the potentially infinite variety of things. Yet this leads to two more difficulties. Once it has been determined *that* the various kinds of matter combine in different ways, one has to give an account of *how* they combine if this variety is to be intelligible. Empedocles' move makes it yet clearer that what is lacking is a cause of change—efficient causality. Second, if the four elements are to be understood as changeable into each other, then clearly they are not the first material causes; yet if there is some other material cause prior to them, we once again need to understand how variety is possible.

Anaxagoras must have sensed this difficulty—if dimly—when he asserted the first principles to be infinite. In this way he made the fact of variety intelligible by reproducing on the level of causes and principles the same multiplicity manifest on the level of appearances. The cost, however, is high, for while variety is now possible, its articulation is unintelligible.

This is the point in the argument where Aristotle first makes it clear that the plot of the philosophical story he has been telling is not arbitrary but "compelled by the *pragma* itself" (984a18). The movement he has been tracing has the structure of philosophical wonder outlined earlier in the first book (982b11–983a23). A puzzle presents itself that leads to a solution out of which a further puzzle is generated. We begin by wondering about what causes change. This leads us to understand the necessity for some permanence or oneness. This, in turn, leads to a new need to explain the variations within permanence—a need that would never have come to sight had not our first experience of change become problematic to us. We are struck by change. To explain it we posit something stable that undergoes change—matter or the underlying. But we then must resist the temptation to end by ignoring the very thing that struck us in the first place—change. Reflecting on material causality thus leads willy-nilly to reflection on efficient causality.

The introduction of more than one material cause has as its unacknowledged purpose the introduction of efficient cause. If, for example, two kinds of matter exist and are understood as contraries they could be understood to bear some relation to each other, whether attraction or repulsion. This, however, also turns out to be inadequate, for if efficient cause is not in any way separate from material cause, will it not always be at work in matter? And if it is always doing its job, will not its job be over? That different forms of matter have been once attracted to one another is scarcely an account of why things continue to move. Change that is already in effect at the beginning is not really change. Accordingly,

> [a]fter these men and such principles (*archas*), because they were not sufficient to recognize the nature of beings, they sought the next principle, just as we said, being compelled once again by the truth itself. For perhaps neither fire nor earth nor any other such thing is either likely to be or to have been considered by them to be the cause that some of the beings are disposed and some come to be well and beautifully. (984b8–14)

The notion that truth itself forces the investigation of why beings come to be and are beautiful and good seems to involve the introduction of final causality. When Empedocles claims that strife is responsible for separating out the four elements from their mixtures with one another so that all of the earth is located in one place and similarly with the other three elements, it is not clear why this single large mixture of the four elements should be inferior to and less a cosmos than the small mixtures that it dissolves. Is it because no human beings can exist in the former state? If so, a tacit preference for the human would have entered Empedocles' argument. What is good is what supports the human. This is perhaps why Anaxagoras seems like a sober man among drunks when he says that mind rules the whole (984b15–18). The "rule of mind" hides his preference for the human.

While truth seems to compel the question of final causality, it is curious that Aristotle never speaks of the good (*agathon*) or end (*telos*) as cause here. Instead, having just raised a question that ought to have received the answer "final cause," Aristotle says the following:

> These men, then, just as we say, even up through him [Empedocles] appear to have grasped two of the causes that we defined in the *Physics*—matter and that from which movement comes—dimly, however, and with no clarity, but as those do who are untrained in battles. For, rushing about, they often strike beautiful blows, but they do not do it with knowledge. Nor are the former likely to know what they mean. (985a10–17)

Truth itself may force the question of final causality, but the way of truth is seen so dimly that the answer given is efficient causality. The sort of order or cosmos that makes things good or beautiful does not appear as a cause in itself but as something that needs to be explained by some other cause. Apparently philosophy did not have to wait for Bacon, Hobbes, and Descartes to have difficulty conceiving that the end of motion could somehow initiate motion. The cause of movement is therefore confused with the goal of movement. Not order, but what brings about order, is understood as the good.

It is not an accident that this confusion should have to do with love, for in love efficient cause and final cause are invariably difficult to distinguish.[9] Love is a cause of movement that is rather frequently taken to be a goal of movement. As lovers we move in pursuit of a beloved that, as the object of our longing, cannot be simply present to us. What we love makes its presence powerfully felt to us in being absent. In one sense, then, being in love is our intimate experience of the working of final cause. Yet we eulogize not only the beloved but also love itself. We fall in love with love. In doing so we mistakenly attribute to what is present (love as efficient cause) the causal power of what is absent (the beloved as final cause). Accordingly, Parmenides, Hesiod, and Empedocles all seem to point to love or desire as the principle that joins things together.[10] Love is the bond between the parts of a complex whole and makes the whole a cosmos. It is altogether natural that it should seem that an order not yet present before the conjunction cannot be the cause of the coming to be of the conjunction. The cause would be what brings the parts together; love would then be what puts beauty and goodness into the whole. As this is good for us, love would then itself be the best and most beautiful; it would be the *telos* or final cause. Still, the real question is whether it is in some way possible for the order to precede the ordering. Although in its cosmic form love may seem only the attractive power that draws things together, on the human level, what is love but the dimly anticipated togetherness that serves as the cause of movement? This, however, is not so very different from what moved the first philosophers.

> For if one should follow and grasp in relation to its thought and not in relation to what Empedocles mumbles when he speaks, one would discover love (*philia*) to be the cause of good things and strife of bad things. (985a4–6)

As we have seen, this language is typical of the way Aristotle refers to his predecessors. It suggests that in thought, as in love, something makes it possible for the end to be "dimly" present before it is fully present and for this presence to serve as a cause of the motion toward its full presence. Empedocles mumbling is perhaps the crucial example for Aristotle of the presence of final causality.

When Aristotle moves to the material atomists Leucippus and Democritus at 985b he seems to regress to a discussion of material cause alone. There is nevertheless an advance in thought. Leucippus and Democritus are the first to make matter officially imperceptible. Everything is understood to be made up of differently shaped, ordered, and positioned atoms. The variety in the world can be understood in terms of the variety of ways in which atoms can connect to one another. Leucippus and Democritus also introduce the void or nonbeing as a principle. Since their goal is to give an account of change and variety, they must avoid the oneness of the whole. Accordingly, they must separate the parts of the whole from one another; the whole is not a continuum or homogeneous but a hooking up of things having discrete natures. But these natures would not be discrete unless they were separated by something, and for this, the void is necessary. However, this void that separates things must at the same time be a principle of their connection. By connecting some things, it in principle connects all things. But this means that all atoms are really one—we are back where we started.

The material atomists were dimly aware that to give an account of the world, a principle was necessary to separate things from other things, but their principle—the void—was unintelligible. At the very least, if beings are constituted by the void plus various atoms, then atoms cannot simply be beings. Some one hundred years before Democritus and Leucippus, the Pythagoreans had already seen that the world must be articulated. Aristotle places them after the material atomists because they move a step beyond them.[11] By identifying the being of things with number, the Pythagoreans tacitly ask what it is that makes each discrete thing one. They ask why being is countable or why there are beings rather than being. And their answer—number—comes very close to making a connection between being and account giving or thinking. Having made the heterogeneity of the whole intelligible by reducing it to numbers and ratios, however, the Pythagoreans make it too intelligible. If the number two is the cause of the being of a certain kind of thing, why is everything that shares in the number two not the same thing?

To all of this Plato adds one thing. According to Aristotle, Plato's principles are the one and the "indeterminate dyad" or "the great and the small." The Pythagoreans had ensured the discreteness of things by making number their causes. Heracleitus had seen that nothing we experience manifests this discreteness. We experience continuity— "everything flows." Plato, according to Aristotle, sees that these two insights must be combined. He mixes the purity of number with the realization that what is formed or limited, and so enumerated, is always only more or less formed. It is a one that is only more or less one and so participates as well in the great and the small. The Pythagoreans give us an intelligible diversity—ones—that would have to be totally intelligible. This, however, would make our beginning point—our puzzling about the diversity of things—unintelligible. Accordingly, Plato introduces a principle of indeterminacy. The Pythagoreans were not moved to distinguish with clarity form and matter because their matter was conveniently all too formal. Plato sees the need to differentiate the two.

Even this brief summary makes it possible to reflect on the place of Aristotle's history of philosophy in the structure of the first book of the *Metaphysics*. Roughly speaking, the book divides into a part about wisdom that involves a digression on the origin of philosophy in wonder and a part about the four causes of things and the history of how they have been understood. As we have seen, the obvious connection between the two—that wisdom consists in knowledge of causes—does not explain the role of the apparent digression about wonder. The not so obvious connection becomes clearer once we reflect that within his history of philosophy Aristotle traces a logical progression from material to efficient to formal cause but never really shows how final cause emerges.[12] This omission is repeated in Aristotle's causal account of causality in which the views of his predecessors provide the matter of the account, these thinkers themselves are the efficient causes of the transformations of this matter (see especially 984b20), the species of cause are its formal cause (see, e.g., 987a7), but there seems to be no obvious final cause.

In both cases final cause is disclosed by the way truth governs. Anaxagoras perhaps comes closest to articulating final causality when he introduces mind as ruling everything, but mind for him is just a way of naming an unknown efficient cause—it is indistinguishable from necessity. Still, Anaxagoras sees that it is in thought that it is most obvious how an end can govern before one has reached the end. Mumbling is not simply a mistake—an inadequate articulation. It is a directed mistake—an in-completeness. It points one to a further perplexity. But this is simply the structure of wonder Aristotle had introduced in chapter 2. It governs the whole of the first book of the *Metaphysics*, a causal account of causality that does not say but shows that the end of the argument, its goal or good, causes the movement of the argument before it is known to be the end. Our experience of being puzzled, or knowledge of ignorance, is the sign that the movement of thought at least is governed by a final cause. The true is governed by the good.

Even granted that all of this is the case, have we not simply reduced

Aristotle's account of final causality to a mere psychological necessity? That the mind operates teleologically does not mean that the world does so, and that all thinking might be wishful thinking seems a powerful argument for finding a new method for thinking about the world. No wonder Aristotle was treated with such contempt by the founders of modern philosophy.

Still, is there no connection between being and thinking? In the *Metaphysics* Aristotle attempts to discover "a science which contemplates being as being" (103a21). While "being is said in many ways" (1028a10), one of these ways has priority over the others.

> For, on the one hand, it signifies the "what is" (*ti esti*) and this particular (*tode ti*), while, on the other hand, [it signifies] the quality or quantity or similarly each of the other categories. Although being is said in these various ways, it is apparent that of these being is first the "what is," which signifies the substance [*ousia*]. (1028a11–15)

While there may be a single sense of being to which all the other senses are related, it is nevertheless characterized doubly as "what is" and as "this particular." The first forms a question that can only yield an answer in principle applicable to more than one being. The second points to a concrete individual—in principle, to only one being. Together the two are called *ousia* or substance, but their togetherness remains the deepest puzzle of the *Metaphysics*.

That this single sense of being remains a question is no accident. Of the ten categories (or ways in which things can be) mentioned in various places by Aristotle (e.g., *Categories*, chapter 4), only this one is characterized in more than one way and by a question. It is called substance (*ousia*), the underlying or sub-ject (*to hupokeimenon*), "the what it was to be" (*to ti ên einai*), this particular (*tode ti*), and "What is?" (*ti esti*). The interrogative form is crucial, for it points to the fact that what is usually a subject (*hupokeimenon*) gets thrust into a predicate position in the question "What is it?" For the most part substance is taken for granted as whatever can be named. To make it a predicate like all the other categories (it is, after all, one of them) is to problematize what is ordinarily taken for granted. Now, to make "What is it?" a predicate amounts to putting a "the" in front of it (*to ti estin*; 1028a14), thus making it a subject or substance able to be a predicate only in a question. This is equivalent to asking "What is 'what is'?" The movement from "What is it?" to "What is 'what is'?" seems fundamental to the primary category of being; *ousia* is what provokes a question about itself by virtue of being taken for granted. It is the most fully revealed and most fully concealed thing, at once the determinate "the" and the indeterminate "What is it?" This is the reason for its double characterization.

Ordinarily a substance is a subject—that of which all else is predicated and which is predicated of nothing else. When we say the dog is black, we must assume that we know what the dog is—it is what we are calling black. Yet to name it makes it possible to ask "What is dog?" Accordingly, dog as substance is both determinate and indeterminate. To ask what it is means that we do not know what it is. At the same time, to ask what it is means that we must have been able to single it out as a being about which it is possible to ask. It is not simply determinate, or we would not have to ask what it is; it is not simply indeterminate, or we would not be able to ask what it is. The being of something then seems to be that which makes it possible to ask what it is. Our experience of being as being—and not as a kind of being—is therefore intimately connected to our experience of questioning. This is the connection between being and philosophy. If philosophy is first about being, it is at the same time about itself—it is autobiographical.

> And indeed what was of old, is now and will always be sought and always be perplexing—What is being?—this is What is substance? (1028b2–4)

To see what Aristotle has in mind, one need only remember that he has characterized substance as the "what is" of a thing. The question of being reduces to the question of substance, but the question of substance is the question of the "what is." Accordingly, what never ceases to perplex us is the question "What is 'what is'?" Being is that which calls itself into question. It is whatever makes the ongoing activity of questioning possible in the world.

This sheds light on some peculiar features of the *Metaphysics*. Aristotle begins the book about being with a claim about the human longing to know because the power of being is revealed in our longing to know. The digression to the origin of philosophy in wonder is really no digression at all, for philosophy is merely the most distilled version of that spirit of questioning distinguishing human beings as such. In a way, the true subject of the *Metaphysics* is simply to point to and articulate as far as is feasible the grounds for the possibility of philosophy. The structure of wonder underlies the philosophical history of causality that Aristotle offers in the remainder of the first book of the *Metaphysics*. Its possibility is rooted in what enables us to ask questions; this is what Aristotle ultimately means by being, *ousia* and the "what is." Its doubleness as at once most available and always hidden is what makes "the beholding of the truth on the one hand hard and on the other hand easy" (993a30–31). Aristotle's second beginning in the *Metaphysics* (the discussion of seventeen *aporiai* in Book B), in articulating the necessarily aporetic structure of our most fundamental questions, therefore in its way articulates the structure of being—what ensures that the question "What is 'what is'?" will always be perplexing. The exploration of these perplexities occupies the remainder of the *Metaphysics*.

The *Metaphysics* is concerned with what Aristotle calls first philosophy.[13] At the end of the first book Aristotle seems to make a remark about the first philosophy—that is the philosophy that first emerged historically. Yet if we understand the phrase *hê prôtê philosophia* to mean here what it means everywhere else in Aristotle, it would be a reference to first philosophy understood as theology or metaphysics. "For first philosophy is like one mumbling about everything inasmuch as it is fresh (*nea*) and in accordance with first principles (*archas*)" (993a15–16). It is the very being of first philosophy to mumble insofar as it articulates what is always perplexing and has power as that which is always perplexing. The object of first philosophy as that which makes it possible to ask questions of beings in the world is at the same time what makes it reasonable that all men by nature desire to know. The experience of putting a question to the world is at the same time the experience of expecting an answer. There is something about a world that supports the possibility of questions that also leads us to expect answers. If this something is being, then for the being who most of all desires to know, being is good. That Aristotle's *Metaphysics* as a whole is a thinking through of this sense of final causality is first apparent in the history of philosophy presented in the first book, with its emphasis on the causal power of truths incompletely present in the mumblings of first philosophy. The fact of questions is the evidence for teleology in the world; the goodness of being is manifest in the nature of philosophy. Accordingly, first philosophy is autobiographical philosophy.

NOTES

1. The central role played by the *Metaphysics* is perhaps most obvious when one reflects on the passion with which it has been attacked by modern philosophers.

> When dealing with natural things we will, then, never derive any explanations from the purposes which God or nature may have had in view when creating them <and we shall entirely banish from our philosophy the search for final causes>. (René Descartes, *Principles of Philosophy* in *The Philosophical Writings of Descartes*, John Cottingham, Robert Stoothoff, and Dugald Murdoch, trans. [Cambridge: 1985], vol. 1, section 28)

In appealing to final causes the human mind "mixes up its own nature with the nature of things" (Francis Bacon, "Plan of the Great Instauration," in *The Works of Francis Bacon*, J. Spedding, R. L. Ellis, and D. D. Heath eds. [Boston: Little, Brown, 1861], vol. 4, 27). For the founders of modern science, final causality, a result of wishful thinking, tells us more about our own natures than about nature. In a watered down form, it may yet belong to psychology (we are goal directed), but, as Descartes foretold, it has been banished from physics.

Now, of the ancient philosophers, "Aristotle," according to Bacon, "is more to be blamed than Plato" (*Works*, vol. 4, 364). It is Christian Aristotelianism—"the speculative philosophy that is taught in the schools"—that Descartes proposes to replace with his new scientific method (Descartes, *Discours de la Méthode* [Paris: Vrin, 1946], 122). Thomas Hobbes, like his fellow founders, is critical of the Greek philosophers generally.

> The natural philosophy of those schools was rather a dream than a science, and set forth in senseless and insignificant language. . . . Their moral philosophy is but a description of their own passions. (Thomas Hobbes, *Leviathan* [Oxford: Blackwell, 1957], fourth part, chapter 46)

Yet Hobbes, too, singles out Aristotle for the most blame. "And I believe that scarce anything can be more absurdly said in natural philosophy, than that which is now called *Aristotle's Metaphysics* . . ." (Hobbes, fourth part, chapter 46). For the founders of the modern scientific project, then, final causality is the enemy, Aristotle its champion, and the *Metaphysics* the primary theater of the war between ancients and moderns. One cannot help wonder at the uniformity of purpose present in this angry rejection of final causality. Its very passion tempts us to take a second look at its cause.

2. For an account of the beginning of the *Metaphysics*, see Seth Benardete, "On Wisdom and Philosophy: The First Two Chapters of Aristotle's Metaphysics A," *Review of Metaphysics* (1978): 205–15. What follows is an account of the rest of book A, but it is deeply indebted to Benardete's analysis of the first two chapters.

3. See *Physics*, 184b24–25 as well as 194b16–23.

4. *Physics*, 194b24–25.

5. *Metaphysics*, 982b11–17.

6. Aristotle goes out of his way to emphasize the chronological order by noting an exception, saying that he will treat Anaxagoras after Empedocles because "while he [Anaxagoras] was with respect to age prior to him, he was with respect to deeds later" (984a12–13). The exceptions begin with Parmenides, who is first introduced after Empedocles and Anaxagoras, although he precedes them by fifteen years. Aristotle also discusses the Pythagoreans and Alcmaeon after his discussion of Leucippus and Democritus although they may have come as much as one hundred years before. Finally, of the three monists—Parmenides, Melissus, and Xenophanes—Xenophanes is mentioned last although he seems to have come first by at least fifty years.

7. See 980b27–981a12.

8. Aristotle, therefore, tentatively links him to Homer, who made Ocean and Tethys "parents of coming to be" (983b30–31)—that is, as gods they are alive and so have an inner principle of motion. And, although Aristotle disparages Hippo "on account of the simplemindedness of his thought" (984a4–5), he links him with Thales as well. At *De Anima* 405b2–6 Aristotle cites Hippo as one of those who identified soul with water because seed or semen is moist.

9. For the following interpretation of 984b23–985a10 I am indebted to Seth Benardete. See also 1072a27–b5 where, in connection with the unmoved mover as final cause, Aristotle makes it clear that our thinking is not separable from our longing—from *erôs*. Only the desired and the intelligible move without being themselves moved.

10. For Hesiod the cosmos originates in sexual coupling; there is a connection between such copulation and the copula.

11. That they can do so even while coming before suggests that the order of philosophical development outlined in *Metaphysics* A is only one possible order, for the urge to reduce things to material causes might have been an urge to reduce things to formal causes.

12. Aristotle acknowledges that this is the case at 988b5–20.

13. The phrase occurs rarely in Aristotle. In the Metaphysics it occurs five times: 1026a16, 24, and 30 in book H, 1061b19 in book K, and in a what seems to be an altogether different way at 983a16 in book A. It also occurs at *De Caelo*, 277b10, *Meteorologica*, 700b9, and *Physics*, 194b14.

4

PHILOSOPHY AND FRIENDSHIP:
THE QUESTION OF THE GOOD IN
PLATO'S *LYSIS*

Platonic dialogues border between the alien and the familiar. While death is a subject of common human concern, in the *Phaedo* the truth of what most men understand by death turns out to be philosophy. The *Philebus*, *Symposium*, and *Republic* begin with the everyday, but the proper understandings of pleasure, love and justice prove likewise to be philosophy. The *Lysis*, familiar to us as the dialogue on friendship, is also not simply about what it seems, for friendship, properly understood, is philosophy. If this is true, the verb *philein*—to love—ought, in the end, to be a synonym for the verb *philosophein*—to philosophize. In our ordinary experience the object of philosophy—wisdom—is incorporated into its process. Accordingly, philosophy becomes the love of philosophy, which, in turn, becomes the love of the love of philosophy and so on in an endless progression. Thinking is necessarily inseparable from the ultimate object of thought. The dialogue on friendship is, not accidentally, devoted to articulating this necessity.[1]

The *Lysis* is an aporetic dialogue; in the end we have examined a series of unsatisfactory versions of what a friend is and are left to wonder whether friendship is even possible. There seems nothing for human beings between the isolation of absolute selfishness—love of one's own—and the isolation of absolute selflessness—love of something altogether other.[2] But perhaps the question should rather be whether these two extremes out of which Socrates, Lysis, and Menexenus repeatedly fail to compose an understanding of friendship are possible in their own right. Perhaps *philia*, which looks to be derivative from self-love and

67

love of the good, is really their antecedent. To see what this might mean requires a closer look at some of the details of the *Lysis*.

The traditional puzzle of the dialogue is the relation between *erôs* and *philia*.[3] The *Lysis* begins with a long prologue concerned with Hippothales' *erôs* for Lysis that provides the frame for Socrates' subsequent conversations with Lysis and Menexenus about what a friend is. Walking along outside the city wall, Socrates is accosted by Hippothales and encouraged to join the group of young men hanging out at a new palaestra. Socrates seems altogether uninterested, until Hippothales blushes at one of his questions. The blush makes public in a way that language never can that Hippothales has private motives, and that he has these private passions makes him interesting to Socrates.

Socrates agrees to converse with Lysis for Hippothales' benefit, to show him how to hunt a beloved. Naturally, one does not hunt a beloved by being perfectly straightforward.[4] Accordingly, Socrates' conversation with Lysis will have throughout a concealed motive; it will be ironic. At the same time, within this conversation Socrates will agree to attempt to refute Lysis' friend Menexenus in the way he had just refuted Lysis. Now, to Menexenus this conversation seems to be a dialogue in which he and Socrates are simply pursuing the true answer to the question "Who is the friend?" Socrates' and Lysis' secret plan to humble Menexenus is contained within Socrates' and Hippothales' secret plan to humble Lysis. Lest we be tempted to stop the regress here, the conversation with Hippothales is not without its dissimulation. The *Lysis* is a dialogue narrated by Socrates to an unnamed auditor. It is a dialogue (if a rather one sided dialogue in which Socrates talks and another simply listens) in which the conversation with Hippothales is shown to be worth repeating and so in some way exemplary. That is, it has a purpose other than the one it first appeared to have. Just as Hippothales' blush reveals that he has secrets, Socrates has his own reasons for talking to Hippothales.

Narration is always concealed dialogue. It seems addressed to no one in particular and so seems simply an account of what is as it is with no accommodation to an audience. And this narration to an anonymous auditor is in principle not different from Plato's presentation of Socrates' narration. Both appear to hold nothing back; it is as though they were addressed to perfect friends—so interested in what is being said as to lose sight altogether of their own interest (compare 206c–d and 213d).

However, to take a narration or a book in this way is to miss half the whole. Had Plato named the auditor of the *Lysis* or even given him some personality by dint of what Socrates addresses directly to him, then we would have had some clue of Socrates' ironic distance in this conversation. As it is, Socrates might almost be talking to himself. The form of the *Lysis* allows him to converse with a person with an indeterminate personality. We know *that* his speeches are directed toward another, and so *that* there will be a discrepancy between what he thinks and what he says, but, as we are unable to say who that other is, we are unable to specify the discrepancy. The *Lysis*, therefore, gives us only half a conversation; the other half is a silence in principle meaningful but in fact indeterminate. There is an other present whose sole purpose is to be other. Still, this anonymous auditor may be the most important character in the dialogue.

After finishing his first conversation with Lysis, Socrates looks over to Hippothales and is about to say aloud that this is the manner in which one should speak to a beloved. He remarks to the auditor that he almost erred—he almost spoke openly to Hippothales in the presence of Lysis, collapsing the two levels, narrative and dramatic, of his conversation. Socrates catches himself when he sees how embarrassed Hippothales is already. In the scene that follows, Menexenus returns to sit down next to them, and Lysis, whispering, tries to convince Socrates to humble his friend. Since neither Menexenus nor Ktesippus, who are sitting close by, hear what is said, clearly Hippothales, some distance off, cannot hear. So Hippothales, already quite unnerved, sees Socrates look over at him, suppress a remark, and begin whispering to Lysis. What is he to think? What are we to think? Everything conspires here to show us how exclusive a thing intimacy is. Socrates has a secret arrangement with each of these young men. It is as though he says, "What I share with you I will share with no other." But he cannot really do that with more than one person. Is it possible, then, when Socrates goes on to announce to Menexenus that he has always been erotically disposed toward the possession of friends (211e), that the whole point might be the plural? Most friendships are founded on a principle of exclusivity: you are my friend because I will tell no other what I am telling you. Socrates' impulsive desire to collapse narrative and dramatic levels seems to be nothing other than his erotic longing for more than one friend. It is his thus far unfulfilled longing to be able to speak unironically. The existence of the anonymous auditor—the other in principle—points to what thwarts the satisfaction of this longing. If one can even imagine another to whom a conversation can be narrated, complete openness with one's interlocutor is foreclosed. And, of course, to the extent to which thinking is simply talking to ourselves (i.e., a relation in which part of us listens to what the other part says), no speech will be altogether in the open. Accordingly, the *Lysis* begins with a series of dramatic actions that move the scene progressively further inside the palaestra until we are in an undressing room. We are pursuing the naked truth, but the difficulty is that what is from one point of view revealed in its nakedness, from another point of view simply conceals something else from view. The awareness that speaking (*legein*) in every case presupposes dialogue or conversing (*dialegesthai*) is what distinguishes those Socrates calls "most wise" from the poets, whom he calls "like fathers of wisdom for us and guides" (214a).

> "Have you not then happened upon the writings of the most wise, saying these things—that it is necessary for like always to be friend to like? These, I suppose, are those conversing and writing about nature and the whole?"
> "You speak truly," he said.
> "Then," I said, "do they speak well?"
> "Perhaps," he said.
> "Perhaps," I said, "with respect to half of it, but perhaps also with respect to all, but we do not understand." (214b)

Why does Socrates introduce the poets as our guides only to cast doubt on their wisdom by comparing them immediately to those who are "most wise"? The two differ in at least two ways. While the poets are said to speak (*legein*), the most wise are said to converse (*dialegesthai*)—only their writings speak. Second, the poet makes a god responsible for always bringing likes together while, according to the most wise, like must always be friend to like.[5] But if the two must be forced together by a god, then they must be able to exist apart from each other.[6] Poets guide us by vividly articulating the elements of certain problems. But they also reify what were at first only elements of a problem arrived at by analysis. Poets animate and personify; they create gods to stand as magnificent metaphors for the necessary relations among things (see

211e). They thus present as separable in fact what are only separate in thought. To make the necessary connections among things visible—to speak them—the poets present the necessary togetherness of things as though it were only contingent. They take what is the result of a question—a part of a conversation—and treat it as though it has a being independent of the question, presenting a part as though it were the whole. Only by recovering the question to which their *logos* is a reply—i.e., only by coming to see that it is only a part—do we discover the larger whole that it implies. This is why Socrates specifies that the most wise converse (even if their writings speak) while the poets only speak. The beings celebrated by the poets are artificial; the discovery of this artifice is what it means to converse (*dialegesthai*) about nature and the whole.

The *Lysis* teaches us that despite appearances *dialegesthai* is prior to *legein*. Socrates' conversations seem always to have an ironic distance—*legein* as private thought seems to precede *dialegesthai*; however, in the *Lysis* every ulterior motive distancing Socrates from his interlocutor presupposes a prior conversation in which it is articulated to another interlocutor. This whole issue arises in a similar way in Plato's *Timaeus* (48ff.). Timaeus is in the midst of giving an account of *khôra* or place (it is what he will call the receptacle of being—where being comes to be) as the only thing about which we can say "this" (he uses both *touto* and *tode*). Everything else is a "such"—a *toiouto*. That in which attributes inhere can never be said because, as particular, it necessarily escapes speech, which points to what is common or comparable. It is something like this that makes it so difficult for Hippothales to tell what the "here" is to which he invites Socrates at the outset of the *Lysis*. "Here" like "this" cannot be articulated without destroying the difference between itself and the class of which it is an instance.

Now, having said something like this, Timaeus recognizes that he has in some way not gone far enough and so begins again (50a-b). Yet nothing in this second sailing in search of *khôra* appears particularly new other than the fact that it is presented as a dialogue: if someone were to model all possible figures out of gold and someone else were to ask what one of the figures was, and so forth. This imagined conversation allows Timaeus to show that *khôra* is only intelligible as an answer to the question *ti esti*—what is it? This indeterminate something that has, and can have, no attributes is made manifest only by virtue of our questioning what makes the attributes of something hang together. Timaeus' second version thus reveals that there can be no account of the coming to be of particular things—of nature—apart from him for whom they come to be. But this is once again the priority of *dialegesthai* to *legein*. Timaeus' first account of *khôra* is poetic; it treats the receptacle as though it were a being in its own right. But on reflection one sees that this is only a part of the story; the most wise realize that *khôra*, the universal principle of particularity, is, in a way, a psychic phenomenon. *Sein* shows itself by way of *Dasein*, *ousia* by way of the question *ti esti*. Trees and *khôria*, by themselves, refuse to teach Socrates anything (*Phaedrus* 230d). The nature we thought to be altogether apart from us is unintelligible except as an answer to a question that we put. Our feeling of alienation from nature, which makes us the hunters and it the hunted, only makes sense in the context of a more fundamental kinship with it. The world is user-friendly. Just as *dialegesthai* is prior to *legein*, *philia* is presupposed by the alienation at the heart of our experience of *erôs*.[7]

The *Lysis* makes clear that the poles of the discussion of friendship are love of one's own—*to oikeion*—and love of the good. Even before directly raising the question of who the friend is, Socrates has had a long conversation in which he weans Lysis from his attachment to his kin (*oikeioi*) by arguing that he who is most good in the sense of useful will be most loved (*philein*). It seems one does not love one's own because it is one's own but because it is good. On the other hand, the contentious Menexenus, whose name means "remains a stranger" and who is the one with whom Socrates first explicitly raises the question "What is the friend?", is treated to a flurry of arguments that make it quite impossible for him to settle on a single account of friendship. By the end of the dialogue Socrates has not only purified the question—the last two arguments point to *the* good and *the* kindred as the friend; he has also done something possible only in narration. At 217a Socrates addresses both Lysis and Menexenus, but only one of them answers; we have no way of knowing which. Not until 218b, when both reply, is the ambiguity clarified. This collapsing of the distinction between Lysis and Menexenus is repeated at 219c–221e. In both instances it points to the collapsing of the principles of friendship for which each of them seem to stand. Lysis may be inclined to love his kin, but since he traces his family back to Zeus, there is obviously some confusion in him between love of the good and love of his own. Menexenus, who tends to the divine matters—the altogether other—having to do with the sacrifices for the Hermeia, and who can be said to remain a stranger, seems to be involved in a relation with one of his kin—Ktesippus. No wonder, then, that Socrates should wonder at the friendship between the two, for the underlying puzzle of the dialogue is not so much whether *philia* is love of one's own or love of the good but rather how it is possible for it to be both simultaneously.

That friendship is love of one's own seems simple enough. Because my own is my own by virtue of its relation to me, there must be some unambiguous me to which things are related. Socrates can undermine Lysis' rather conventional attachment to his kin only because Lysis has not understood this. The whole first argument, while purporting to show that Lysis is only loved by his family to the extent that he is useful and is only useful to the extent that he is wise, in fact is unintelligible unless there is a deeper level of attachment to one's own. If all are *philoi* and *oikeioi* to the one who is wise (210c-d), the neighbors will prefer even the anonymous gifted and talented to their own children. Accordingly, Socrates argues that the rule (*horos*) that one's father uses to judge when to give over control of himself and his property to his own child will be the same as the rule used by his neighbor. Yet it can hardly be coincidental that *horos* has as its primary meaning the boundary line *separating* one's property, and with it the place of one's ancestral gods, from that of one's neighbors.[8] Neighbors are distinguished by *not* having the same *horos*. Our ownness is defined by our place; *horos*, like *khôra*, has something to do with the fact that we say "this" and "here."

The problem is yet clearer when Socrates asks Lysis whether the Great King would let his eldest son and heir treat a disease of his own eyes or allow the two of them to do whatever they wanted if he thought they were doctors. Does not the king's preference for competent doctors for his son have to do with the fact that he *is* his son? This emerges in yet another way when we see what the lure in all of this is for Lysis. Socrates has said that if the Great King thought they were doctors they would be allowed to do what they wanted, however whimsical, to his son the patient. Now, Lysis is attracted by the possibility of putting salt in the soup and ashes in the prince's eyes not because it is wise to do so—he possesses the arts of cookery and medicine only by hypothesis—but rather as a sign that he can do anything he wants. From the beginning, Lysis has been unsettled by a series of examples designed to show him how little freedom he possesses. He now understands wisdom to be good because, as a universal instrument to allow him to do whatever he wishes, it will release him from slavery. At the end of the argument Socrates shows him that he cannot "think big" or be vain in matters about which he does not yet think. Lysis is thus encouraged to think for the sake of being able to thing big, for the sake of being able to love himself. However, unless he already loved himself such an urging would fall on deaf ears. We want wisdom for ourselves.

> But we ourselves will be free in these things [those in which we have become prudent men (*phronimoi*)] and rulers of others. And these things will be ours, since we will profit from them. But in those things which we do not possess sense [*noun*], no one will turn it over to us to do the things seeming [best] to us, but all will impede us to the extent of their power, not only strangers but also father and mother and if there is anything [*ti*] more akin [*oikeioteron*] than these. . . . (21b–c)

There is apparently some *ti*, a neuter "something," that is more akin or his own than what Lysis at first understood to be the object of his love. This *ti* would be that in the name of which I call everything else my own. As my proper self, it is what I would have to share with another in order to be genuinely intimate. However, as it is neuter, indeterminate, and rather a sign of my referring everything to myself than an indication of what the self is to which I refer everything, such intimacy is something of an illusion. Socrates' various secret arrangements are intimacies not by virtue of any revelation of his innermost nature but rather because of the act of will involved in intimating that "I will share with you what I will share with no other." Put somewhat differently, if it is the case that intimacy is in principle possible only with one other, and if the existence of some *ti* more intimate than either father or mother means that I am ultimately most intimate with a part of myself—i.e., that there is always for me some unnamed interlocutor closer to me than the one to whom I am speaking—then, of course, this friendship with myself will preclude any friendship with another.

It looks at first as though we can only ever love ourselves. But what is this self that I love? To give it a content would mean to give it attributes and so make it comparable to other things. I love myself not because I am tall or short, beautiful or ugly, wise or silly. As Socrates' argument with Lysis shows, if I love myself because I am wise, then I must love those who are wiser more than I love myself. The *ti* is thus what makes me a "this here," which can only be known to be a this here because it is not a that there. I know this core of me only insofar as I am aware that I am not another. This is the equivalent of the priority of *dialegesthai* to *legein*.[9] I may love only myself, but I can never get hold of this self that I am supposed to love. Insofar as this most intimate something shows itself, it does so negatively; it impedes my attempts to exercise control in matters where I am not *phronimos*.[10]

The unavailability of myself to myself is confirmed in a different context later in the dialogue. In order to show that the neither good nor bad is friend to the good because of the presence of the bad, Socrates must explain what it means for something to be neither good nor bad. In the course of his argument he uses an example in which he compares hair that has been made to appear white by being rubbed with lead with hair that has become white by aging. An attribute can be either real or apparent. Either it altogether saturates the thing to which it is attributed, or it is only superficial. Now, the language of the section is quite difficult, and the boy (we do not know whether it is Lysis or Menexenus) does not quite understand. Socrates seems to rub him with an argument that he does not absorb. This last is interesting, for it suggests that to say "I do not understand" means that one is between knowledge and ignorance in the way that superficial attributes allow for something to be in between the good and the bad. This would seem to be a model for self-awareness. The you that attaches some attribute to yourself always has to think of that attribute as impermanent—something that could be otherwise. To talk to oneself means that a part of oneself speaks and so assumes knowledge (as the poets who spoke appeared to know), but another part must listen and so assume ignorance.

If self-awareness means talking to oneself, it requires positing some core of one's being that is necessarily indeterminate because never simply possessing saturating attributes. This is even clearer from the manner in which the example is presented. Socrates asks the boy to imagine what it will be like to grow old and so have hair that is naturally white. But to make sense of this example the boy must imagine himself as the same self first young and then old. The self, then, must be essentially neither. Without saying it, Socrates has thus introduced a notion of the self as something for which change over time is not essential. Now, if not even age is a saturating attribute of soul, then what about that for which aging was previously used as a metaphor—i.e., maturity, character, and, ultimately, wisdom? Soul or self cannot be essentially either good or bad, for no character is ever so completely formed that its corruption or restoration is altogether unthinkable. This is what it means to be a person. Character that had become so powerful as to leave no doubt whatsoever as to any outcome would be utterly mechanical. Good and bad would be done by instinct, and the same would hold of thinking. The gods cannot be said to philosophize because their thinking would have to be *legein* and not *dialegesthai*. Without containing some sense of the questionable or provisional, answers cease to be answers and become as mechanical as morality without temptation.

What is rubbed on in time is never simply rubbed in; this seems at first a defect. But it reveals the significance of the indeterminacy at our core for our natures as moral and thinking beings. Socrates indicates as much in the sequel. He likens himself to a hunter who has captured his prey, but then "from whence [he does] not know some most absurd [*atopôtate*—literally, most placeless] suspicion came to [him]" (218c) that their conclusion had been wrong. Their "final" conclusion fails because the final is not available to us in time or in space. It conditions our experience and so cannot be itself experienced. That we are always one step behind ourselves means that there is always some other self looking over our shoulder at what we are doing. There is always someone to whom we are talking, and so our *legein*, never altogether free of irony, is always *dialegesthai*. Like *Dasein*, the soul cannot be a part of the world even as the world cannot be apart from it.

Granted that if we are never objects of experience to ourselves, we cannot understand ourselves as the straightforward objects of our love, it is equally difficult to understand any object external to us as the real object of our love. The *Lysis* contains an explicit account of this problem, but before we even get to it we have been given a preview by the way in which the argument about saturating and superficial attributes, which seemed so final, was called into question by a voice out of nowhere. By placing it into a larger context, the inadequacy of the argument—its character as instrumental or conditional—becomes clear. If each "friend," each thing loved or held dear, is loved for the sake of something else, then that for the sake of which it is loved will be yet more dear, loved, or friend than it. But then the first friend at the beginning of this regress will be the only true friend; all the others will be mere shadows of it. This analysis reminds one of Aristotle's account of the good in the first book of the *Nicomachean Ethics* where everything is done for the sake of happiness, but happiness, as an experience of the whole of life, is unavailable from within life.[11] It reminds one as well of the account of the good as beyond being in *Republic*, book 6 (509b). The good is that which makes it possible for us to single out certain things as good for us, as in our interest. It therefore makes it possible for us to pull them out of their contexts and look at them for their own sakes while at the same time placing them in a context insofar as they are for a purpose beyond themselves. Put differently, that I have needs moves me to question and so for the first time make the things in the world questionable. However, that these questions are born of my needs skews them. The good focuses our interest by allowing us to single things out as interesting. At the same time, it can do this only by attaching the thing in which we are interested to a new context—a new whole. The good, then, which conditions everything else, could never itself be subject to conditions. But since, unlike the beautiful or the just, the good is not good unless it is real—there are beautiful illusions and just lies but not goods known to be false (*Republic* 505d)—our experience of the reality of things is linked to our experience of them as good. This means that we can never experience as real that which conditions our experience of everything else as real. The good is beyond being.[12]

When Socrates asks whether that for the sake of which something is *philon* is not also *philon*, and then whether it is more truly *philon*, he is pushing toward just such a regress. The experience of the *philon* seems to be an experience of something as "good for." Now, that in the name of which everything else is a friend could therefore not be experienced as a friend because it would be quite literally good for nothing. But why does Socrates not simply do the analysis in terms of the good? Why introduce friendship at all? When we have a friend, we have experience of something as simultaneously good in and of itself and good for. Friends are the impossible experience of the good in the world; this is what moves Aristotle to say that "without friends, no one would choose to live."[13]

Insofar as we have experience of the good in the world, we experience it as a person; this is the connection to the question of friendship.

It is no accident that Socrates' first argument with *Lysis* concludes with the view that the wise *man* is the universal object of love. Nor is it accidental that Socrates' earlier argument about whether the *philon* had to love back leads us to wonder about the construction of the word *philosophos*. Are lovers of wisdom always, in fact, lovers of wise men? Finally, that the good is experienced as a person has to do with the recurrence of the gods as an issue in the *Lysis*. That the good should appear as a person, a friend, is simply a sign of the double demand we place on it—that it should be both good for itself and instrumentally good as well.[14]

Of course, the problem with all of this is that asking why something is *philon* begins the regress. If you answer, your answer is *philon*; if you cannot answer, the reality, and therewith the goodness, of the friend is undermined. Still, it is necessary to see that since the question "Why?" itself is a form of *dialegesthai*, it presumes some interest. The undermining of one *philon* is always the positing of another. One cannot call the goodness of something into question without tacitly affirming the goodness of something else. Care is the character of our being in the world, even when apparently inauthentic.

The discovery of the "first friend" serves to undermine one's love of those shadow friends that are merely in the service of the first friend. While this is true, Socrates' own example shows that it is also problematic. It may be true that when a man's son is sick, his first love is his son—the medicine that will cure him as well as the cup that contains it are loved only instrumentally. Yet it is also true that there is no way for the father to show his love for his son apart from these signs of affection. One cannot dispense with the shadow friendships upon getting the real thing. It is not even clear that the father can experience his love for his son apart from his concern for such things as cups and medicine. The content of real love seems inseparable from shadow love.

Accordingly, the argument of the *Lysis* contains two regresses. The one points to the principle of the *oikeion*, the neuter something more akin than either mother or father, but altogether beyond experience. The other points to the good, the first friend in the name of which all others are friends, but also altogether beyond experience. These two poles of friendship have something to do with the two dramatic foci of the dialogue. Hippothales begins with a view according to which love, *erôs*, is of the beautiful, understood as an altogether unapproachable object. Socrates therefore tries to teach him that any beloved is for the sake of oneself—that *erôs* is a species of hunting. Lysis begins with a view that love means love of one's own, one's *oikeioi*, and so, finally, of oneself. Socrates tries to teach him that ultimately the *oikeion* is unintelligible without the "other." According to the *Lysis*, these first principles, the *ti* and the first friend, are not so primary as they seem but are derivative from a prior experience—*philein*. The experience of things and people as being dear, when analyzed, forces us into the language of the first friend and the self. Verb gives way to noun. When these results of analysis are taken as self-subsisting beings (in the way of the poets), they destroy the possibility of that from which they are derived. The absolutizing of the good necessary to understand the existence of good things undermines the existence of those good things. It is in this sense that the good is our enemy (220e). And the absolutizing of the privacy of the self necessary to understand "true" as opposed to superficial *philia* (i.e., the demand that you love me for my*self* and not my attributes) makes any *philia* as communication impossible. The *Lysis* is an attempt to reveal the original phenomenon, *philein*, without being forced to explain it solely in terms of these things that ultimately undermine its possibility.

Put somewhat differently, Socrates shows that to experience oneself means to experience oneself as a focus of interest—that by which other things are measured. However, this is nothing but the experience of the world as good for—i.e., *philein*. Similarly, to experience the good, the first friend, is nothing but the experience of the world as good for. Neither the good, the principle of being in the world, nor the self are really beings; they do not exist independently as causes. They are results of analysis; the primary phenomenon is *philia*, the experience of something as dear for me. Were it not the case that we were connected in some fundamental way to the world—to nature—the experience of ourselves as alienated would be altogether impossible. Thus, the argument of the *Lysis* is aporetic—the tension within *philia* between one's own and the good is never resolved. But the action of the dialogue traces the dependence of Hippothales' alienating *erôs* on what is more fundamental—*philia*.

In the first sentence of the *Lysis*, Socrates describes his movement by saying that he was making his way "from the Academy directly toward the *Lyceum* (*euthu Lukeiou*)." *Euthu* plus a genitive occurs only six times in all of Plato's writing, thrice on the first page of the *Lysis*.

The use of a genitive to express motion toward is uncommon in Greek; one would ordinarily expect an accusative. This peculiarity in the language seems connected to the peculiarity of the motion it describes at the outset of the *Lysis*. Having begun the narration by telling us that he was making his way directly toward the Lyceum, Socrates repeats himself in the conversation he proceeds to narrate. Hippothales asks him where he is going, and Socrates replies *"euthu Lukeiou"* (203b2). After this Hippothales urges him to come instead directly to us—*euthu hêmôn* (203b3). We are at first startled by Socrates' reaction " 'Where,' I said, 'do you mean, and whom are you with?' " Apparently it is not so simple to come *euthu hêmôn*, for although Socrates clearly sees Hippothales, he finds it necessary to ask where "here" is. Hippothales proceeds to show Socrates a door opposite the wall. But even this is not *euthu hêmôn*, for we then follow him progressively further inside the palaestra. So "directly to us" turns out to mean not where Hippothales is but where he is drawn and intends to take Socrates. He is at first directing Socrates to a way to a place and not to the place itself. "We" are apparently hard to get to "directly." Coming to what is "of us" is not coming to us. Similarly, although Socrates was headed *euthu Lukeiou*, he was apparently content to stop at this new palaestra. If his initial movement was actually toward the things belonging to the Lyceum, such things might be available wherever young men congregate to exercise.

In the *Lysis* Socrates seeks an answer to the question "What is the friend?" But if *philia* is what makes all seeking possible, what we seek in the *Lysis* will not make its appearance directly, for to do so is to risk losing its character as a way. In becoming a noun, it ceases to show itself as a verb, or, to follow the philosophical grammar of the *Lysis*, in becoming accusative, it would cease to show itself as a genitive and less determinate object of motion. For when we seek the first friend, we always perforce seek what belongs to the first friend even as we want more. Socrates' desire from childhood, his "holding erotically toward the possession of friends," is the same as his longing to make an end out of the way to the end without destroying its character as a way. This is what would be necessary to grasp the nature of philosophy. One can no more set as a goal to make friends, *philein*, than one can set out as a goal to hold a conversation, *dialegesthai*. Both are always of something else. But *dialegesthai* and *philia* are not for this reason less important than the ends they seem to serve. The account in the *Lysis* of *philein*—the verb to love, befriend, or hold dear—in its way, then, points to the strange, but by now familiar, fact that the ultimate object of philosophy is double, and in neither guise can it be approached directly. On the one hand, it is the activity of philosophy itself; on the other hand, this is just to say that the object of philosophy is being. To the extent that "it is the same thing to think and to be," philosophy is the autobiography of philosophy.[15]

NOTES

1. The importance of friendship for Greek thinkers generally cannot be overstated. According to Aristotle, *philia* is that without which no one would choose to live even having all the other goods (*Nicomachean Ethics*, 1155a5–6). It is the cosmic binding principle in Empedocles' poem *On Nature* (see fragments 17 and 26) and the one word that Sophocles' Oedipus claims has made all of his suffering worth it (*Oedipus in Colonus*, 1611–19). While friendship has not ceased to be of practical concern, it has clearly lost for us the theoretical import it once had.

2. A reflection of this sort must have moved Francis Bacon to say that "those who want friends to open themselves unto are cannibals of their own hearts" ("Of Friendship").

3. For an account of the controversy surrounding this issue, especially between Pohlenz and von Arnhim, see David Bolotin, *Plato's Dialogue on Friendship* (Ithaca, N.Y.: Cornell University Press, 1979), 201–5.

4. Compare *Sophist*, 219b.

5. Socrates quotes a singularly inappropriate passage from Homer's *Odyssey* (17.218): "Always a god leads like to like." The two in question, Odysseus and Eumaeus, are explicitly said to be alike in being bad. In the context there are layers of ambiguity. Odysseus is disguised as a beggar, and Eumaeus claims to be a swineherd only in appearance but really to be the son of a prince.

6. This distinction is found elsewhere in Plato. At *Phaedo*, 60b, Socrates comments on how strange pleasure and pain are so that pursuing the one and getting it will generally necessitate that one take the other as well. It is as though the two were suspended from one head. He then goes on to say that if Aesop had thought to, he would have made a story about how the two were at war and the god, wishing to reconcile them, fastened their heads together. Once again a poet is responsible for an account according to which two things, otherwise quite separate, are put together by a god. And the story is meant to be a poetic explanation for how these two things are in principle inseparable.

7. In the *Lysis*, beauty is identified from the outset as the object of erotic

love. Early on (204b) Hippothales states the principle of erotic attraction as *allos allôi hemôn doikei*—a different one seems [beautiful] to each different one of us. *Erôs* is therefore presented as something differentiating us from others; in emphasizing our otherness, *erôs* alienates us—it assures that we remain a stranger (*mene-xenos*).

8. See *Laws*, 842e-43a and Numa Fustel de Coulanges, *The Ancient City* (New York: Doubleday, 1956), II.6.

9. This negatively determined "something" bears comparing to something never mentioned in the *Lysis* but prominent in the *Republic*—*thumos*. *Thumos* is a sense of anger against the violation of oneself, of one's integrity or wholeness. As essentially reactive, it is without positive content. *Thumos* is clearly what moves Lysis to reject his parents in this dialogue; his resentment at being enslaved is clear from the fact that Socrates is able to engender in him "desires" to do things he heretofore has been altogether unconcerned with (e.g., driving the family mules) solely because they have been forbidden him. In light of this, it is interesting that Aristotle says of *thumos* that "this is the power of the soul by which we love [*philoumen*]" (*Politics*, 1328a1). See also *Republic*, 439e ff.

10. Compare *Apology*, 31d ff., and *Theages*, 128d, with *Lysis*, 211d-212a. The *Lysis* and *Theages* are connected in several ways at first hard to understand. Along with the *Meno*, the two are the only Platonic dialogues in which neither *nomos* nor any word cognate with it occurs. And along with the *Gorgias* they are the only dialogues in which the word *euthu* occurs followed by a genitive. This occurs six times in Plato—in the *Gorgias* (525a6), in the *Theages* (129a3, d6), and thrice on the first page of the *Lysis*.

11. See especially *Nicomachean Ethics*, 1100a-1101b.

12. For this account of the good in the *Republic* see Seth Benardete, *Socrates' Second Sailing* (Chicago: University of Chicago Press, 1989), 153–56.

13. *Nicomachean Ethics*, 1156a.

14. This is connected to another issue present from the outset of the *Lysis*, the relation of the beautiful to the good, as well as to the relation of *erôs* to *philia*.

15. *to gar auto noein estin te kai einai*—Parmenides, fragment 3 in *The Presocratics*, M. R. Wright, ed. (Bristol, Great Britain: Bristol Classical Press, 1985), 14.

PARABASIS

H eidegger begins with the question of being in a degenerate, although perhaps naturally degenerate, form. Its restoration requires
that our ordinary understanding of being as objective—as *vorhanden*—be
replaced by an understanding of it as ready to hand or for us—as *zuhan-
den*. This, in turn, leads us to realize the importance of this "us"—of
Dasein—for the question of being. The meaning of *Dasein* shows itself
finally as care. Being, as that which appears, cannot show itself apart
from a simultaneous showing of that being to whom it appears. As all
appearing to such a being is for the sake of some end or purpose, the
twin concerns of philosophy, the true and the good, are somehow one.
And since openness to being is inseparable from being, the question of
being and the question of philosophy are also one. Philosophy is the
autobiography of philosophy.

Nietzsche begins with the question of the good and seems at first to
disparage the question of being. We are located in the world in such a
way that each of us has an a priori that reveals itself in the questions we
bring to the world. By calling our questions into question, we may lay
bare this a priori and reveal to ourselves the good, the system of value,
that constitutes us and thereby reveal to ourselves the world constituted
by our being in the world. Yet Nietzsche does not stop here. By raising
the question of the value of values as such, *On the Genealogy of Morals*
seeks to lay bare the conditions for every a priori. If the good is the
condition for being, to ask after the being of the good is to ask after the
condition for all being in its relation to that being open to it and for
whom it is good. For Nietzsche, too, philosophy is the autobiography
of philosophy.

In their different ways, both Heidegger and Nietzsche are aware of the difficulty of saying what they say. As being cannot be understood as an object, it does not admit of an objective account. Somehow, the peculiar character of the proper account of being must be a part of its proper account. For the Heidegger of *Being and Time*, this way of giving an account is named doubly phenomenology and fundamental ontology; for the Nietzsche of *On the Genealogy of Morals*, it is called genealogy. Heidegger must therefore provide us with a phenomenology of phenomenology and Nietzsche with a genealogy of genealogy.

Aristotle's *Metaphysics* has a double beginning: in the desire to know, which leads ultimately to the question of philosophy, and in the question of being. The two come together in the first book in final causality; once again it is the good that calls our attention to the fact that "being and thinking are one" so that an inquiry into one cannot escape being an inquiry into the other.

The *Lysis*, not obviously about either being or philosophy, nevertheless reveals the togetherness of the two. Socrates' question about the friend leads in two directions. It points, on the one hand, to the self that is so singular that it cannot be known as anything other than whatever it is that gives me a single point of view—that makes the world my world and thus open to me. On the other hand, it points to what is good universally, simply, and not for the sake of anything else. Both poles prove to be "beyond being" in the sense that, as conditions for the possibility of my experience of anything, they are never themselves objects of my experience but appear always already in combination in experiences like *philein* and *dialegesthai*. Because they show themselves by what they do—as verbs—they are revealed by *logos* only in its action—*dialegesthai*, conversation or dialectic. Like all Platonic dialogues, the *Lysis* raises a question that is answered only when one realizes why it cannot be answered in the form in which it was initially raised. This Platonic reflection on the necessarily indirect character of any account of what is most fundamental is apparent in the action of philosophic dialogue, the importance of which every Platonic dialogue is in some way about. All specific beings called into question in Platonic dialogues (friendship, justice, love, etc.) lead back to philosophy as their truth. To reflect on this fact is to reflect on what it means for them to be. Being and thinking are one.

It is not immediately obvious what any of this has to do with Rousseau, who is certainly much less openly metaphysical than any of the thinkers we have thus far discussed. Rousseau does not begin with being but with a human being—himself. At first this seems not to distinguish his thought from Heidegger's turn to *Dasein* or Nietzsche's insistence that each of us has our a priori or Aristotle's beginning an account of being with the human desire to know. Yet it is one thing to announce the importance of the particular and another thing to do justice to it in its particularity. It may be that "*Dasein* is determined altogether through mineness,"[1] but to show adequately the meaning of this mineness in general would be possible only by way of a powerful example of it in particular. *The Reveries of the Solitary Walker* at first appears straightforwardly autobiographical. Rousseau makes explicit claims only about his solitary nature and the unique situation of his soul. But if every soul is constituted by uniqueness and isolation, and if all experience of things and of other human beings can be understood only in light of this isolation, then Rousseau's examination of his own soul is a paradigm for an examination of soul generally in its relation to the world. It is as though, before the fact, Rousseau had attempted to represent *Dasein* prephilosophically on one level in order to understand it philosophically on a deeper level. Part one traced the discovery of the soul, and hence philosophy, in all things. Part two will trace Rousseau's discovery of the ground for the togetherness of soul and world in the paradigmatic character of his idiosyncratic soul. The story of this discovery is *The Reveries of the Solitary Walker.*

NOTE

1. *Sein und Zeit*, 43.

Part Two

ROUSSEAU'S LIFE

5

SOLITUDE AND SOCIETY

1. SOLITUDE AND SOCIETY IN THE *SECOND DISCOURSE*

The Reveries of the Solitary Walker is Rousseau's autobiographical account of his exile from civilization to a life of solitude and of the unexpected contentment that results from this exile, a contentment elsewhere characterizing only man in the state of nature. The primary problem of the book is therefore Rousseau's peculiar nature. What is it that allows for his return to wholeness?[1] The impediment to understanding the *Reveries* in this manner is the *Discourse on the Origins and Foundations of Inequality among Men*,[2] where human beings, by nature born equally innocent and happy, are characterized by a simple, unreflective self-love—*amour de soi-même*.[3] We are also alike in being essentially adaptable. But as we realize this nature (our freedom) in the activity of changing ourselves to meet the needs of new situations, we make our equality manifest only in the act of distinguishing ourselves.[4] Each adaptation narrows our options; having made ourselves something, we are not something else. As we move along a path with various forks, each choice necessarily excludes others, and each exclusion has consequences, sometimes tragic, for how we will be able to adapt in the future. One path proves decisive, for when we fall into the twin peril of political life and rationality, our once finite desires become comparative and so infinite. Now governed by a self-love constituted by our sense of how we measure up to others—*amour-propre*, we are no longer capable of innocent happiness because there is always potentially an other in comparison with whom we are wanting. We become rational and political but also necessarily miserable, and there is no return to what we once were.

When we look at our own behavior as though through the eyes of others, we are not genuinely free, and, since our happiness consists in the experience of our own freedom, we are doomed to unhappiness. We are divided against ourselves—our self-awareness at odds with innocent happiness. We cannot even think our way back to wholeness, for thinking is what rends us in two.

There are various reasons within and without the *Second Discourse* to think that this tragedy is not Rousseau's final word on the question of human nature. It is not difficult to see that there is a discrepancy between the body of the *Second Discourse*—its account of the incurable misery of man's fallen state as political and rational—and the exaggerated praise in the introductory letter of the happy condition of citizens of Geneva. How can political life be so bad if Genevans have it so good?[5] Furthermore, Rousseau indicates to the Genevans that

> as for you, your happiness is complete; it is only necessary to enjoy it, and you have no further need in order to become perfectly happy than to know how to content yourselves in being so.[6]

This is surely strange advice from one who is about to say that civil society makes us miserable and that its true founder was the man who first said "*c'est à moi.*"[7]

Rousseau points to the difficulty of the Genevans' situation by emphasizing the ambiguity of his own situation. He is and is not a Genevan citizen. As he completes the introductory letter, Rousseau is on his way back to Geneva to have his citizenship restored.[8] Accordingly, he combines in himself being an outsider, and so having an objective perspective on Genevan life, with being an insider, and so at the same time participating in this life. This is precisely the conflict of perspectives that a book at once attacking civilization as such and dedicated to a city would have to overcome.[9] But how is it possible to be simultaneously insider and outsider, natural man and civil man, innocently conscious and self-conscious?

As the *Second Discourse* is primarily concerned with stating this tension in all its intractability, it provides only hints of a possible resolution. One hint comes directly after the preface in the *Avertissement sur les notes.*

> I have added some notes to this work according to my lazy custom of working by fits and starts. These notes sometimes stray sufficiently

from the subject as not to be good to read with the text. I have therefore thrown them back to the end of the *Discourse* in which I have tried my best to follow the straightest path. Those who might have the courage could amuse themselves the second time with beating the bushes and trying to go through the notes. There would be little harm if the others do not read them at all.[10]

Now, elsewhere he speaks with some contempt of "those who want only one agreeable and quick reading."[11] And, as we shall see, Rousseau is an especially careful writer.[12] It is unlikely that he would have increased the length of his book by almost a third if he did not wish his readers to read what he had written. This seems especially true given his habit in the *Second Discourse* of using the notes to introduce radical revisions of what he has said in the text proper.[13] At the same time, no one who has read the *Second Discourse* can have failed to notice how awkward a book it is to read. Just as one begins to follow the thread of the argument, one is directed to a note, supposedly a gloss on what one has been reading but frequently so long as to make one forget what it was supposed to be glossing.[14] This movement is accentuated by the physical difficulty of being tossed repeatedly from the front of the book to the back. We know that Rousseau could have organized his text differently. In the *First Discourse* the notes are at the bottom of the page. Since the conventions of footnotes and endnotes were still in the process of being formed in the middle of the eighteenth century, Rousseau had considerable freedom in using notes. Why, then, make it so difficult?

The effect of the notes in the *Second Discourse* is to split the reader's activity. The text proper is a reflection on reality; the notes are a reflection on the text. The one is a thinking about things, the other a thinking about what has been thought. Rousseau claims that this is his own custom—he works in fits and starts, going back over what he has already done. The *Second Discourse* as a whole, of course, presents reasoning as the death of the simple innocence that makes us content. Yet our own experience, artfully engendered by Rousseau, is not so simple. We know, because we have read his book, that it is possible to lose ourselves in thought. We are reminded of this especially in Part I of the *Second Discourse* because while thinking about the simple innocence of man in the state of nature we are constantly vexed by notes that pull us out of our innocent reflection on innocence and make us aware of ourselves.

Ironically, Rousseau scarcely interrupts our train of thought in Part II, allowing us an almost uninterrupted and untroubled reverie on our now essentially alienated natures. In these two ways Rousseau demonstrates the possibility of losing oneself in thought and so indicates that there is an analogue to the wholeness, freedom, and contentment of man in the state of nature not only on the political level in an idealized Geneva but on the level of thought itself. What the *Second Discourse* only hints at indirectly, *The Reveries of the Solitary Walker* makes thematic. In some way the state of nature exists in men always, but intermittently—there are always notes.

2. SOLITUDE AND SOCIETY IN THE FIRST WALK

Rousseau is quite explicit in saying that *The Reveries of the Solitary Walker* is only "a formless journal" in which

> I will say what I thought just as it came to me and with as little connection as the ideas of the day before [or of wakefulness—*la veille*] ordinarily have with those of the day following. (I.13)[15]

A commentary on such a journal might be open to the charge of excessive voyeurism. What is to be gained philosophically from prying into the private affairs of a man who frequently seems to have had a rather unstable and grandiose view of the importance of those affairs? On the other hand, the manuscripts of the *Reveries* clearly seem to be a final copy of the first seven walks and a much reworked draft of the last three.[16] Is it really possible to believe that Rousseau would make such elaborate revisions in what is supposed to be a haphazard collection of unrelated thoughts? One begins to wonder just how disconnected Rousseau believed the thoughts of the day before (of wakefulness) to be from the thoughts of the following day (of reflection?). While it is perhaps not so shocking that Rousseau would misrepresent his true intentions, it is still necessary to ask why he would dissemble.[17] Presumably something is to be gained from this appearance of formlessness. The appearance of a private or idiosyncratic writing seems essential to the teaching—that is, to the public or general meaning—of Rousseau's *Reveries*.

The First Walk divides in two. Its first part (paragraphs 1–11) is a description of Rousseau's condition. After an introduction (paragraph 1), Rousseau turns to his position relative to present society (paragraphs 2–8) and then to his position relative to future society (paragraphs 9–11). Its second part (paragraphs 12–15) is an account of his book, the *Reveries*, first relative to his present condition (paragraphs 12–14) and finally in relation to the future (paragraph 15). The First Walk is thus concerned with two issues. The first is Rousseau's isolation, which turns out to be social in the extreme and leads to a certain indifference that looks like autonomy. The second issue is the literary form of the *Reveries*—if it is not for publication, why write it at all? Both issues are organized on the basis of a distinction between the immediate situation and the future relative to the immediate. This common form suggests that there may be a unity underlying the dualism of the First Walk. Its two issues may turn out to be one. To see whether this is the case, we must turn to the text.

The full title of Rousseau's "journal" is *Les rêveries du promeneur solitaire. Rêveries* are a wandering of the mind—daydreaming. A *promeneur* is one who goes for a walk (*se promener*)—one who walks without necessarily having a fixed destination. From the beginning, then, Rousseau has as his aim to fix our attention on aimlessness, the principle allowing him to put together body and mind, acting and thinking, without setting them at odds with one another. They are bound together in the title of his book by their mutual aimlessness. The book's title also calls attention to its ambiguous status. The *Reveries* presumably consists of a collection of reveries. But the record of these aimless thoughts is not the same as the aimless thoughts themselves. To come into being, the record had to be recorded, in this case written down, and such writing requires reflection. Reverie might be compatible with aimless walking around, but the author of the *Reveries* can only figuratively speaking be a *promeneur*. It seems, then, that either the wandering of the *Reveries* is metaphorical (Rousseau is really at his desk) and the real "doing" here is writing, or the *Reveries* are not reveries but reports of reveries. The difference is important, for if reverie, as essentially aimless, has something to do with losing oneself, what does it mean to recommend it in writing as a cure? Following Rousseau's model, are we to make aimlessness our goal?

This doubleness of thought and action is continued in the first paragraph.

> Here I am [*me voici*], therefore, alone on the earth, having no longer
> any brother, any neighbor, any friend, any society than myself. The
> most sociable and loving of humans has been proscribed from it by a
> unanimous accord. They have sought, in the refinements of their ha-
> tred, the torment which could be cruelest to my sensible (sensitive)
> soul, and they have violently broken all the bonds that attached me to
> them. I would have loved men despite themselves. Only by ceasing
> to be it, could they have escaped my affection. They are [*les voilà*] thus
> strangers, unknowns, finally nothing for me since they have wished it.
> But I, detached from them and from everything, what am I myself?
> That is what remains for me to seek. Unhappily this seeking [*recherche*]
> must be preceded by a glance at my position. It is an idea through
> which I must necessarily pass in order to get from them to me. (I.1)

The first word of the *Reveries* is *me*—*I* in the objective case. Rousseau's
attempt to discover who he is begins by making him an object. He
looks at himself, as he had looked at Geneva, from the outside. Even his
understanding of his solitude will be social.[18] In more than one way
society and solitude are correlative terms. On the one hand, Rousseau
defines his situation as a negation of the various forms of society—he is
a man without brothers, neighbors, friends, or society. He needs what
he is not in order to recognize what he is; this is no state of nature. On
the other hand, Rousseau does not say that he has no society; he says
rather that he has none other than himself.[19] And, although he certainly
emphasizes his solitude, he also asserts that he is still the most sociable of
men. Perhaps this is the case not despite his solitude but because of it.
Perhaps the most sociable and loving man must be alone. In any case, it
is clear that only the social self can "be alone." *I* is a word never said
except in the presence of another.

Rousseau tells us that he has been proscribed or outlawed by universal accord. Now, on the one hand, this means that his isolation has a
practical cause. On the other hand, even if we had not peeked ahead to
see that Rousseau's "solitude" does not preclude frequent visitors, not
to mention the companionship of his wife, it would be clear that exile
by "unanimous accord" is an exaggeration. Since Rousseau is not even
universally known, he can scarcely be universally hated (in the Second
Walk a number of people will behave rather decently toward him). Yet
as Rousseau repeats the phrase in paragraph 3, the exaggeration seems
to be intentional.[20] Now "*un accord unanime*" is reminiscent of "*la volonté*

générale"—the general will. It is the principle upon which all political society is founded.[21] Is it possible, then, that Rousseau's isolation is not an unfortunate accident but is paradigmatic for something (see II.23–24)? Does society unify itself in its hatred for whatever Rousseau represents? One might almost say that this refined hatred (the expression is also used in I.5) that by unanimous agreement seeks to bury him alive (I.3) is something like a definition of society. If this is the case, then the *Reveries* will be about more than the sufferings of an unfortunate man. These sufferings will be meaningful, and their meaning will depend on what Rousseau represents.

Rousseau says that he would have loved men in spite of themselves—that they could only avoid his affection by ceasing *"de l'être."* One expects *d'être,* with the infinitive used as a noun, so that men could only avoid Rousseau's affection by losing their being, presumably by dying. But *l'être* seems to imply an object of the infinitive. Does it anticipate *l'affection,* the only singular noun in the neighborhood? This rather forced reading would mean that only by ceasing to be his affection can men escape it. The most natural, and least grammatical, possibilities are that only by ceasing to be men or by ceasing to be themselves can they escape Rousseau's affection. In no case is the meaning really clear, but taken together the readings are suggestive. *L'affection* has the same doubleness in French as in English, meaning either tenderness or perception—affect. Men cease to affect Rousseau when they cease to act upon him as selves. Accordingly, his love for men is contingent upon their remaining perceivable to him as selves—as agents, or, as he will later suggest, as *sujets* (I.12). Of course, for men to cease to be *sujets* is for them to cease to be men—that is, for them to cease to be. Solitude, then, is what keeps others from being real men, selves, or *sujets* for Rousseau. The fundamental question of the *Reveries* is what Rousseau is when he ceases to see other human beings as like him, as *sujets* with whom to sympathize, and begins to see them only as objects. Unhappily, Rousseau can get to himself only through them, but the preoccupation with them is what gets in the way of his knowing himself. There is no other access to himself because, for human beings, to seek (*chercher*) always means to seek again (*rechercher*); it is only the alienated self that seeks itself. The only motive for seeking oneself is the feeling of having lost oneself.[22] Accordingly, society of some sort is a precondition for solitude.[23]

In the second paragraph Rousseau turns to the strange position he has been in for almost fifteen years. In saying that it appears to him to be a dream, perhaps caused by indigestion, Rousseau suggests that his condition originates from within rather than from without. He imagines that were he to awaken from this sleep, he would find himself without pain and with his friends again. Now, later (I.12) *amis* (friends) will be replaced by *semblables*—literally, "similars." To be with friends means to be with similar beings; real solitude means there are no *semblables*. This is so painful that for the first time Rousseau compares his situation to death.[24] As a state of total indifference, death suggests the suppression of subjective distortions in our understanding and so the possibility of complete objectivity. Yet as a condition where nothing matters, in death there is no "order of things," no cosmos. Being "dragged out of the order of things" means being thrown into a world in which nothing is for anything else; it therefore does not matter how things are connected. Such a world is a little like a jigsaw puzzle that has no picture on the front and that can be put together in more than one way. You need the picture, the hope for and divination of some final solution, in order to have a motive to put the puzzle together. Without hope of some kind, understanding is not possible, even if hope itself ensures that fully objective understanding is also not possible. In a condition of total indifference, then, the world is for us "an incomprehensible chaos" (I.2) in which it is not possible to come to any understanding of oneself. Without hope the self vanishes.[25]

Rousseau begins the third paragraph by wondering how he might have foreseen his fate, but, of course, such foresight was impossible; he needed the alienating experience of being in society to understand what it means to be an outcast, an alien. Rousseau is especially perplexed that he who is so much one, who was always and is always the same, should have multiple appearances and seem to others monstrous and so not a genuine whole. Rousseau is particularly shocked that by unanimous accord an entire generation takes so much delight in burying him alive. This is their idea of the supreme torment—living death. Ironically, it will turn out to be Rousseau's idea of salvation. As a combination of opposites, it looks monstrous. Rousseau must show it to be a genuine whole.

But the real cause of Rousseau's fate is not his enemies; it is his anger. Rousseau had already made the singular significance of anger clear in the first book of *Emile*.[26] Anger differs from being hurt or sad by imputing a will to the cause of hurt. It is one thing to stub your toe; when you kick the offending stone, however, you blame it and so personify it. For Rousseau, this is the first sign of religion—imputing a will to the objects around us, we make subjects of them. Now, in Rousseau's case, his enemies can, of course, hurt him, but they hurt him much more deeply because he is unwilling simply to suffer these hurts without adding to them the much more powerful hurt of the indignity of being hurt by another.[27] Anger is a passion inextricably linked to *amour-propre*—vanity or pride. It is the result of a wound to one's sense of oneself. Thus, by attributing his fate to the conscious machinations of "enemies" and not simply to necessity, Rousseau makes things much worse for himself. He gives his enemies a hold over him.

> My agitation, my indignation plunged me into a delirium that has had no less than ten years to calm itself, and in this interval, having fallen from error to error, from fault to fault, from foolishness to foolishness, by my imprudences I have furnished to the directors of my destiny as many instruments as they have ably put to work so as to fix it [my destiny] irreversibly. (I.3)

Now, if Rousseau's destiny turns out to be reversible, then, of course, his anger will not have been so fatal as it seems here. In addition, Rousseau's conclusion is rather peculiar. If the problem is anger, then by ceasing to be angry he would break the hold of his enemies over him. But if his motive is to break the hold of his *enemies* over him, does he not still understand them as his enemies, and so is not a more fundamental anger still at work?

The solution to Rousseau's problem seems to be resignation—freedom consists in recognizing that you cannot do anything (I.4). Only in hopelessness can one gain tranquility. However, this "solution" is not so straightforward as it seems. The last sentence of the third paragraph contains the phrase "as many instruments as they have ably put to work." The fourth paragraph begins with the sentence "I struggled/ debated for a long time as violently as I did vainly." It concludes with the following sentence:

> I found in this resignation compensation for all my ills through the tranquility it provides me which could not mix with the continual toil of a resistance as painful as it is fruitless. (I.4)

This formula—as X as Y—is repeated throughout the First Walk.[28] It always leaves more in question than it seems to. Here it indicates that a nonvain struggle will not be violent and a nonfruitless resistance will not be toilsome. Tranquility is not something for which one can work. Just as the "plot" of the fall of man in the *Second Discourse* involves seeing that toiling to maintain the simple inarticulate sentiment of one's own existence—what Rousseau calls *amour de soi-même*—leads to frenetic activity incompatible with the sentiment of one's existence, in the *Reveries* Rousseau's indignation ensures the impossibility of overcoming the object of his indignation. The suggestion beginning to emerge is that out of this resigned hopelessness another sort of hope can be generated—a hope originating in what Rousseau will call "profound indifference"(I.15).

What sort of hope will this be? The "refined hatred" of Rousseau's enemies proves to be self-contradictory. They do not see that their hatred cannot be absolute. One has to keep one's enemy alive and hoping in order to keep hurting him. To be wounded means still to have hope. Enemies, therefore, can never be total enemies; perhaps without realizing it, they always have a stake in the minimal continued well-being of those they hate. If politics requires something like the distinction between friends and enemies, and if this distinction is something like "refined hatred," then politics does not admit of final solutions. Accordingly, in leaving Rousseau nothing, his enemies deprive themselves of their hatred. Had they known this in advance they would not have been much better off, however, for then they would have had to acknowledge that their hatred could not be absolute, thus also depriving themselves of it. In either instance, Rousseau indicates that without this enmity they would not be what they are.

This impossibility of total enmity points to the underlying issue in the section: hell.

> The defamation, depression, derision and opprobrium with which they have covered me are no more susceptible of augmentation than softening. We are equally out of position—they to aggravate them and me to avoid them. They were so pressed to bring the measure of my misery to its peak that all human power aided by all the tricks of hell could no longer add anything to it. (I.5)

The various ills are no more susceptible of being increased than they are of being mollified; only if they are increasable are they mollifiable. Hopelessness presupposes hope, and where there is hope there is some reason for hope. Accordingly, there is no utter deprivation, no complete unhappiness. Yet the same argument necessarily applies to happiness as well. Where you are happy you are necessarily potentially unhappy. There is no hell, but there is also no heaven. Rousseau's position, therefore, must be less perfect than he imagines it to be. How that is the case begins to become clear in the sequel.

The surface argument of paragraphs 6 through 8 is fairly straightforward. Pain is by itself not so bad. Worry (*l'inquiétude*) and fear or terror (*l'effroi*) are the real culprits. Anticipation of hurt is much worse than the actual experience; human beings are generally tyrannized by their imaginations. In a state of hopelessness we can only feel pain, not its anticipation. By rendering his position hopeless, therefore, Rousseau's enemies have really done him a favor. And habituation makes even genuine nonanticipatory pain subside. Thus, Rousseau can laugh, and so be pleased, at his enemies' attempts to hurt him.

This surface argument is not without difficulties. The relief Rousseau feels, and in which he takes pleasure, depends on the anticipation of the possibility of greater suffering. His exultation in his own freedom—that they are not able to have *l'empire* over him (Rousseau exploits the pun; *empirer* means "to hurt")—presupposes a prior worry about not being free. To the extent that Rousseau does not worry, therefore, he will approach feeling nothing rather than feeling free. He will approach the indifferent neutrality of death. This is brought out in paragraph 7 where it becomes clear that for all Rousseau's "tranquility," "unforeseen events" still have the power to make him sad. Now, that an event is "as sad as it was unforeseen" means that were it foreseen, it would not have been sad. But not being sad is not the same as being happy. Perhaps it is fortunate that Rousseau's condition proves to be less permanent than he makes it out to be.

The general issue emerges in paragraph 8 by way of Rousseau's reflections on his contemporaries. Rousseau knows them and so expects nothing from them. However, that they "will never be anything" for him is only true if they remain always as they are. Since our lives are unpredictable—the future is unknowable—Rousseau cannot be sure. That there is a future means that fundamental change is possible, and this, in turn, means that hope is always possible. The problem for Rousseau's "hopelessness" is therefore the future, and this is where the argument turns in paragraphs 9 through 11.

While it is true that his contemporaries have been poisoned against him, why is there no hope that future generations will see Rousseau as he really is? Twice in paragraph 9 Rousseau alludes to his *Dialogues*, which along with the *Confessions* and the *Reveries* constitute Rousseau's autobiographical writings. The full title of the *Dialogues* seems to have been *Rousseau juge de Jean-Jacques: Dialogues*.[29] The book contains three dialogues in which a character named Rousseau and one called "the Frenchman" discuss the discrepancy between the public reputation and the true character of an author named Jean-Jacques. This splitting of Rousseau is partly a reflection on the plot against him. Still, somehow the difference between the public and private Rousseau is not simply a function of the hostility of his age; it is a necessary condition of human existence. In a way, insofar as they can never be seen altogether as they are, all men can be said to have a plot against them. Recognizing the necessity of this gap between inside and outside releases Rousseau from any hope. As his enemies cannot get at him by means of any wish on his part to transform the world, Rousseau will not be a frustrated idealist. He therefore claims a period of absolute repose that he does not think will change.

And yet if very few days pass without thinking of the public (I.10), how absolute can his repose be? Only by locating the cause of his own condition in something abiding and not simply in an accidental plot could Rousseau know that the split between his authentic inside and his outside appearance reflects the fundamental and unchanging human predicament.

> Individuals die, but the collective body does not die at all. The same passions are perpetuated there, and their ardent hatred, immortal as the demon who inspires it, has always the same activity. (I.10)

The issue has now become metaphysical. Who is this demon who inspires hatred? Strictly speaking, it is Rousseau, or at least the public appearance of Rousseau. He would then stand for something immortal. In any case, what is at stake is more fundamental than the fate of an individual man. Rousseau goes on to say that it is the oratorians and doctors who make up the immortal bodies that will never forgive him.[30] He admits to having offended the doctors; his attack on medicine along with science generally was real. Yet perhaps they will come to forgive him in another age when they realize that at a very deep level his attack on science was in the service of science. The oratorians are another matter. They will hate him always. While he does love what they claim to love, virtue, he shows the defect in their love and so offends their vanity. Science, on the other hand, is built on the assumption that it is better to know when one is wrong. Rousseau's immortality would seem to have to do with this relation between knowledge and virtue.

The movement of the first part of the argument of the First Walk culminates in paragraph 11.

> All is finished for me on the earth. Here one can no longer do me either good or ill. There remains for me no longer anything either to hope for or to fear in this world, and here I am tranquil at the bottom of an abyss, poor mortal but impassible/unmoved as God himself. (I.11)

Rousseau has from the outset been moving toward a comparison of himself to God. By becoming as imperturbable as God, he becomes autonomous (notice what this implies about God's love of men). And yet, thus far this autonomy is entirely negative—it is freedom *from* torment, not freedom *for* anything. Rousseau therefore needs external confirmation of it. Having disposed of his contemporaries and of future generations, he needs God—an external being who unlike all others can see Rousseau as he really is.

The connection of all of this to the remainder of the First Walk is at first unclear. In paragraphs 12 through 15 Rousseau turns to the status of the *Reveries* themselves. His beginning is startling.

> Everything external to me is henceforth strange/alien to me. I have no longer in this world either neighbor, or fellows [*semblables*] or brothers. I am on the earth as on a strange planet onto which I have fallen from the one where I lived. If I recognize anything around me, they are only objects [*objets*] afflicting and rending my heart, and I am unable to cast my eyes on what touches me and surrounds me without finding there some object [*sujet*] of disdain which makes me indignant or of pain which afflicts me. (I.12)

Rousseau first sharpens the issue. Now not just men but everything external to him is strange. To be like God means that he will have no attachments at all. Only then will he be invulnerable. This is what underlies the collapsing of *objet* and *sujet*. To be sure the two can be used as synonyms, but doing so here highlights the overall movement of the argument. To treat everything as an object is to deny that one has any *semblables* in the world.

At the same time Rousseau once again hints at some doubt.

> Let us therefore separate from my mind all of the painful objects with which I occupy myself as sadly as I would uselessly. Alone for the rest of my life, since I find only in myself consolation, hope and peace, I neither ought nor want any longer to occupy myself other than with myself. . . . I consecrate my last days for myself to study myself, and to prepare in advance the account I will not delay to give of myself. Let us give ourselves up entirely to the sweetness of conversing with my soul, since it alone is what men cannot take away from me. (I.12)

The occupation with external objects is as sad as it is useless. If it were useful, then, it would not be entirely sad. Rousseau, then, might have some hope that has to do with studying himself by himself, but not altogether independent of what is external to him. He is, after all, writing a book. Granted that *livrons-nous* can mean "let me be delivered," more literally it means "let us deliver ourselves." In fact, Rousseau is inviting us to examine his soul with him. By treating himself as absolutely unique and unconnected to anything else in the world, he makes himself available to others as a model for their own condition. He makes himself as *sujet* an *objet*. The experiment of the *Reveries* is therefore to make the necessary split between the internal and the external—the split that alienates us from the world—the means to get inside the soul and so overcome human alienation. Rousseau affirms himself to be our *semblable* even as he is in the act of denying it.

The *Reveries* is an autobiographical writing in which Rousseau calls attention to his uniqueness for the sake of showing us what all human beings share. His position is thus paradoxical but not unlike the position of the man whose life is most frequently taken as a representation of philosophy—Socrates. The Socrates of Plato's *Apology* on the one hand places himself on a continuum with all human beings. What makes him distinct, his "human wisdom" consists simply in knowing that, like all other men, he does not know. He presents the life he pursues—philosophy—as the consequence of the command of a generally acknowledged god—Apollo (*Apology of Socrates*, 23b). On the other hand, Socrates gives as the cause of his way of life something absolutely unique to him—his *daimonion* (*Apology* 31c-d). The core of Socrates is at once unique and universal. Plato, of course, has a name for this core. Philosophy is both the nature of man and the practice of only a very few men. As we have seen in the case of the *Lysis*, philosophy is both the truth of the everyday and that which is perhaps most rare. Rousseau rarely mentions philosophy in the *Reveries* and then only to disparage it.[31] He seems wary of the consequences of naming what makes him simultaneously normal and exemplary, as though to do so would necessarily deflect attention from what is most important about it. To call the activity philosophy is potentially to lose sight of how it saturates everything we do; it is to make it seem academic. Yet to call the core of our being *Dasein* is perhaps to lose sight of its authentically philosophic character.

When Rousseau gives a name to what all human beings share, he calls it freedom.[32] This is what it means to attempt to give a picture of his soul "in the strangest position a mortal was ever in" (II.1). Rousseau means to depict perfect freedom. This is the connection to the aimlessness of action and thought in the title—a total lack of constraint. Yet one constraint remains. Rousseau has in mind some good to be accomplished by this depiction. The *Reveries* therefore has a moral purpose; as governed by some need, it is not the expression of perfect freedom. One could say that the *Reveries* are Rousseau's attempt to justify himself as not needing to justify himself. This issue emerges as the problem of the status of reverie in paragraphs 13 through 15.

What do Rousseau's dreams consist in? "I would forget my unhappiness, my persecutors, my opprobrium, while dreaming of the prize that my heart merited" (I.12). Reverie is thus born out of prior unhappiness. Rousseau dreams of the prize his heart merits as a way of overcoming his unmerited suffering. But somehow dreaming about unhappy events does not make him unhappy. Does this internalizing of events make *objets* out of *sujets*? Rousseau says he will fix these memories in writing (*l'écriture*), although he adds

> I will say what I thought just as it came to me and with as little con-
> nection as the ideas of the day before (or of wakefulness—*la veille*)
> ordinarily have with those of the day following. (I.13)

Rousseau himself seems to be the connection between the walks. His
periods of immediate wakefulness or experience can be followed by reflection only because the one reflecting is somehow the same as the one
who experienced. While Rousseau says that the *Reveries* will be unlike
the *Confessions* because there is nothing left for him to praise or blame,
he is surely praising this condition. Success in his project will require
two things: both the order and method characteristic of science and the
spontaneity of reverie. But how will both be possible? What exactly is
reverie? Is it the thinking of the thought? The writing down of the
thought? The writing down of something independent of its previously
having been thought? Is reverie itself an action, a thought about an action or a pure thought? And how can Rousseau claim this writing down,
which is an act of publication in some sense, to be so guileless, immediate, and spontaneous? Rousseau's complete contentment seems to depend on spontaneity (II.1); it depends on the unitary character of the
self—being imperturbable like God himself. This is what it would really
mean to be a solitary. But Rousseau ends the First Walk by pointing out
that there are two of him present in reverie.

> If in my old days at the approach of my departure I remain, as I hope,
> in the same disposition as I am, reading them will recall to me the
> sweetness that I taste in writing them, and, thus, making the time past
> be reborn for me will double, so to speak, my existence. Despite men
> I would still be able to taste the charm of society and, decrepit, I
> would live with myself at another age, as though I were living with a
> less old friend. (I.14)

This is in a way perfect society—to live with one who knows you as
you really are—yet it is identical with perfect solitude. Human autonomy requires that one live with oneself without either losing oneself
(life in the state of nature) or giving oneself up to others (*amour-propre*).
However, this does seem to involve a certain resurrection of hope on
the narrative level. Rousseau hopes to remain in the same condition.

That Rousseau knows his announced program has not simply succeeded is clear from the final paragraph of the First Walk. His statement

of "profound indifference" with regard to the fate of his writing and his sense of the utter hopelessness of any transmission to future generations does not square well with the fact that we are reading his book over two centuries later. But perhaps he means rather that even if we do receive his books, we will necessarily misunderstand them. That we see this possibility, however, once again suggests that he was too pessimistic. The logic of his conclusion is rather queer. If he had known at the time of his first calamities not to become angry at his fate, Rousseau says all the contrivances directed against him would have been to no effect. And yet to know about necessity means to know it as painful. To foresee the evils of resisting, Rousseau would have to have invented them in his imagination. Does this amount to avoiding them?

The First Walk depends on what might be called the dialectic of anger. Rousseau begins by describing a real situation in which there is little doubt that he had a great many enemies. In his anger—his *amour-propre*—he exaggerates and "idealizes" his situation, understanding it as a result of a unanimous agreement. This is, of course, the ordinary consequence of anger, a passion that regularly speaks the language of "never," "always," and "everyone." However, Rousseau sees that when this universalizing character of anger is allowed to run its course, anger turns on itself, for it implies that one is completely isolated from the world and without *semblables*. This, however, deprives anger of any appropriate object and saps its power. The reverie that was to have moved from "them to me" literally ends with the word *them* and, more precisely, with a tacit comparison between his persecutors, who enjoy Rousseau's disgrace *à leur gré*—at their will—and his finishing his days in peace *malgré*—in spite of them (or bad will to them). His whole understanding of his freedom derives from this *malgré*.

The First Walk addresses two issues that are really one. On the one hand, Rousseau's solitude, and with it his newfound happiness and freedom, is problematic. This solitude is defined in remarkably social terms and, in the end, seems to be understood as the perfect society—the togetherness of I and me. Yet it is not clear that even this society avoids the problems of the soul split against itself. The intransigence of alienation emerges in the complicated relation between hopelessness and hope. Rousseau is not vulnerable because he has no hope, but this is precisely what gives him hope on a deeper level and so seems to make him once again vulnerable. There is no life without hope and no hope without being vulnerable. The first problem of the First Walk is how happiness is compatible with life. Why is Rousseau's description of his ideal state not simply a description of death?

This leads to the second issue—reverie. What exactly is it, and how is the total spontaneity of reverie compatible with the writing of the *Reveries*? Strangely, this issue is the same as the first. If to write a book is at least potentially *publi*cation, what does it mean to write a book for oneself? The true solitary—for example, man in the state of nature— would not write. To write is to split the soul between experience and reflection on experience. The single issue of the First Walk, therefore, is the split soul of the book's title—*The Reveries of the Solitary Walker/ Wanderer.* Reverie and wandering, while alike in their aimlessness, nevertheless do not fit together easily. The problem of the Second Walk is thus set by the First Walk: What is reverie, and how does it overcome that tension between doing and thinking at the very core of the human soul?

NOTES

1. "But I, apart from them and from everything, what am I myself?" All references to Rousseau are to *Oeuvres complètes*, edited by Michel Launay, 3 vols. (Paris: Editions du Seuil, 1967). Translations are my own. The passage cited here is from vol. 1, 501.

2. Hereafter the *Second Discourse*.

3. *Oeuvres complètes*, vol. 2, 260.

4. This begins to become clear in the note to the first sentence of Rousseau's preface. Having declared the most useful, but least advanced, human knowledge to be self-knowledge, Rousseau glosses his claim with a quotation from Buffon. Buffon argues that we are not designed for self-knowledge but rather know everything better than we know ourselves. Nature designs us to "seek only to be spread without and to exist outside ourselves" (*Oeuvres complètes*, vol. 2, 248). Only our "internal sense" separates us from all that is not part of us. Our internal sense is thus the faculty responsible for such self-knowledge as is available to us, and, according to Buffon, it must be cultivated. Yet, what does our internal sense sense? To know ourselves means to know what we are. As we are essentially beings who extend ourselves beyond ourselves, sensing ourselves would require that we sense ourselves in the act of sensing other things. But then the internal sense must necessarily be derivative. How could it be possible to sense our sens-

ing purely—that is, not colored by external concerns? Sensing of sensing must always be reflective, and so self-knowledge must be secondhand—indirect. (It is interesting that Rousseau should begin to make all of this clear in a note. He relies on an external authority—Buffon—to make the argument for the primacy of inner sense.)

According to Rousseau's explicit account in the preface, self-knowledge is so little advanced because the self (here he calls it the soul) is like the statue of Glaucus, which was so long in the sea that it was disfigured by various accretions. In the passage of Plato's *Republic* to which this seems a reference (611b-d), it is soul's association with body that obscures its true nature. Rousseau indicates this, too, when he refers to "the changes happening to the constitution of bodies" (*Oeuvres complètes*, vol. 2, 208). He, therefore, agrees with Buffon, whom he has just quoted as saying

> "How to disengage our soul in which it [the internal sense] resides from all the illusions of our mind? We have lost the habit of using it; it has remained without exercise in the middle of the tumult of our bodily sensations. . . ." (*Oeuvres complètes*, vol. 2, 248)

If it is thus body that is responsible for obscuring the soul, it would seem to be body that must be stripped away in order to make self-knowledge possible.

At the same time, Rousseau identifies the corruption of the soul with the fact that it no longer acts "always by certain and invariable principles" (*Oeuvres complètes*, vol. 2, 209). Apparently our corruption is connected to our unpredictability—our freedom. The mixture of body and soul that leads to the corruption of reason by passion and of understanding by delirium is at the same time the birth of our humanity. This is confirmed in what follows.

> It is easy to see that it is in these successive changes of the human constitution that it is necessary to seek the first origin of the differences that distinguish men, who, by common avowal, are as naturally equal among themselves as were the animals of each species before diverse physical causes had introduced in some of them the varieties that we notice there. (*Oeuvres complètes*, vol. 2, 209)

But when exactly is it that all men, dogs, and so on, are equal by common avowal? Rousseau seems to imply that equality exists within a species only when they are pure. Yet Rousseau admits of a "natural or physical" inequality among men and other animals (*Oeuvres complètes*, vol. 2, 211). Equality within a species would then seem to exist only prior to its members having bodies. Or it exists logically, in the way all common nouns refer to the same thing by "common avowal." Our "natural equality" seems to be something we discover only in the act of losing it, and we lose it upon being embodied—that is, at the moment of birth.

5. This is, of course, only a preliminary version of the larger tension between the accounts of freedom in *On the Social Contract* (book I, chapter 8) and the *Second Discourse*, part I. Rousseau had already alluded to this problem in the account of virtue in his earlier *Discourse on the Arts and Sciences*. See Leo Strauss, "On the Intention of Rousseau," in *Hobbes amd Rousseau*, Maurice Cranston and Richard Peters, eds. (Garden City, N.Y.: Doubleday, 1972), 254–90.

6. *Oeuvres complètes*, vol. 2, 206.

7. *Oeuvres complètes*, vol. 2, 228.

8. See Roger Masters, ed., *The First and Second Discourses* (New York: St. Martin's Press, 1964), 229.

9. From the outset the letter calls attention to this dual perspective.

> While seeking the best maxims that good sense could dictate about the constitution of a government, *I* was so struck at seeing them all fulfilled in *yours* that, even without having been born within *your* walls, *I* would have believed myself unable to dispense with offering this picture of human society to that people who of all the rest appear to me to possess its greatest advantages and to have best prevented its abuses. (*Oeuvres complètes*, vol. 2, 204; emphasis added)

In the letter as a whole, there are repeated versions of this duality. On the one hand, Rousseau treats the Genevans as though, although living in civil society, they possess the innocence of simple unreflective natural men. As the state of nature is to the state of civil society so are the Genevans to Rousseau. On the other hand, after articulating the conditions necessary for Geneva, and so for any city, to be whole (paragraphs 1–6), Rousseau goes on to give an account of the internal articulation of Geneva into citizens and magistrates—that is, a part that initiates and a part that approves (paragraphs 7–11). Accordingly, he introduces self-consciousness into Geneva. And in the second half of the letter (paragraphs 13–22), Rousseau reveals alternative sources of authority within political life— religion and the family—that tend to undermine the experience of it as complete and whole. The letter thus maps a continuous proportion: paragraphs 2–6 : paragraphs 7–12 :: paragraphs 1–12 : paragraphs 13–22 :: *Second Discourse*, part I : *Second Discourse*, part II :: body of the *Second Discourse* : Letter to Geneva. The template for these proportions is the relation between consciousness and self-consciousness. Accordingly, the simple unreflective life of man in the state of nature is mirrored by the simple unreflective life of the citizen in the good regime just as the alienating effect of self-consciousness is already present in some form in the narrowing effect of adaptation in the state of nature. Looked at in this way, for Rousseau, the fall from innocence may not be a one-time event but rather something persistently repeated.

10. *Oeuvres complètes*, vol. 2, 211.

11. *Oeuvres complètes*, vol. 1, 380. See also Masters, *The First and Second Discourses*, 234.

12. Consider, for example, the following from the preface of a letter to Charles Bordes.

> Some precautions were, at first, necessary, and it is in order to make everything understood that I did not want to say everything. It is only successively and only for a few readers that I have developed my ideas. It was not myself that I spared but the truth, so as to make it pass more surely and render it useful. Often I was at great pains to try to conceal in a sentence, in a line, in a word tossed off as if by chance the result of a long series of reflections. Often the greater part of my readers must have found my discourses badly connected and nearly entirely disjointed for want of perceiving the trunk of which I showed them only the branches. But that was enough for those who knew how to understand, and I have never wanted to speak to the others. (*Oeuvres complètes*, vol. 2, 192)

13. Consider, for example, *Oeuvres complètes*, vol. 2, 213 with 250.

14. Consider, for example, note i, which glosses a sentence that is itself a gloss on a word Rousseau has just coined to describe the distinctive feature of human beings—*perfectibilité*:

> It would be sad for us to be forced to agree that this distinctive and nearly unlimited faculty is the source of all the misfortunes of man; that it is this which, by force of time, draws him from that original condition in which he would glide through tranquil and innocent days; that it is this which, over the centuries, hatching his enlightenments and his errors, his vices and his virtues, renders him in the long run the tyrant of himself and of nature. (*Oeuvres complètes*, vol. 2, 218)

The note divides in three: a part that deals with the various ways in which civilization makes men miserable while appearing to promise happiness (paragraphs 1–8), a part concerned with luxury as the "remedy" that is really the greatest evil of civil society (paragraphs 9–13), and a part concerned with whether the true solution is the return to the state of nature (paragraph 14). The importance of the note is signaled early when Rousseau describes his activity as a return (*remonté*—*Oeuvres complètes*, vol. 2, 251) of man to man directly after having made clear in the text that this is what all animals do naturally or mechanically, for he sees "in every animal only an ingenious machine to which nature has given senses to restore [*remonter*] itself" (*Oeuvres complètes*, vol. 2, 218). The underlying question of the note is, Why, if we were originally happy and it is such hard work to make ourselves miserable, do we do it? The answer seems to be our pride, but what is the source of this pride that drives us out of paradise?

In the first paragraph of the note, Rousseau gives a series of examples of the wickedness of men. Men strive serially to realize the possibilities of "man." This desire to be man leads to civil society—a pooling of our resources designed to make up for the defects of individual men. This is no doubt admirable. However, it also serves as a constant reminder for each of us of our individual incompleteness and therefore engenders not only hatred of those with whom we join together but self-hatred as well (Rousseau makes beautiful use of the ambiguity of *s'entre-haïr* and *se croisser*, *Oeuvres complètes*, vol. 2, 251). Thus, the very goal that moves civil society is also the reason to abuse it ("there is no profit so legitimate that it may not be surpassed by one made illegitimately"; *Oeuvres complètes*, vol. 2, 252). Rousseau refers here to Montaigne (*Essais*, vol. I, no. 22), who argues that men do take advantage of the ill fortune of others but that this is true of anything useful. Any service is possible only because there is someone in need. Underneath it all we therefore want others to need and do not want to need them. Montaigne concludes with a quotation from Lucretius to the effect that the coming to be of one thing is always the death of another. Lucretius uses it at least four times as a general principle that applies to atoms, men, color, and so on—that is, it applies to everything. In other words, the being of anything is necessarily purchased at the expense of something else. It is this principle that the desire to be "man" is at once a rebellion against and an instance of.

According to the part of the *Second Discourse* on which this note is a gloss, man in the state of nature possesses two instincts: compassion and self-preservation. The one suggests a perception of equality—our heart goes out to any of our kind. The other suggests that I think of myself as fundamentally different from and better than others. Together the two constitute an actual equality that engenders a perceived inequality—we are alike in seeking to preserve ourselves at the expense of others. This sense of my own specialness is at the heart of civil life. We are totally unsuited for civil life because our selfishness has been unleashed by civil life. Savage man, on the other hand, is the "friend to his fellow" because he has no friends and so does not know that he can gain at their expense. Civil society is thus one of those useful institutions that lead unexpectedly to consequences quite the opposite of what was originally intended.

This is the general tenor of note i. Of course, note i is a gloss on natural man. The destruction of natural man seems already built into his defining feature—perfectibility. Human beings can alter the world and even themselves to satisfy their "needs." What drives this movement is ultimately not utility, as Rousseau's account of the longing for luxuries because they are useless indicates. We want unnecessary things precisely as a sign of our liberation from necessity—our freedom. Yet, that some should be able to ignore necessity means that others will have to bear its burden. Luxury leads to poverty, and luxury comes to be inexorably not from the desire for wealth or ease but rather for a sense of one's own freedom.

It is no accident that what began as a gloss on making oneself "tyrant of oneself and of nature" should end with the issue of God. In the final paragraph, Rousseau makes it clear that going back to the state of nature might be an option if human beings had not heard the divine voice. Yet, clearly it is pride and the desire for excess that make the return to the state of nature impossible. Are we meant to identify the two?

15. References to the *Reveries* (*Oeuvres complètes*, vol. 1, 501–43) will be placed in parentheses. The Roman numeral, which comes first, indicates the walk cited; the Arabic numeral, which follows, indicates the paragraph. Translations are my own, although I have frequently consulted those of Charles Butterworth, *The Reveries of the Solitary Walker* (New York: Harper & Row, 1979), and Peter France, *Reveries of the Solitary Walker* (New York: Penguin, 1979).

16. See Butterworth, *The Reveries*, 243–44.

17. For Rousseau's willingness to dissemble, see *Emile*, book 2, paragraph 68 (*Oeuvres complètes*, vol. 3, 64), *Jugement sur la polysynodie* (*Oeuvres complètes*, vol. 2, 364), and *Préface d'une seconde lettre à Bordes* (*Oeuvres complètes*, vol. 3, 192).

18. Consider Rousseau's repeated use in the *Reveries* of words like *l'état*, *l'empire*, and *la révolution* to describe his own condition. It is not accidental that they also bear political meanings.

19. In the opening paragraph and throughout the First Walk, Rousseau repeatedly doubles himself by using reflexive verbs and making an object of himself. See especially I.14.

20. See also *Rousseau juge de Jean-Jacques*, in *Oeuvres complètes* vol. 1, 378.

21. See *Du Contrat social*, I.6 and II.1–4, in *Oeuvres complètes*, vol. 2, 522–23 and 525–29.

22. Similarly, in the *Second Discourse*, natural man makes sense only as that for which civil man longs. That natural man has no real existence apart from this looking back seems clear from the difficulty Rousseau has finding appropriate examples, all of which prove to be either animals or already in some measure civil.

23. *Dasein* is always already *Mitdasein* (*Sein und Zeit*, 117–30).

24. In a way the *Reveries* is a variation on Plato's *Phaedo*, apparently a reflection on the goodness of death but really a reflection on the queer connection between death and the highest activity of which the human soul is capable. Thus, philosophy can be understood as the practice of dying and being dead. See Plato, *Phaedo*, 63e–64c.

25. This is a version of the good as the governing principle of all knowing, of the dependence of understanding on final causality, and of care as the being of *Dasein*. Completely objective awareness is incompatible with awareness.

26. See the Introduction to Allan Bloom's translation of *Emile* (New York: Basic Books, 1979), 10–15.

27. See *Oeuvres complètes*, vol. 2, 230.

28. In addition to these cases in I.3 and I.4, see I.5, I.7, I.10, I.12, and I.13.

29. See *Rousseau Judge of Jean-Jacques: Dialogues* in *The Collected Writings of Rousseau*, Roger Masters and Christopher Kelley, eds. (Hanover, N.H.: University Press of New England, 1990), vol. 1, xxix-xxxi.

30. The oratorians were a society of secular priests. See *Les Confessions de J.-J. Rousseau* books 10–11, in *Oeuvres complètes*, vol. 1.

31. See III.5.

32. See, for example, the famous first sentence of *On the Social Contract*, book 1, chapter 1: "Man is born free, and everywhere he is in chains" (*Oeuvres complètes*, vol. 2, 518).

6

THE FALL

The Second Walk divides into three parts. In the first four paragraphs Rousseau raises the question, What is reverie? The second and longest part (paragraphs 5–22) concerns Rousseau's accident—being run down by a Great Dane—and subdivides into three sections. The first (paragraphs 5–6) is concerned with Rousseau's walk before the accident. In paragraph 5 he discusses his observation of specific plants, and in paragraph 6, his meditation on the whole of the country scene.[1] In the second (paragraphs 7–12), Rousseau discusses the accident itself, and in the third (paragraphs 13–21) its consequences—first in general (paragraph 13), then in the specific instances of M. Lenoir (paragraph 14) and Mme d'Ormoy (paragraphs 15–19), and finally with regard to the premature reports of his death (paragraphs 20–21). The third part (paragraphs 22–24) of the Second Walk consists of conclusions drawn from this experience, especially with regard to God. The structure of the walk proves to have something to do with the structure of reverie itself.

The Second Walk begins with a puzzling claim.

> Having therefore formed the project of describing the habitual state of my soul in the strangest position in which a mortal could ever find himself, I saw no simpler or surer manner of exercising this enterprise than to keep a faithful account of my solitary walks and of the reveries that fill them when I leave my head entirely free, and my ideas follow their bent without resistance and without limit. These hours of solitude and of meditation are the only ones of the day in which I may be fully myself and for myself, without diversion, without obstacle, and in which I may say truly that I am what nature wished. (II.1)

It is by no means clear at the beginning of this walk what Rousseau means by the strangest state possible for a mortal. That this state is habitual means that it has been formed. Accordingly, whatever Rousseau's strange state, it is something he has grown to be, not something he always was. Perhaps Rousseau means that, unlike most mortals, he is not preoccupied with his mortality—he has been released from any concern with death. This would be a state in which one's ideas are not governed by pressing needs. In the absence of necessity one's thoughts would wander altogether freely and without constraint. At these times one could be truly oneself and for oneself, and so only during such times could Rousseau *say* he is what nature meant him to be.[2] Freedom—the truth of the self—is only possible when alone, and one can say it only by meditating on this solitude. Rousseau's project is to describe himself when he is most fully himself. To give a faithful account he must describe his solitary walks, when he is most himself, and describe the reveries that filled them, when he is most for himself. These dualisms will, of course, create problems. How can he be entirely free when he is watching himself *in order* to give a faithful account of how nature wanted him to be? How is it possible to give an account of one's own spontaneous activity without undermining its spontaneity? It is all a little like being placed in front of a camera and told to be natural. Can one give an account of oneself without alienating oneself from oneself? Is it possible to be oneself and be for oneself at the same moment, to combine reverie and meditation? Is this combination "the strangest position in which a mortal could ever find himself"?

The immediate problem for Rousseau's project is that he has grown old. He admits that his situation has declined since he first discovered it to be hopeless. Because his imagination is becoming dull, reverie has begun to become memory. Reverie seems to require a mixture of youth and old age (compare I.14). To walk—that is, to move somewhere other than where one is or to "thrust oneself" beyond one's "decrepit exterior"—is the work of the young; to write down—that is, to look back and reflect—is the work of the old. But walking, for all of the aimlessness of the promenade, must always be walking somewhere.[3] It requires a goal, however playful or provisional; it requires some hope. The fading of Rousseau's imagination leads to a tepid languor; this indifference threatens to kill him. The soul is nothing if it is not alive. But the spirit of life is creation and the inflamed imagination (II.2). When this spirit is extinguished in him by degrees, Rousseau no longer has a motive for recollecting. The success of the First Walk, Rousseau's hopelessness, is the problem of the Second Walk, Rousseau's indifference.

Something stands in the way of death, however. That he still lives means that Rousseau must still have hope.

> [O]nly with trouble does my soul any longer thrust itself beyond its covering, and without the hope of the state to which I aspire because I sense myself to have a right to it, I would no longer exist other than in my memories. Thus, in order for me to contemplate myself before my decline, I must climb back at least a few years to a time during which, losing all hope here below and no longer finding food for my heart on the earth, I accustomed myself little by little to nourish it with its own substance and to seek all its fodder within myself. (II.2)

The eating metaphor is important for understanding what Rousseau has in mind. Food in general does not provide sustenance; one must eat *something*. Rousseau does eat; he is not really indifferent to everything. He has a hope for a perfect justice that makes it possible for him to live. This sense of perfect justice is possible, however, only because nothing particular in the world has a hold on him any longer. If, for example, Rousseau were to be attached to his children, he would not be able to escape the natural, but strictly speaking unjust, preference of a parent for its own offspring. Rousseau finds nourishment in himself by feeding in particular on his hope for justice in general, a hope that, in turn, depends on his denial of the importance of the particular.[4] In the First Walk Rousseau suggested that the human condition of being alienated from all others could in fact provide the foundation for human society. Our sense of being cut off from others leads us to realize that all men feel cut off; in sympathizing with this plight we connect ourselves to others. Similarly, in the depths of hopelessness, Rousseau finds hope. This is how the soul can thrust itself out of itself (i.e., live) while still remaining within itself.

This ability to feed on himself compensates Rousseau for everything. In a way he is simply gaining the world by renouncing the world; he has been born again. But this time he is born into a state of neutrality that enables him to be content because he does not feel his ills and in fact scarcely remembers them. The difficulty with this compensation is that memory of experience is no more neutral than experience. Accordingly, it is from "[his] own experience" that Rousseau understands that the source of happiness is to be found in ourselves. He sees this because he experiences the gradual diminishing of his own unhappiness, but the price is that experience also threatens to disappear. His memories, after all, are the memories of what he has suffered. This problem of being reduced to willing the particular in general is similar to a difficulty with the general will in the *Social Contract*. One is to will it because it is general not because of its particular content. Thus, the motive for willing legislation to build a bridge can never really be the particular advantages resulting from building the bridge. The motive is, rather, that it is the general will that the bridge be built, for if the general support for the bridge were to erode, one should will not to build it with the same fervor as one previously willed to build it. While the particular object is the necessary occasion for the general will, it is not really its content. Realizing this fact, however, makes it difficult for the particular object to serve as an occasion for the expression of the general will.

The problem becomes clearer in a strange sentence in the third paragraph.

> The habit of returning to myself made me finally lose the sentiment and almost the memory of my ills, I thus learned by my own experience that the source of true happiness is within us and that it does not depend on men to render truly miserable the one who is able [*sait*—knows how] to want [*vouloir*—to will] to be happy. (II.3)

At first Rousseau seems to have introduced a kind of stoicism—our happiness depends on ourselves because we alone determine how we will respond to things. And yet this really cannot be the case. The sentence means, rather, that the one who wants to be happy cannot be perfectly miserable. The heart of living men is this wanting to be happy, which, because he has been deprived of everything else, Rousseau represents in its pure form—the desire for justice. The wish to be happy is the hope that by deserving to be happy we will be happy—it is a longing for theodicy. If pure willing or pure freedom were possible, this is what it would will. The truth of all the particular desires men have, of all their hopes, is this willing to be happy. Rousseau, in his decline and having renounced all particular objects of will, hope, and desire, can for a moment realize this pure willing. But it always threatens either to turn into indifference, and so an absence of any willing at all, or into a preoccupation with revenge against his persecutors, that is, against a particular object of will.

This rapture and ecstasy are radically unstable, and their instability is identical to the instability of reverie. Why keep a faithful account of your state if you are perfectly content? Paragraph 3 ends by once again raising the difficulty of this dualism within reverie. In describing a reverie one characteristically falls into it again. Now, either the memory of a reverie leads to experiencing it again, in which case there can be no question of giving a faithful account of it, or the memory of a reverie does not lead to experiencing it again, in which case there is also no possibility of giving a faithful account of it. A state that is spontaneous and so admits of no distance cannot be described. Accordingly, the soul, while in the very act of separating itself from itself, falls back into itself and becomes one.[5]

Reverie is only possible where nothing matters—in a world without cares, without final causation, without *philein*. Only in such a condition is aimless musing or free thinking possible. However, this necessarily involves forgetting the conditions leading to this aimlessness—in Rousseau's case, hopelessness born of total persecution. This, in turn, means forgetting that nothing matters and so once again potentially being caught up in hopes. Reverie, this state that is possible because Rousseau is not susceptible to any external event, thus makes Rousseau totally susceptible to external events. In his pure openness, Rousseau is just about to be bowled over by a Great Dane.

> I experienced this effect a good deal on the walks that followed my project of writing a follow-up to my *Confessions*, especially on the one of which I am going to speak and on which an unforeseen accident came to break the thread of my thoughts and give them for some time another course. (II.4)

Reverie seems to be a strange combination of complete invulnerability and complete vulnerability.[6] Paragraph 4 therefore announces an external event that shifts Rousseau's thoughts altogether. But it is still more complicated. Rousseau says there is a tension between experience (or walking) and description (or thinking), but he also says that he experienced this same tension on his walks. Accordingly, in a single sentence he uses cognate words—*suivirent* and *suite*—to refer first to his walks and then to his writing. Despite their differences, experience and reflection are alike. Reverie somehow unifies them.

Rousseau's accident with the Great Dane is certainly the most startling event of the Second Walk and perhaps even of the *Reveries* altogether. Just as the Second Walk divides into three parts so that there is a general account of reverie, a particular example and conclusions drawn from the example, the particular event itself is divided into a prologue concerned with reverie, an account of Rousseau's fall and an account of the consequences of the fall. The prologue consists in a reflection on nature. In the Seventh Walk Rousseau will distinguish two kinds of science, using botany as an example (VII.12–16). One may study plants as a pharmacologist does for the sake of their uses, or one may study plants as a true botanist does with no view to the use of what one learns. Rousseau claims to do the latter and also claims that it is this very uselessness that makes botany worthwhile. This is connected to Rousseau's activity prior to his accident.

> On Thursday, October 24, 1776, after dining I followed the boulevards as far as the Rue du Chemin-Vert, through which I gained the heights of Ménilmontant, and from there, taking paths across the vineyards and meadows, I crossed as far as Charrone the cheerful countryside that separates the two villages. Then I made a detour in order to come back by the same meadows, but taking another way. I amused myself by going through [*parcourir*] them with that pleasure and that interest that agreeable sites have always given me, and by sometimes stopping to gaze [*fixer*] at plants in the greenery. I perceived two of them that I saw rarely enough around Paris, but that I found very abundant in that district. The one is *picris hieraioides* of the family of composite plants, and the other *bupleurum falcatum* of that of umbelliferous plants. This discovery made me rejoice and amused me for a long time and ended in [the discovery] of a plant yet more rare, especially in high country, to wit *cerastium aquaticum*, which, despite the accident that happened to me the same day, I found again in a book that I had with me, and placed in my herbarium. (II.5)

Most shocking, of course, is the fact that the solitary man is wandering around not on some desert island but in the outskirts of Paris. As we soon discover, he is far from an outcast in any conventional sense. It is also interesting that the date is cited with such precision. Rousseau takes great pains to make the incident as particular as possible with respect to place and time. In making a detour to avoid returning the same way, he makes aimlessness the purpose of his walk. His categorizing of the plants he encounters is quite careful—hawkweed and chickweed look a good deal alike—but not altogether objective. Rousseau takes an interest in certain plants only insofar as they relate to his situation—they are rare around Paris. What is only implicit here becomes explicit in the following paragraph—in studying nature Rousseau is really studying himself. Finally, we are informed that Rousseau carried a book with him on his walk. Does he stop to read? Can one lose oneself in a book in the way Rousseau has lost himself in the contemplation of nature?

In the sixth paragraph Rousseau's relation to nature undergoes a subtle change.

> Finally, after having gone through [*parcouru*] in detail several other plants that I saw still in bloom, and of which the aspect and the enumeration, which were familiar to me, nevertheless always gave me pleasure, little by little I left off these minute observations to give myself up to the impression, no less agreeable but more touching, that the whole of it made on me. . . . The countryside, still green and cheerful, but partly defoliated and already nearly desolate, offered everywhere the image of solitude and of the approach of winter. There resulted from its aspect a mixture of sweet and sad impressions too analogous to my own age and my fate for me not to make the connection to it. (II.6)

Rousseau uses the same verb, *parcourir*, that he used in the fifth paragraph to describe his movement through the field; he will use it again in paragraph 17 to indicate his perusal of Mme d'Ormoy's book. Here *parcourir* is used to indicate how he observed plants in detail. Is there a parallel to be drawn among walking, classifying, and reading? The movement from the fifth to the sixth paragraph is from minute observation to what touches him more—contemplation of the whole scene. Rousseau is moved because he sees it as an image of his own condition. In fact, that is what makes the scene a whole. Rousseau's situation has given an order to nature, not vice versa. The way he goes on to embroider the example shows that he is using the external scene to make his internal condition visible. It is as though he were using walking to make thinking visible.

Now, it is by examining this external world that Rousseau makes his inside—his purity of will—clear to himself. In this context he uses the phrase "the author of my being."[7]

> Sighing, I said to myself, "What have I done here below? I was made to live, and I die without having lived. At least this wasn't my fault, and I will carry to the author of my being, if not the offering of the good works that I have not been allowed to do, at least a tribute of good intentions frustrated, of sentiments pure but rendered without effect and of patience proof against the contempt of men." (II.6)

God is introduced as author just as Rousseau unifies his vision of the countryside so as to make it a whole and give it a purpose—at that moment when Rousseau acts like an author. He carries with him a book that will later be used to turn a piece of nature into a display.

In a way Rousseau's reverie consists in thinking about writing—thinking about what life looks like when made whole by way of some external metaphor. The landscape makes this unification possible. It makes clear that in a way all of us were made to live but die without having lived. The perfect tense, "having lived," is unavailable except through the sort of musing and imagining (i.e., authorship) in which Rousseau is engaged. At the very end of paragraph 6 Rousseau says that he was returning to himself and was very content with his journey. This return is, of course, a return in thought. Rousseau proceeds as though walking and thinking were the same, as though *parcourir* were univocal. He also indicates that this coming back to himself was the peak of his reverie. Coming back to oneself (paragraph 6) after having lost oneself (paragraph 5) seems to be the heart of reverie. Reverie is not a simple static condition but rather requires time for something like the rediscovery of oneself in one's aimless activity. Clearly a condition so dependent on external events cannot last. At the peak of his reverie, Rousseau is about to be run over by a dog.

It is no accident that Rousseau chose as a paradigm for reverie an event that he refers to as *la chute*—the fall. Its queer combination of innocent immediacy and reflection is a reminder of the problem of the Fall of Adam and Eve from paradise. It also points back to Rousseau's own alternative to the Fall—his account in the *Second Discourse* of the corruption of natural man. The plot of the fall in the *Reveries* is fairly straightforward. Rousseau had just reached the peak of his reverie (II.6) and was going down a hill when some people ahead of him moved quickly out of the way, and he saw a Great Dane rushing toward him. He had just enough time to think that his only hope was to jump up and hope the dog passed beneath him, but the thought took the time the deed would have needed, and Rousseau got hit without enacting his plan. He did not feel the blow and did not experience anything that followed; his direct experience stops here until "I returned to myself" (II.7).

> It was nearly night when I regained consciousness. I found myself in the arms of three or four young people who related to me what had just happened to me. The Great Dane, having been unable to restrain its bound, hurled itself against both my legs, and striking me with its mass and speed made me fall head first; my upper jaw, bearing all the weight of my body, hit a very rough pavement, and the fall had been so much the more violent as, being on the descent, my head had gone lower than my feet. (II.8)

All of this Rousseau gets secondhand. He has no direct experience of his leap into selflessness.

> The carriage to which the dog belonged followed immediately and would have passed over the body if the coachman had not instantly restrained the horses. That is what I learned from the account of those who had picked me up and who supported me still when I returned to myself. The state in which I found myself at this instant is too singular not to describe it here. (II.9)

Rousseau signals his detachment from himself by referring to himself as *le corps*—the body. In the sequel things begin to get rather queer. It should be kept in mind that the return to himself here parallels the movement from paragraph 5 to paragraph 6 and from hopelessness to hope.

> The night was advancing. I perceived the sky, some stars and a little greenery. This first sensation was a delicious moment. I sensed myself still only over there. I was born in this instant to life, and it seemed to me that I filled all the objects I perceived with my light existence.

Entirely in the present moment, I remembered nothing; I had no distinct notion of my person [*individu*], not the least idea of what had just happened to me; I knew neither who I was nor where I was; I sensed neither ill, nor fear nor worry. I saw my blood flow as I would have seen a brook flow, without in any way dreaming that this blood belonged to me. I sensed in all my being a ravishing calm, to which each time I recall it to myself I find nothing comparable in all the activity of known pleasures. (II.10)

Rousseau's experience, upon coming to, begins with externals and gradually moves closer to himself—from the sky and stars, to greenery to himself. In this instant he "was born to life"—precisely what he had denied was true of himself in paragraph 6. Being born seems to mean filling objects with his own existence, animating other beings or being an author of beings.[8] This moment is delicious—a rapturous calm—because he has all of his faculties but none of the history of their acquisition. It is like being born complete. Rousseau sees himself and his pains and pleasures as he would an object; he is totally detached from himself. And yet this total detachment is a ravishing calm to which no pleasure in life compares. He thus simultaneously affirms and denies himself. And yet is not the pointedly secondhand account of Rousseau's knowledge of his fall meant to point to the "memory" of this delicious moment as an invention—a limit case that Rousseau constructs out of his decline from the moment? This event is in many ways *the* example of reverie in the book, and yet it seems to be necessarily experienced as a memory. This peak of spontaneity emerges only in the third person. At the moment when we are about to experience *amour de moi-même*, it turns into *amour de soi-même*.

Rousseau's account in paragraphs 11 and 12 of what happens as he gradually makes his way home contains some signs of this difficulty. He does not know where he is and so asks. They tell him the location is Haute-Borne—literally, "upper limit." The significance of this meaning is confirmed by Rousseau's subsequent remark that they might as well have told him he was on Mount Atlas. Mount Atlas is, of course, the traditional meeting point of heaven and earth. Rousseau asks, "Where am I?" They answer that he is at the place where it is possible both to be himself and not. As he begins to get his bearings, to come to himself and make his way home from this "upper limit," he progressively loses

his sense of exhilaration. Returning to oneself is necessary to make plea-
surable the sensation of not being a self, but at the same time, to come
back to oneself is to begin a descent from that pleasure. It is on the way
home that Rousseau begins to feel pain.

Rousseau first notices his own hurt through the responses of others
and especially through the cries of his wife. He returns to himself fully
by seeing himself through the eyes of others. When he wakes up the
next day and takes stock of his injuries (with the same sort of detailed
observation that he had used on plants), he refers to the good luck of his
fall. By "the fall" he apparently understands the whole event. It was in
la chute that he was born; the two are coextensive. To be born anew
means not knowing where one was born but having all the abilities of
having been born somewhere. The disembodied Rousseau seems able
still to speak eloquent French. And yet this ravishing pleasure of reverie,
of experiencing oneself as not being a self, is available to us only as a sort
of limit case. Each actual example of it seems already to represent a fall
away from it. We long for the experience of freedom, but, as every
exercise of freedom must be a particular action necessarily bringing with
it the limitations accompanying all particular actions, freedom is an experience we cannot have. Reverie is the attempt to capture as a moment
of pure freedom that instant at which the limitation, decline, or fall
begins, but the moment proves accessible only as a construction of memory. Memory, of course, had previously been a faculty that waxes as our
lives wane (II.2). Here the very peak of living is impossible without it.
Reverie seems to be available to us only as the authors of our own lives.
All experience of reverie comes by way of secondhand accounts. What
this means becomes clearer when we turn to the series of secondhand
accounts that distort Rousseau's experience.

Rousseau begins the section in which he complains of the distortion
in the various accounts of his fall by saying "There, very faithfully, is the
story of my accident" (II.13). And yet, if so much of his account is
second hand, how can he know that it is faithful? That he "should have
counted in advance on this metamorphosis" (II.13) suggests that secondhand accounts are necessarily distorted. Rousseau himself has given an
account of the cause of these distortions. All of us tend to see ourselves
in the world; we unwittingly animate the world with ourselves.[9] While
Rousseau clearly knows this, the motives underlying the various distortions to which his story was subjected first worry and then terrify him.

"I have always hated darknesses; they naturally inspire in me a horror that those with which I have been surrounded for so many years have not been able to diminish" (II.13). Whatever it is that causes the necessary distortion of stories is the obstacle to removing the darkness so feared by Rousseau. Not knowing destroys his tranquility, and the very existence of others guarantees that he will not know. This is why "others" generally are such a torment to him; they are the source of the darkness in the world. Accordingly, what follows (paragraphs 14–21) is an account of assorted others and their hidden motives.

It is no accident that the first of these should be M. Lenoir (Mr. Black) whose secretary is sent to offer Rousseau what seem to him various useless services.

> This great earnestness and the air of confidence connected to it gave me to understand that there was beneath it all some mystery that I sought vainly to penetrate. So much was not necessary to frighten me, especially in the state of agitation which my accident and the fever connected to it had put my head. I gave myself up to a thousand worrisome and sad conjectures, and about everything that occurred around me I made commentaries that marked rather the delirium and fever than the *sang-froid* of a man who no longer takes any interest in anything. (II.14)

The real cause of Rousseau's worry was not M. Lenoir but uncertainty combined with the heightened imagination resulting from his fever. The issue then is not how "they" persecuted Rousseau but how the existence of others in itself persecutes him. Fever or delirium consists in knowing that there are everywhere others who have their own purposes and that these purposes remain necessarily dark. This obviously has some connection to the way anger causes us to attribute purposes to inanimate things in the world. The world does not seem meaningful to us on the surface; we are willing to entertain the possibility that it is altogether hostile to us if only it can be understood to be governed by intentions. At the same time, we are tormented by the opacity of these intentions. Our sense of justice requires that we know what "others" intend; their insides cannot remain closed to us. Ultimately the problem of others becomes the problem of seeing God in everything, for this is, of course, where the Second Walk will conclude. The purpose of the Second Walk as a whole is to transform the tension between "me" and "them" into the tension between "me" and "God." What does it mean to be human, and so by nature free, in a world governed by purposes? What will it mean to be both the author of one's own life and a character in someone else's story? Or, what can it possibly mean for nature to want or will human beings to be free?

Rousseau's account of his relations with Mme d'Ormoy (paragraphs 15–19) reveals the extent of the problem of others. Once again he sees ulterior motives: "Mme d'Ormoy had sought me out for some years without my being able to divine why" (II.15). She gave him little gifts, visited him at home, tried to get his advice about her novel, and finally, what unsettles Rousseau the most, she included exaggerated praise of him in the preface of her novel. Several things are revealing about all of this. First, as in the case of M. Lenoir, it is not just open hostility that unnerves Rousseau. Because he is so certain of the enmity of others— that is, of what he elsewhere calls their *amour-propre*, their preference for themselves over all others—Rousseau seems even more suspicious of expressions of support and admiration than of expressions of hostility. Because all admiration is suspect, particular instances of it remind Rousseau of the gulf between what seems to be and what is. The hidden intentions of others are signs of the darkness surrounding him. This, combined with the fact that M. Lenoir's secretary (once) and Mme d'Ormoy and her daughter (frequently) visit him at home where he lives with his wife, Therese, makes it clear that Rousseau's solitude is not of any ordinary sort. It seems rather metaphysical than actual. Rousseau's underlying understanding of human nature forces him to assume that the flatteries expressed by Mme d'Ormoy in her book are not just the exaggerations of a silly but good-hearted woman. He must find a motive that reveals some good to her by way of some ill to him. He concludes, therefore, that the praise of him in her preface is meant to call attention to a note that appears later in the book. The note glosses an interchange between a woman named Emily and a nun that, of course, recalls the speech of the Savoyard Vicar in *Emile*; its content could easily have been offensive to the aristocracy and to the king.[10] Rousseau concludes that Mme d'Ormoy is attempting to avoid danger by deflecting blame onto him, although it is not clear why she could not simply be imitating him. In any case, he breaks off relations with her by sending a note: "Rousseau, not receiving any authors at his home, thanks Mme d'Ormoy for

her kindnesses and begs her no longer to honor him with her visits"
(II.18). In the sequel Rousseau criticizes the seeming honesty of her
reply to this note in comparison with his own frankness and then generalizes his self-satisfaction.

> It is thus that rectitude and frankness in everything are terrible crimes
> in the world, and I appear evil and ferocious to my contemporaries
> having no other crime in their eyes than not being as false and perfid-
> ious as they. (II.19)

One has to wonder about this. How frank is Rousseau? His note
does not really confront Mme d'Ormoy with his suspicions; it rather
cleverly excludes her from his home on a general principle—she is an
author. Of course, Rousseau too is an author. Does his note mean that
he is no longer receiving himself? Is the problem of otherness exclusive
to the hidden motives of other human beings, or does it also apply to
our own motives? This section is concerned with what it means to know
another. To be human means to be an author. We each spin out our
own worlds and do not really connect with one another. At the same
time it is also concerned with what it means to know oneself. In the last
section of the Second Walk, Rousseau asks how the existence of a common author for all of our lives would affect our isolation. He turns to
God.

Rousseau had thought himself to be indifferent to "them," but the
aftermath of his accident proves him wrong. The concealed motives of
M. Lenoir and Mme d'Ormoy, the false reports of his death followed by
unflattering anonymously authored obituaries summing up Rousseau's
life (II.20) and the possibility that he would not even be safe as an author—that writings not his would be attributed to him (II.21)—all
served to reinforce his sense of the "black darknesses" (II.22) surrounding him. They reanimate his fear of solitude and with it cause the rebirth
of his "deadened imagination" (II.22). Rousseau begins to think about
his world again; he is reborn as an author out of a need to make sense of
his world. But this time he goes further. He concludes that the agreement enforcing his solitude is too uniform and universal to be accidental.
A plan so intelligible must have a purpose. In other words, where there
is so much bad, there must be purposes beyond the wills of men. Such
a combination of fate or necessity and will indicates the presence of God.

Rousseau, therefore, finds purposiveness in the universal evil surrounding him and is cheered by it.

The argument thus far seems to have several stages. Rousseau presents us with a series of ambiguous examples of concealed motives. He overinterprets them as hostile and then concludes that where the plot against him is so universal there must be some more than human purpose behind it. This he calls God. But what exactly does this mean? The absoluteness of Rousseau's isolation will prove to be the means for breaking through his isolation. Universal alienation can become the foundation for a common sense of purpose. Of course, this means that the common sense of alienation must remain for the common purpose to remain. Accordingly, it can never be the foundation for an actual society even though it is in some sense the foundation of all society. The most social man is in principle the solitary man.

All of this naturally leads to some questions. Would Rousseau have seen this purposiveness if only good things had happened to him (and, insofar as it is good to have seen it, is it good that bad things have happened to him)? Would the world have impinged on him at all under those circumstances? If some of the purposes were perceived as good and some bad, then, of course, he could, like the rest of us, easily have attributed both the good and the bad things that happen to chance. It looks, then, as though a sense of divine purpose could only have emerged in this way. The existence of purpose as such, as distinct from various contingent purposes, gives Rousseau hope. A being capable of universal purposes would have to be an author who saw into things and for whom the purity of Rousseau's intentions would be clear. From such a being Rousseau could expect justice. God is an other who overcomes the problem of otherness.

Still, a large difficulty remains. Why would such a being have allowed Rousseau to suffer so much? As Rousseau's fate is not just on the face of it, God too must have ulterior motives. To be an intentional being would seem to entail opacity. Like Mme d'Ormay, God is an author; he is not frank. Rousseau's expectations of future justice thus point to a problem. If taken literally, God does not seem to solve the problem; He is as outside as any other. As an image, God points to the goal of the *Reveries*: to make the nonpurposiveness, injustice, and disorder of the world serve as its purpose so that the very problem of solitude, when properly understood, becomes its own solution.

The first two walks of the *Reveries* are concerned with the relation between solitude and society. Rousseau says that he will move from "them" to "me," but the First Walk, in fact, moves from "me" to "them." To understand himself Rousseau must understand his relation to others—why he is a solitary. But in discovering "what nature wanted [him] to be"—a solitary dreamer—he discovers what disconnects him in principle from all other men. Because he is a *sujet*—an intentional being, he is inaccessible to them. So far he has moved from "them" to "me." Yet this truer understanding of himself as *sujet* leads to a truer understanding of what he shares with all other men—his apartness, strangeness, and individuality. Rousseau has therefore experienced something of the equality that is so central to his political philosophy. Rousseau's total isolation thus proves to be the condition for realizing what human freedom consists in. He can see men as they are only because he is now indifferent to them and does not wish to use them. Only in solitude does he realize the truly social nature of man. He therefore moves from "them" to "me" to "them."

This is connected to the peculiar status of justice (*the* social virtue) as the anchor of Rousseau's remaining hope. The one thing that keeps him alive is "the hope of the state to which I aspire because I sense myself to have a right to it" (II.2). It is not by chance that this is Rousseau's last hope; he can have it only because he has given up on everything else. To say he nourishes himself on himself means that he feeds in particular on his denial of the importance of particular things. Only this could compensate for the loss of everything (II.3). Rousseau cannot be made miserable because he knows how to will to be happy, and this will, independent of the willing of any particular end, is as close as one gets to pure willing, pure freedom, or experiencing one's pure being—the experience of oneself as having a purpose not limited by the particularity of every particular purpose. This seems to be the strangest position a mortal was ever in, and it seems to be what Rousseau means by reverie.

Still, there is a catch; it is signaled by the beginning of the first sentence of the Second Walk: "Having thus formed the project of describing the habitual state of my soul in the strangest position in which a mortal could ever find himself, I. . . ." Does the phrase "the strangest position in which a mortal could ever find himself" refer to "the soul" or to "I"? Is it the condition of the soul that is strange or the fact that it can describe its condition? This is simply the tension between reverie and *Reverie*. Reverie seems to be a condition that of its very nature could never be defined or delimited. To distinguish one example of pure spontaneity from another requires that we make it specific or particular in a way that necessarily detracts from its purity. Any example of a pure condition is thus already a decline from purity. The peak of reverie is only possible given certain surrounding experiences. Reverie is like a durationless boundary representing the limit of hopelessness and with it of pure invulnerability—a boundary simultaneously the limit of hope, pure possibility, and so pure vulnerability. In this sense, freedom and necessity—pure will and reverie—coincide.

Rousseau presented this moment to us by way of his accident with the Great Dane—that is, at a time when he was unconscious. Waking, or coming to himself, proves to be a decline or Fall from purity. Purity therefore seems to be something reassembled out of the fragments it has broken into. But this is simply the tension between spontaneous reverie and an account or reconstruction of spontaneous reverie. It is this problem of being an author to which the Second Walk is particularly devoted. The heart of the Second Walk is the transformation in Rousseau's understanding of his persecution from the accidental enmity of other men to an enmity grounded in their very existence as other. It is a movement from historical to metaphysical solitude. Any being capable of having a view of the world, of having interests or purposes, is by this very fact isolated from his *semblables*—his fellows. We are similar to one another only in our freedom, which shows itself as difference from one another. This is the source of the darkness so dreaded by Rousseau—his author theory of humanity, which at the end extends even to God. Accordingly, in the Third Walk Rousseau will give an account of what it might mean to be the author of one's own life.

NOTES

1. On the difference between meditation and reverie, see VIII.1–2.

2. It is worth noting that Rousseau has understood nature to be teleological here. At least with regard to him, nature has wishes or purposes.

3. See *Emile*, book 4 (*Oeuvres complètes*, vol. 3, 236–37) and book 5 (*Oeuvres complètes*, vol. 3, 310).

4. Compare this with Nietzsche's inquiry into the value of values in *On the Genealogy of Morals*.

5. Rousseau calls attention to this strange feature of reverie by telling us first that to contemplate himself before his decline he finds it necessary to "go back at least a few years" (II.2) and then proceeds to give an account of an event that must be very recent. See Charles Butterworth, *The Reveries of the Solitary Walker* (New York: Harper & Row, 1979),161–63.

6. See II.23 for the identification of will and fatality, and so of freedom and necessity.

7. Consider with this the first sentence of book 1 of *Emile*.

8. Compare with chapter 5, note 4.

9. See II.6 and II.10.

10. See Butterworth, *The Reveries*, 23–25.

7

THE TRUE MORALITY

To say we are the authors of our own lives is, in a way, simply to say the obvious.[1] Human beings necessarily view their lives somewhat arbitrarily as wholes even though they are not yet wholes. We objectify a self that is not exactly an object. Rousseau sets an epigraph over the Third Walk with this in mind, for in predisposing the reader to see what follows in a certain way, an epigraph makes a whole of what is not otherwise a whole until it is finished. An outer seal stands as assurance of an inner unity. The problem of the Third Walk will be that it is one thing to make an artificial whole of one's life unwittingly and quite another to do it while fully self-aware.

The Third Walk divides in three. The first part (paragraphs 1–3) is about learning and old age, and ultimately about the impossibility of learning the most important things. The second part (paragraphs 4–24) is about the necessity of a substitute for learning in life. Rousseau first reflects on how he came to see the need for such a substitute (paragraphs 4–6); he then outlines the nature of his substitute—his private revolution (paragraphs 7–18); finally, he turns to the subsequent test of this substitute (paragraphs 19–24). In the last part (paragraph 25), Rousseau returns to the question of what can in fact be learned and to the epigraph with which he began.

The Third Walk begins with a quotation from Solon, a king of ancient Athens and one of the legendary seven wise men: "I become old in [or 'while'] always learning." Rousseau uses the quotation to argue that knowledge always comes too late for us. If we are always learning, what effect will what we learn have? What we thought we knew will change as soon as we learn something else. We may have thought we knew all there was to know about shoes but then discover something

131

about whole human beings, about vanity for instance, that changes our understanding of feet that, in turn, changes our previous understanding of shoes. If it is not really possible to have knowledge of parts without knowledge of the whole of which they are parts, then Solon's remark will really mean that it is not possible to learn anything. This quotation is therefore frequently linked with another of Solon's famous remarks to the effect that we should count no man happy until he is dead.[2] Our lives become whole only when we ourselves are no longer in a position to judge them. We cannot, therefore, count ourselves happy any more than we can say of ourselves that we know anything. To the extent that learning approaches a whole, and is thus actually useful, what we learn now renders what we did before stupid. Rousseau clearly intends his epigraph to point to the problem of measuring our lives from within our lives, and so to suggest the possibility of a life beyond this one from which this life could be measured—a life that would be potentially happy. All knowledge, then, would be necessarily retrospective or second hand. We could know ourselves only by treating ourselves as other; to be human is to be two. This seems to be the link between the Second Walk and the Third Walk.

Because we can never grasp our lives as wholes, we learn to live only after it is of any use to us. Now, if the goal of life were knowledge, this would not be so bad. Tragic wisdom—*pathei mathos*, learning through suffering or experiencing—would mean that we get closer to wisdom as we grow old. If, however, the goal of life were practical, this tragic wisdom would be genuinely tragic. Learning would mean discovering that we have made terrible mistakes, perhaps without remedy. Rousseau differs from Solon in that he sees the implied sadness of the saying. That learning does not end means that it is never really learning. Yet does not this too imply a view of one's life as a whole? "Solon often repeated this verse in his old age" (III.1); does this not mean that something remains constant in his life? Rousseau implies as much when he claims to know that it is preferable to be an imbecile and ignorant. This is presumably something Rousseau does not expect to change. How, then, does Rousseau know what he knows? Furthermore, of what use is this knowledge that knowledge comes too late? And when did Rousseau learn it?

Rousseau indulges in his own simplification of human life by giving youth and old age different proper activities. Youth, he says, is the time to study wisdom, old age to practice it. Yet, Rousseau has already described himself as a combination of youth and old age (I.14). To make his point here, he makes human life much more linear temporally than it really is. Old age simply follows after youth. Yet, that the two elements are necessarily present at the same time is clear from the beginning of paragraph 4: "I said all this to myself when it was time for me to say it. . . ." One's first thought is that this proper time is Rousseau's old age—when he has learned many things—but a moment's reflection makes it clear that Rousseau made these reflections when he was relatively young. And yet it is not clear that this precocity has affected his practice.

Now, a certain kind of learning does remain to the old. Granted that the activity of the old is *practicing* wisdom, their study is learning to die. Does this mean that practicing wisdom and learning to die are the same? This would not be an unprecedented conclusion.[3] Knowing of and accepting death is what gives us a sense of life as a race or career (*carrière*, III.3). Only because we do not live forever is the problem of happiness a problem. There seem, then, to be three stages of life as Rousseau has described it: first, a blissful ignorance; second, unhappiness owing to the fear of death, which makes us aware of the need to see our lives as wholes (count no man happy until he is dead); finally, accepting death or providing a substitute for death. The first three paragraphs provide an introduction to the issue of the Third Walk—the connection among knowledge, self-knowledge, and happiness. But, as this introduction is a speech Rousseau makes to himself when he is young, it points to some knowledge Rousseau intends to profit from and so undermines its own pessimism.

How, then, did Rousseau succeed in the impossible—learning something in time?

> Ceasing, therefore, to seek among men the happiness that I sensed I would be unable to find there, my ardent imagination leaped readily beyond the space of my hardly begun life as though on a terrain that was foreign to me so as to rest myself on a tranquil seat where I could settle myself [*me fixer*]. (III.4)

Leap has occurred twice previously in the *Reveries*; at I.2 Rousseau used it to describe a leap into death and at II.7 to describe the leap he contemplated to avoid the onrushing Great Dane. The verb *fixer* occurs at II.5 in a slangish way to mean "to stare fixedly." If we follow that usage here, in addition to settling himself, Rousseau would be looking at himself. Rousseau's imagination would make possible a leap into death that is really a way of avoiding death because it provides a vantage point for him to look at himself and so to survey his whole life before he is dead. Learning to die, the study of old age, is the same as practicing wisdom insofar as it means detaching oneself from oneself so as to look after oneself.

This ability to jump outside himself is a sentiment nourished by misfortune. Only when we are unhappy do we seek to take stock of our lives as wholes. There is no self-reflection without unhappiness, no epistemic self-consciousness without being self-conscious in the more ordinary sense of being ill at ease. Now, for Rousseau this feeling "has *at all times* made me seek to know the nature and destination of my being with more interest and care than I have found in any other man" (III.5, emphasis added). He apparently seeks this knowledge even now in his old age.

The remainder of the fifth paragraph—a scathing attack on what we would call professors—is the only place in the *Reveries* where philosophy explicitly emerges as an issue. It is not a pretty picture. The learned "philosophize" as strangers to their philosophy; they study the world disinterestedly. Unlike Rousseau, they conceal their own interests from themselves, never making them objects of study. They pretend disinterest out of vanity, yet

> [s]everal from among them wanted only to do a book, it mattered not what book, provided that it was well received. When theirs was done and published, its content no longer interested them in any way, unless to make others adopt it or to defend it in case it was attacked, and moreover without drawing anything from it for their own use and without even troubling themselves about whether its contents were false or true, provided that they were not refuted. (III.5)

While Rousseau discovers his own interest in being disinterested, the *philosophes* seek to impose a view on the world because it is theirs and not because of its content. Their imperial motives would remind us of Rousseau's reverie in the meadow (II.6) were it not that Rousseau knows that in looking at the world he is really looking at himself and so knows that he studies the world in order to know himself.

This issue comes to a head in a difficult sentence in the fifth paragraph.

> What one ought to do depends very much on what one ought to believe, and, in everything that is not bound by the first needs of nature, our opinions are the rule of our actions. (III.5)

Rousseau does not say that what we ought to do depends on what we believe—that would make a certain sense. Our understanding about what we should do derives from our beliefs about the world. As it stands, however, the two "oughts" operate on quite different levels. When I ask myself whether I ought to believe something, I do not yet, or any longer, believe it. Accordingly, the sentence could make sense only when said of another. I cannot say it of myself since then I do not believe what I "ought to believe," and the connection between belief and action is severed. If I genuinely believe gods ought to be worshipped, I will worship them; if I believe that I ought to believe they ought to be worshipped, who knows what I will do? The learned philosophers do what they do for reasons other than they think; if they knew their real motives, they would not do what they do. Can Rousseau, then, who knows about the relation between what we believe and what we do, and therefore the relation between what we ought to believe and what we ought to do, any longer be affected by what he knows he "ought to believe"? Put very plainly, how can one give a law to oneself? How is it possible to climb out of oneself to "direct" the "use" of one's life so as to know its true end? One needs to know the end or purpose to direct the life, but one cannot really know it without experience of the whole of life and so of its end. Is not the direction a part of the use? This is simply the second and absent quotation from Solon—what one might call the implied epigraph. It describes a dilemma to which imagination seems to be Rousseau's answer.

The problem is how to make a whole out of life before it is really whole so as to avoid the difficulty of never being able to rest content with what one has. To do this Rousseau arbitrarily picks an age (forty) when he will stop questioning and learning. In effect, he divides his life into sections and says that after the age of forty he will consider his life complete. Ignoring for the moment the fact that he does not really do this (he has, after all, claimed to learn things in the first two walks, written after he was sixty, and begins the Fourth Walk with a claim to ask a rather fundamental question), by imagining his life in this linear way (and he does it when he is quite young), Rousseau is able to clarify for himself what is important. It is as though he imagined himself dead and from the prospect of being dead can regulate his life. Now, it is no accident that Rousseau's language almost begs us to make the following analogy (III.15): Rousseau before forty : Rousseau after forty :: this life : the after-life. Rousseau has outlined for us the moral function of an imagined after-life. At the same time, there will be a difficulty. The Third Walk is Rousseau's account of how he discovered what he "ought to believe" so as to discover what he "ought to do." As we have seen, when we say to ourselves that we ought to believe something, we mean that we do not believe it. Accordingly, his protests notwithstanding or even perhaps as witness, the old Rousseau never altogether escapes the worries and doubts of his younger self. His detachment is something of a fiction.

To account for how he came to understand the necessity to change his life, Rousseau turns in paragraph 6 to a brief account of his early years, beginning with something of a lie.

> Born in a family where morals and piety ruled, raised subsequently with gentleness in the home of a minister full of wisdom [or chastity] and religion, I had received from the time of my most tender childhood principles, maxims—others would say prejudices—that have never altogether forsaken me. (III.6)

It is not clear that even Rousseau would characterize the father, who (after his mother's death in childbirth) raised him until he was ten, as a pious man. Furthermore, he lived for only two years with the family of the minister, Jean-Jacques Lambercier, a time about which Rousseau elsewhere indicates that he has mixed feelings.[4] In the *Confessions* he calls his uncle, who became his guardian after the arrest of his father, "a man of pleasure just like my father."[5] Nevertheless, if we accept his account at face value, Rousseau would have claimed that his judgments throughout his life were affected by the principles of Protestant piety engendered in his youth. Others would call them prejudices—pre-judgments—because they were accepted without rational argument.

In the next stage of his moral history, Rousseau converted to Catholicism. Here, too, he is at great pains to show us that he did not think his way to conversion. "Still a child, and delivered up to myself, enticed by caresses, seduced by vanity, lured by hope, forced by necessity, I became Catholic . . ." (III.6). The language of seduction is not inappropriate, as it proves to be his love for Mme de Warens that produces Rousseau's conversion.

This background prepares Rousseau for solitude where he was forced to read books well, meditate, study nature, contemplate the universe, and ultimately "thrust himself incessantly toward the author of things" and search for "the end in everything he sees and the cause of all he feels" (III.6). From within, the world looks altogether turbulent; only from without, from the position of a solitary, is it possible to see the world as purposive. Rousseau's moral disposition is at the heart of this tendency to speculate. In a way his "natural disposition to affectionate feelings" (III.6) is the cause of his intellectual life. Only because Rousseau pre-judges does he judge at all. And since he has just finished criticizing the way the "learned philosophers" feign pure curiosity and philosophize for others rather than for themselves, Rousseau seems to suggest that what is true of him is true simply. There is no such thing as purely speculative or theoretical activity. Behind reason is always "the heart."[6]

The heart is the cause of the activity of reason. From his attachments to the principles and maxims of his youth—the epigraphs of his life—to his conversion to Catholicism, Rousseau's thoughts are always rooted in some passionate attachment. At some times he has simply been luckier than at others. Accordingly, even when he is "thrown back" into the world, Rousseau cannot take its conventions of success and failure altogether seriously. His heart longs for the pleasures of his earlier "solitude." In Rousseau, the contest is never between rationality and passion but rather between the corrupted passions of social life and the purer passions of his heart. Yet, are these passions as pure as Rousseau first represents them? Since they are the foundation of the personal reformation Rousseau is about to undertake, it will be crucial to understand them.

From the time of my youth I had fixed [*fixé*] this period of forty years as the term for my efforts to succeed and for all my pretensions of any sort. Well resolved, after having attained this age in whatever situation I was, no longer to struggle to get out of it and to pass the remainder of my days living from day to day without any longer occupying myself with the future. The moment came, I executed this project without trouble, and, although my fortune just then seemed to want to take a more fixed status [*une assiette plus fixe*], I renounced it not only without regret but with a true pleasure. (III.7)

Rousseau had fixed or perhaps seen (*fixé*) forty years as the span of life necessary to undergo before putting his project into effect. However, he settled on this age in his youth, before he was wise. There is thus something arbitrary about his choice. Why should he be as wise as he will ever be at age forty? Having decided, Rousseau does not really do what he decided. Rather, he immediately changes his life to go back to a way of life he enjoys and does this just before his life is about to take *une assiette plus fixe*. The same language was used in paragraph 4 to refer to a life beyond, to which Rousseau leapt in his imagination in order to find a resting place. He therefore avoids a resting place here and does not accept life as it is but instead calls everything into question in the name of accepting life as it is. A principle that seems to involve sealing off one's life is used here to open it up.

Rousseau's external reforms are thus not to be taken at face value. Forsaking conventional standards, he claims to give up his sword, his watch, his white stockings, and so on, but for what? In substituting "a simple wig" for fancy headdress, he has simply adopted new social standards to demonstrate his new social position. The change from headdress to simple wig marks a shift of prejudice not its annihilation. It is by way of this external shift that we are supposed to see Rousseau's internal shift away from the "cupidity and covetousness" (III.7) of his heart. If this is the only way Rousseau can show his new "inside" to us, he has clearly exaggerated the extent to which internal and external revolutions can be separated from each other (III.8). He has therefore exaggerated the extent to which he can split himself in two, treat himself as an object, examine himself, and finally re-form himself.

Rousseau's self-examination, a "great revolution" that reveals to him "another moral world" (III.9), follows a peculiar sequence. First he notices the madness of others and therefore the worthlessness of their praise. He goes so far as to feel disgust (*dégoût*) or distaste for it. This distaste leads him to want to find a more stable good. For this project Rousseau needs solitude, for which he then finds himself acquiring a taste (*goût*). What was at first only a means to an end thus becomes an end in itself as Rousseau discovers that the condition for asking questions about what bothers him turns out to be the answer to these questions. Thus, the necessity to detach oneself from the world in order to see the purpose of the world turns out to be the purpose of the world. Rousseau refers to this solitude (which in paragraph 6 he already knew that he liked and for which he expressed a "taste" in paragraph 7) as "another manner of life in which subsequently I found myself (*je me trouvai*) so well" (III.10). Treating life as an artificial whole, however exaggerated his claims, thus seems in some way to make Rousseau whole.

The doubleness of Rousseau's new position comes out clearly in his treatment of the superiority of the ancient to the modern philosophers (III.11–12). Rousseau appears to reject modern philosophy as having as its goal to shake all his certainty about what it was most important to know. Unlike the ancients, the moderns do not help him remove (*lever*) doubts and stabilize (*fixer*) irresolution. Now, *lever mes doutes* can also mean "raise my doubts," and, as we already know, *fixer mes irrésolutions* can also mean "look fixedly at my irresolutions." Understood in this way, the dogmatism of the ancients, and of Rousseau, would only be apparent. Morality would be the surface of philosophy. Just as Rousseau's project is only apparently for the purpose of finding *une assiette fixe* and he only appears to acquiesce in the world as it is, he only apparently embraces ancient philosophy as dogmatic and so comforting; in fact, it seems rather to open up the possibility of genuine questioning. At the same time, this possibility has a certain fixity. In his explicit criticism and rejection of the *philosophes* in the Third Walk, Rousseau seems to have rediscovered philosophy. The moderns, only superficially open, are really "imperious dogmatists" (III.11) who become angry when anyone dares to disagree with them. The sign of their natures is their unwillingness to see the importance of the question of God. Rousseau, on the other hand, knows how important the heart is; he is therefore more rational than they.

What seems at first most peculiar about Rousseau's criticism of the moderns is the way he measures their views against his understanding of their motives. If they are not true, their views cannot be true. He does not make clear why bad men may not utter true views. In fact, the whole of the Third Walk proves peculiar in that nowhere does Rousseau really treat the content of his internal reformation. Even when he refers to the speech of the Savoyard Vicar in his *Emile* as "almost" the same as the result of his inquiries (III.17), he refers us to a speech that, in its context, he endorses rather because it manifests a will to be good than for its understanding of the content of goodness.[7] The Third Walk is thus a wholly exterior account of internal reform. Still, Rousseau has a point. Although morality must have a content—something willed—the manner of willing remains decisive. And if a "view" only becomes clear in connection with an author or viewer, then the opacity of the motives of modern philosophers would imply the opacity of their views. Because they exclude themselves and their interests and motives—their *heart*—from their views, because they write for others, they feign a kind of universality and objectivity. True universality and objectivity emerge in the expression "let us seek for it with all my strength" (III.13). While Rousseau begins by acknowledging his selfish concern, this nevertheless involves treating his self as an object. He looks at his intellectual faculties and says, "Now they are at their peak." The irony is that he first makes this judgment long before his faculties reach their peak ("From the time of my youth I had fixed this period of forty years. . . ."; III.7) and then well after their decline (III.22). The view that one's faculties are at their peak is a view that presumes one can stand apart from one's faculties. The problem is once again the epigraph, a problem reproduced in Rousseau's remarks about his inability to embrace the rules of common prudence (III.14). Prudence has the quality of being unself-aware. It is like tradition, which does not understand itself as tradition but as truth. Like tradition, prudence cannot be appealed to without going beyond it. One never does something prudent because it is prudent even though it may be one's prudence that is the cause of what one is doing. Prudence is always adverbial; it is attached to some other activity. Or, once again,

> [w]hat one ought to do depends very much on what one ought to believe, and, in everything that is not bound by the first needs of nature, our opinions are the rule of our actions. (III.5)

This is a rule for others, not for oneself. It may be that when asea in a storm it is best to act prudently, but this prudence consists in striving to behave like a seaman, not in striving to be prudent.

Rousseau's substitute for prudence is "good faith." It is connected to the courage (which he claims to have had for the first time in his life) to persist in his project despite all its difficulties. After the most ardent and sincere of inquiries "ever perhaps having been made by any mortal" (III.15), Rousseau determines the *sentiments* upon which he would base the remainder of his life. They are sentiments rather than principles because they are grounded not in his reason but in his sense that he has tried as much as he could to reason correctly. Rousseau's uniqueness consists in valuing the manner or form of his choice of principles more than their content. He begins by reflecting on the fact that actions consist of a deed and the motive for the deed. While the motive is what is important, there are elements to our motives of which even we are not aware. Motive divides into what we might call conscious and unconscious parts. The philosophers for whom Rousseau has such contempt do not, after all, know that they are motivated by vanity. In weighing one's actions all one can do is to purify one's conscious motives to the greatest extent possible. This is acting sincerely or in good faith— wishing the good in general even though one knows one's motives are probably at some level tainted.[8] This is the best that one can do—to do one's best. Accordingly, Rousseau believes he does not deserve to suffer because his attempt has been sincere. This is the heart of Rousseau's understanding of justice; he provides no account of the content of the principles he discovered because the form is the content.

Still, how do we know when we have acted in good faith? Rousseau is well aware that at some level his childhood prejudices are operating and that the secret vows of his heart threaten to lead him to adopt the most consoling views.

> One defends oneself with difficulty from believing what one wants with so much ardor [to believe], and who can doubt that the interest of admitting or rejecting the judgments of the other life determines the faith of the most part of men concerning their hope or their fear? All that could charm my judgment, I admit it, but not alter my good faith; for I feared to deceive myself about anything. If everything consisted in [depended on] the use of this life, it was important for me to know it, in order to make the best of what depended on me while there was yet time and not be completely a dupe. (III.15)

The "other life" is useful; it gives one an interest in being disinterested and so provides an imaginary content to morality that attaches one to the form—attempting to be disinterested. This holds no matter whether the other life means an afterlife or the life Rousseau has invented for himself after he reaches forty. If everything in the other life depends on the use of this life, then I am moved to be good generally and not to become too preoccupied with the goods of this life, which are, after all, mere means to an end. And if everything in the other life consists in the use of things in this life, then the other life is my life taken as a whole. Here too each individual good thing will have a purpose that points beyond itself insofar as it is part of a coherent whole. In either case, apparent purposes are not to be taken altogether seriously.

It is this sense of his "other life" that assures Rousseau of his own good faith. Still, is not Rousseau's unshakable principle that one is only responsible for trying as hard as possible (III.16) at odds with knowing that one must try or else face terrible consequences? That is, either the content of one's morality matters, in which case trying is not enough, or it is the effort to get at the true principles of morality that matters, in which case the content does not matter, and one knows it. This dilemma emerges clearly in paragraph 16 where Rousseau says, on the one hand, that a dogmatic tone in matters of morality is suitable only to charlatans while, on the other hand, several lines later he announces that he holds it as an unshakable principle that, if we fall into error despite our best efforts, we could not justly suffer any penalty. The problem is once again the problem of Solon. Making the most of this life, because this life is all there is, requires something like making another life depend on this one. The wholeness of one's life is the goal, but it requires taking the parts with the utmost seriousness even though they are merely means to the whole.

It is with this issue in mind that Rousseau once again raises the question of future generations in paragraph 17. Here he claims to write for a future generation that elsewhere he has indicated can never exist (I.9–10). What can this be, then, other than a formal principle? Rousseau thinks in terms of a future generation so as to affect the way he thinks now; the structure is the same as the invention of an afterlife. Both are regulative principles. The ideal "future" audience for which Rousseau writes will combine good sense and good faith. Good faith is not enough because an age may be sincere without realizing the importance of its sincerity. Rousseau would only be understood by an age aware of its own good faith. But this simply restores the difficulty of the curious sentence in paragraph 5 concerning the relation between what one ought to do and what one ought to believe. Lest we seem to have made no progress, however, it seems clear that however much good sense drives out good faith, it is still the case that there can be no good sense without good faith. That good sense, or reason, and good faith, or will, are both necessarily together and at odds with each other is clear from the following remark in paragraph 18.

> No, vain arguments will never destroy the *convenance* [fit, convenience] that I perceive between my immortal nature and the constitution of this world and the physical order that I see rule there. I find there in the corresponding moral order, of which the system is the result of my inquiries, the props of which I have need in order to support the miseries of my life. (III.18)

That *convenance* can mean both fit and convenience is the problem. Reasoning requires the coincidence of reason and will, which in turn undermines the reliability of reason.

In the third part of the Third Walk Rousseau gives an account of how his reformation was tested. It turns out that his decisions seem almost preordained (III.19). What was originally meant for one purpose in retrospect served another. Rousseau had originally planned to evaluate his life at age forty in order to prepare himself for the next life—to assure himself of heaven and avoid hell. In fact, his project served him when his lot was the most terrible of a mortal on *earth*. Now, Rousseau had picked his principles on the assumption that nothing important could change in his life but was then thrown into a situation he admits to have been absolutely unforeseen. Granted that his principles sustain him, still, either his underlying view is proven wrong, or his falls (*chutes*; III.19) are not absolutely unique but are a *kind* of misfortune and therefore comparable to others.

From his account in paragraph 20, it is clear that Rousseau's plan was not altogether successful; he was miserable for years. Insofar as the plan did work, Rousseau implies that life's pains diminish when they are seen as means to an end. The compensation for them, once seen, dwarfs even the greatest pains, and the certainty of compensation was what Rousseau had drawn from his previous meditations. But the compensation comes from the meditation itself and not necessarily from the result.

Or, once again, Rousseau does not say what the further end is to which these pains are the means. He only says that his reflection has led him to see that they are means. In a strange way, then, Rousseau's satisfaction comes from thinking about his life as a whole. Just as the life of solitude, entered into for the sake of thought, proved to be an end in itself, thinking about justice proves to be justice.

This is the heart of the Third Walk and the importance of paragraph 21. Even if Rousseau's principles are illusions, the internal fact that his heart confirms them as sentiments is decisive. The danger, of course, is that this pure willing of a system will lead to the loss of will, that the emphasis on the purity of his intention will undermine particular intentions. It may be that Rousseau never doubts these principles (of which we never in any case get an account), but it is clear in what follows that he scarcely ever *stops* doubting his manner of arriving at them. In paragraph 22 he quite rationally works through precisely why he is no longer sufficiently rational to guide himself. In the process, of course, he guides himself. He is so sure of himself that he claims that any new objections that arise are

> the sophisms of a subtle metaphysics that were unable [did not know how] to weigh the eternal truths admitted at all times by all wise men, known by all nations, and engraved in the human heart in ineffaceable characters. (III.22)

Since all wise men, nations, and human hearts do not agree about the content of fundamental principles (Rousseau has just admitted as much by saying that his principles seem illusory to others), what they all share must be their form. It is the form of morality, not its content, that is important.

Rousseau concludes the third section of the Third Walk with the claim to have forgotten the reasoning underlying his views, although not the conclusions of the reasoning. His system is not like reverie; reimagining it does not reintroduce the initial experience. What Rousseau clearly has not forgotten is his rational critique of reason—that only by doing justice to the heart do we behave rationally.

At the end of the Third Walk Rousseau returns to Solon, criticizing him for having thought that knowledge is limitless (III.25). Still, Rousseau thinks that he can learn something more about virtue in his old age.

This seems to involve favoring the practical over the theoretical life. Yet, since pure disinterested knowledge is not possible, perhaps Rousseau's turn to virtue is something like Socrates' turn to the human things after his disillusionment with the pre-Socratic philosophers. Perhaps Rousseau means only to turn our attention to the knower when something is known. This would lead us to the Fourth Walk where the heart of the argument will be the identification of lying and harming—i.e., doing injustice. What might this mean? If knowledge always presupposes a whole, where do we get such a whole? Where does the impulse to provide epigraphs come from? While the Third Walk seems at first to present Rousseau's plan of life as uniquely his, in fact it is simply the structure of morality generally. Human beings are put together in such a way as to have to jump outside of themselves in order to be themselves. By emphasizing the priority of the heart to reason, Rousseau suggests that the experience of rightness in moral matters provides us with a sense of what it means to be right that then gets transferred to theoretical matters. Whereas we tend to think our moral views need to be validated by theory, this notion of validation is the experience of morality that we never leave behind. Only because we are moral beings could we have a sense of truth. Knowledge of the content of morality, therefore, varies, but the sense of the possibility of wholeness or rightness is necessarily present in our prejudgments or prejudices. The argument of the Third Walk is therefore an attempt to show that any theoretical view is false unless it goes "through" our "knowledge" of virtue. This is the bridge to Rousseau's reinterpretation of lying, and so of truthtelling, in the Fourth Walk. Good faith is the underlying principle of all thought.

NOTES

1. See *Rousseau Juge de Jean-Jacques*, in *Oeuvres complètes*, vol. 1, 382–83.
2. See Herodotus, I.32.
3. Plato's Socrates defines philosophy as the practice of dying and being dead at *Phaedo*, 64a.
4. See *Les Confessions de J.-J. Rousseau*, in *Oeuvres complètes*, vol. 1, 121–27.
5. *Oeuvres complètes*, vol. 1, 129.
6. The word *heart* occurs at least nineteen times in the Third Walk in paragraphs 2, 4, 6 (four times), 7, 10, 12, 15, 18 (twice), 19, 21, 22 (four times), and

24. Five times it is coupled with *reason* (paragraphs 12, 18, 21, and twice in paragraph 22).

7. See *Emile* book 4, in *Oeuvres complètes*, vol. 3, 182, 204.

8. See *Oeuvres complètes*, vol. 3, 182.

8

THE GOODNESS OF TRUTH

That the Third and Fourth Walks make a pair is clear from the last sentence of the Fourth Walk.[1]

> In this, therefore, and in all similar things, the maxim of Solon is applicable to all ages, and it is never too late to learn, even from one's enemies, to be wise, true, modest and to presume less of oneself. (IV.42)

Solon is the thread that runs through the two walks but in the double way of the epigraph to the Third Walk and its unmentioned companion. We do grow old learning many things, but we cannot make our lives whole until we are dead. We, therefore, cannot be happy despite what we learn and, apart from some sense of a whole, cannot even learn what we think we are learning. Morality provides an alternative to this dismal scenario. It is the sign that we do have a view, however provisional, of our lives as wholes. One can only learn many things if one has a view from the outside of what one is learning. Morality, as our sense of detachment from the immediate, allows us to judge the immediate. Our concern for what ought to be is our release from what is.[2] Accordingly, like the Third Walk, the Fourth Walk is concerned with the relation of morality to truth—specifically, with whether lying can ever be moral.

The relation between the two walks is complicated by the fact that the issue of lying arises at all. At the time of the writing of the *Reveries*, it is over twenty-five years since, supposedly at the peak of his cognitive powers, Rousseau was to have settled all of the fundamental questions of morality. Now, since this question of lying is surely such a question, either Rousseau did not settle everything in 1750 (and what he said in the Third Walk was a lie), or he did settle everything (and what he says here is a lie). In either case, we know in advance the outcome of Rousseau's inquiry in the Fourth Walk: he believes that lying is sometimes justifiable. Thus, while the two walks are obviously connected, it is not clear that they are compatible. The Rousseau of the Third Walk was skeptical about the possibility of knowing anything at all, but lying seems to presuppose the possibility of speaking the truth. How can someone lie who never believes himself to know anything?

The structure of the Fourth Walk is fairly straightforward. Rousseau first gives an account of why he came to ask himself about lying (paragraphs 1–5). He then turns to a general examination of the morality of lying (paragraphs 6–24). After applying his general conclusions to himself (paragraphs 25–38), Rousseau concludes by explaining why he more than others is obliged to tell the truth (paragraphs 39–42).

The introductory section begins with a reference to Plutarch.

> Among the small number of books that I still sometimes read, Plutarch is the one that grips and profits me the most. It was the first reading of my childhood, it will be the last of my old age; he is [*c'est*] nearly the only author that I have never read without drawing from him some fruit. (IV.1)

Why does Rousseau begin with Plutarch? Plutarch's *Life of Solon* is almost certainly the source for the epigraph of the Third Walk. Rousseau elsewhere claims to have read his series of lives—*bioi*—of famous Greeks and Romans beginning at the age of six.[3] *Bios* suggests the problem of the Third Walk. A life is something that belongs uniquely to human beings because only they can survey their lives as wholes. Plutarch, then, is concerned with this issue. Rousseau begins by conflating Plutarch and his books. This is not so absurd and, in fact, is an ordinary figure of speech, although Rousseau does not really read Plutarch unless he has identified the man completely with his writings. There is an old joke to the effect that Shakespeare did not really write his plays but that they were really written by another man of the same name. The joke is funny to the extent that all we have of authors are their books. Rousseau says that Plutarch was the first author to appeal to him and will be the last; he thus represents a continuity that cuts across the apparent division in Rousseau's life between young and old. Plutarch is apparently one from whom it is possible to learn while growing old. But Plutarch is not a man; he is a book.

Rousseau cites in particular one of Plutarch's moral writings, *How One Could Draw Utility from One's Enemies*. The book contains the following passage:[4]

> Whenever something untrue is said, one ought not to despise and have no care for it because it is false, but rather to inquire which of the things said or done by you or of your endeavors or associations has produced the greatest likeness to the slander and to guard against this and flee it. For if others are taught useful things by becoming involved in involuntary matters . . . what prevents one from taking one's enemy as a teacher without a fee and profiting and learning from the things one failed to notice? (89F-90A)

Plutarch argues that the lies of one's enemies cannot originate from nothing at all. As they must have some foundation, one need only discover their grain of truth to profit from them. Rousseau begins the Fourth Walk supposedly with Plutarch but really with his book. In doing so, he tacitly points to the problem of lying and truth telling in books. In a book we are confronted with the manifestation of an other, a *sujet*, but with no illusion that we will ever be in the presence of this other. The Shakespeare who did not write the plays and the man of the same name who did write them are not really distinguishable from one another. "Shakespeare" is only a placeholder for whatever author lies behind the plays. Learning from a book is thus learning from someone from whom we are in principle alienated. Authors are enemies—Rousseau no longer accepts visits from them (II.18). Profiting from the lies of enemies therefore has something to do with reading books. To learn to do the one is to learn to do the other. This is particularly important since, as we have seen, the *Reveries* is a book in which the author lies.

The immediate cause of Rousseau's reflection on lying is a journal sent to him by its author, Father Rozier, and inscribed "*Vitam vero impendenti*"—to the one who dedicates his life to truth (one who grows old learning many things?). Rousseau takes this to be a sly insult. Rozier does not believe that this motto that Rousseau had taken for his own was accurate; the dedication is thus ironic.[5] But why is Rousseau so certain of Rozier's hostile intent, especially since the whole of the Fourth Walk might be understood as an attempt to show that Rozier wrote the truth, that Rousseau does dedicate his life to truth? Apparently the suspected sarcasm changes everything. Rozier says what is true, but in the context he makes it clear to Rousseau that he means the opposite. Therefore, he lied or said a *contre-vérité*. Rousseau thus begins with an extreme case of what he will treat explicitly later in the walk. In a lie, the words are unimportant; the intention is everything. This is the equivalent in the Fourth Walk of the *bon foi* or good faith of the Third Walk.

Still, how is it possible to know Rozier's intentions from the written inscription alone? The key to Rousseau's intention is the fact that he consistently misspells Rozier's name—he spells it *Rosier*. Now, while it may be that a Rosier by any other name would smell as sweet, still, Rousseau has apparently just looked at the inscription on the journal. Could he have misspelled the name intentionally, showing that he can make Rosier anything he wishes? This is the fate of authors—of Plutarch who was identified with his book, of Rozier whose name was misspelled, and of Rousseau himself, who foresees that no future generation will understand him. The intentions of another are only really knowable to him who made him up; to make his point, Rousseau makes up Rosier. And what does this made-up Rosier do? He insults Rousseau, but "What reason (*sujet*) could I have given him?" (IV.1). To be justified in his imagined sarcasm, Rosier would have had to imagine some motive equally inaccessible for Rousseau's actions. Rousseau as *sujet* is as fictional for Rozier as Rosier is for Rousseau. All of this highlights the underlying difficulty of interpreting the Fourth Walk. One cannot automatically expect an account that justifies lying under certain circumstances to be entirely truthful. Everything depends on the intentions of Rousseau as *sujet*.

At the end of the first paragraph Rousseau alludes to the problem of self-knowledge.

> In order to put the lessons of the good Plutarch to profit I resolved to use the walk of the following day to examine myself on lying, and I came to it well confirmed in my already held opinion that the "know thyself" of the temple of Delphi was not maxim so easy to follow as I had believed in my *Confessions*. (IV.1)

Since there turns out to be some truth in Rozier's *contre-vérité*, and since Rousseau had claimed in his confessions to be the most frank of men, Rousseau must have mistaken himself.[6] Is Rousseau's relation to himself, then, like one's relations to one's characters or like one's relations to others?

Rousseau begins his self-questioning with a phrase—*mettre en mar-che*—that is the perfect combination of the literal and metaphorical. It means both "to walk" and "to set out." The first thing he thinks of is the famous lie of the *Confessions*.[7] Rousseau was employed as a personal secretary to the dying Mme de Vercellis. At her death, in the confusion of the dismantling of her household, Rousseau stole a piece of pink and silver ribbon belonging to a Mlle Pontal. Confronted with his theft, he claimed that Marion, the pretty young cook, had given it to him. Rousseau says that he did not lie out of any intent to harm. He lied out of shame and fear of being discovered for what he was. Plutarch remarks in *How One Could Draw Utility from One's Enemies* that

> this is peculiar to vice, being ashamed for our errors before enemies rather than before friends. Whence, when some thought and said the affairs of Rome to be safe since the Carthaginians had been annihilated and the Achaeons enslaved, Nasikas said "Now indeed our position is precarious, having left for ourselves neither those we fear nor those before whom we are ashamed." (88A)

Shame and fear point to our awareness of others in the world and so to our need of the other, or the enemy, to keep ourselves honest. Lying and truth telling are social phenomena.

Rousseau claims that the memory of this event and, worse still, imagining what it might have cost Marion have kept him from lying throughout his life. Remembering what his natural timidity cost him makes him more afraid to lie. His shame triumphs over his shame because his capacity to imagine or remember consequences is stronger than the fear and shame of the present. Still, while Rousseau knows he does not intend to lie, he begins to wonder about the connection between this will or intent and what he actually does. Looking at himself as Rozier would—i.e., through an imagined enemy's eyes—helped Rousseau to do this.

Rousseau is somewhat startled by what he discovers. He, who

prides himself on love of truth, tells lies all the time, and it does not even bother him. How could this be, and why, in particular, does he lie when nothing is at stake and tell the truth when everything is at stake? Rousseau concludes that truth telling must be important only when things are at stake, or *justesse* (rightness as correctness) in some sense depends on *justice* (rightness as justice). Since truth telling is a social act, it will be measured not by an abstract standard but by its consequences—its justice. Rousseau is thus slowly moving toward an understanding of lying that makes *justesse* depend on *justice*. It could be true that after death there is nothing for us other than being put in a coffin underneath six feet of earth, but the mother I once knew who told her four-year-old daughter this "truth" was not really telling her the truth. A four-year-old will think of herself as buried alive in a coffin; death for her becomes hell.

The general question of the introductory section of the Fourth Walk is simple: How is it possible to be dedicated to truth and yet say so many things that are not true? Lurking in the background is the thought that such falsehoods may be not only possible but obligatory. Rousseau's move to the next section—the general account of lying—is motivated by a particular problem: the insult from Father Rozier. However, to make this particular problem the appropriate introduction to his general reflection on lying, Rousseau may have tinkered with its details. Rosier is a particular invention of Rousseau for the purpose of a general reflection on lying.

The second part of the Fourth Walk also begins with a book. "I remember having read in a philosophy book that to lie is to hide a truth that one ought to show" (IV.6). Rousseau introduces an anonymous author who makes a claim to an anonymous audience. This definition of lying seems at first to be a truth without a context, but if Rousseau really means that *justice* is prior to *justesse*, these bookish anonymities cannot really be possible. According to the anonymous definition, concealing a truth one is not obliged to tell is not lying. However, is it lying to say what is not the case when one is not obliged to say anything? Rousseau's own example points to the problem: "for if he gives fake money to a man to whom he owes nothing, he deceives this man, without a doubt, but he does not rob him" (IV.6). Yet this may not be so harmless as Rousseau indicates. If you give another counterfeit money, and, thinking it is real, he uses it to pay his bills, have you not harmed him? It is not so easy to know when one is obliged to reveal a truth. All of this leads to two questions.

> The first, when and how one owes the truth to another, since one does not always owe it. The second, whether there are any cases where one may innocently deceive. This second question is already decided, I know it well: negatively in books where the most austere morality costs the author nothing; affirmatively in society where the morals of books pass for chatter impossible to practice. Let us therefore leave these authorities who contradict each other, and let us seek to resolve these questions for myself by my own principles. (IV.7)

Having himself just begun from a book, Rousseau now says something about books. The bookish rule is that we never ought to deceive another. Society finds this ridiculous; only when nothing is at stake can one afford to say lying is always bad. Only in a context indifferent to context can *justesse* have a meaning independent of *justice*; otherwise truth has no meaning apart from what Rousseau calls *utilité*—usefulness. Yet, just as we are about to conclude that this book does not take books very seriously, we come to paragraph 8.

> General and abstract truth is the most precious of all goods. Without it man is blind; it is the eye of reason. It is by it that man learns to conduct himself, to be what he ought to be, to do what he ought to do, to tend to his true end. Particular and individual truth is not always a good, it is sometimes an evil, very often an indifferent thing. The things that it is important for a man to know and of which the recognition is necessary to his happiness are not perhaps great in number, but in whatever number they may exist, they are a good that belongs to him, that he has a right to claim everywhere he finds it, and of which one cannot defraud him without committing the most iniquitous of all thefts, since it is of goods common to all of which the communication does not deprive the one who gives them of anything at all. (IV.8)

Could general and abstract truths do all Rousseau says that they do and still not strictly speaking be true? After all, one must begin as Rousseau has in fact begun here. He begins with a definition from a philosophy book and proceeds to develop it to show how it does not fit in his case. Abstract truths seem at once the most precious of goods and useless.

> In this, as in all else, my temperament has had much influence on my maxims, or rather on my habits; for I have scarcely acted by rules, or scarcely followed any other rule in anything than the impulses of my nature. (IV.26)

Yet,

> [a]s to truths that have no sort of utility either for instruction or in practice, how will they be a good owed since they are not even a good, and since property is founded only on usefulness, where there is no usefulness possible at all, there cannot be any property. (IV.9)

Abstract truths, being of no use at all, are in no way owed: "they are not even a good." At the same time they are "the most precious of all goods." Perhaps this contradiction can be resolved if we understand abstract truth to be good precisely because it is not of any use; it is good not as an end but as Rousseau uses it here—as a beginning point. Rousseau hints at this possibility when he says that "in the moral order nothing is useless, no more than in the physical order" (IV.9). What else is there other than these two orders? "But are there any truths so perfectly sterile that they are in every way useless for everything?" (IV.10). If there were no sterile truths (even the color of the sand at the bottom of the ocean would be a pregnant truth), concealing the truth would always either benefit or harm others. Then it would be impossible to say anything true or false even with the best of intentions without simultaneously helping some and harming others. If a completely innocent lie is hard to imagine, so also is a completely innocent truth. Accordingly, *justice* proves as difficult as *justesse*, and lying proves to be something one has no choice but to do. The only question would be how to do it. This is the analogue in the Fourth Walk to the problem of solitude in the Third Walk, where Rousseau forsook society by changing his style of wig.

By the end of the eleventh paragraph, Rousseau seems to have reduced truth to useful truth—*justesse* to *justice*—and so seems to have answered the first of his two questions (when and how one owes another the truth) explicitly and the second (whether there is such a thing as innocent deception) implicitly. However, a problem remains. This general rule of utility does not solve the problem of what is useful when and to whom. In seeking a "pure application for practice" (IV.12), Rousseau indicates that thus far he has only formulated an abstract principle (even if it is about what is not abstract). The principle of utility is like those useless truths found in books. More particularly, since utility or interest is always particular, and since speech is always a public or general act, how can we ever isolate and individualize our acts of speech? To know what is useful would mean to know what is good; this would require knowing perfectly each of the souls I address and their relations to other souls and things, as well as perfectly knowing my own soul. To make the sort of judgment Rousseau demands, I would have to be an all-knowing god.

In the face of this difficulty, we are tempted simply to formulate a general rule: Do not lie. We would then act as though the world were such that justice could be identified with truth. We would have finessed the problem of when to lie for the sake of the good by making truth telling a paramount good. However, such a solution is possible only by virtue of a lie to ourselves. We think we have "put nothing of our own" (IV.13) in our truths when, as a matter of fact, our motive for always telling the truth is cowardice and despair. We know that we need to take into account variables that we fear can never be determined, and so, making a virtue of necessity, we determine that it is a virtue to ignore these variables. Accordingly, our general rule always to tell the truth does not really settle matters.

> But that is to settle the question without resolving it. It was not concerned with declaring whether it would be good always to say the truth but whether one was always equally obliged to do so. . . . (IV.14)

There is a difference between what would be good and what one is obliged to do; one is only obliged to do what is possible. If it is not possible for us always to tell the truth, given that we cannot know all of the particulars we would need to know, the serious question is whether it is possible to formulate a rule that makes it possible to determine when to lie and when not. We need something to mediate between knowable but useless generalities and the infinite, and so unknowable, particulars.

Rousseau knows into what a difficult corner he has painted himself.

How is it possible ever to prove the infallibility of a rule that can only be measured by particular results? His reply is instructive.

> In all difficult questions of morals like this I have always found myself better off resolving them by the dictates of my conscience rather than by what is brought to light by my reason. (IV.15)

Rousseau will rely, rather, on what he hears than on what he sees. Still, this does not mean that he will let his conscience judge particular cases; it is his rule of which his conscience will be the judge. It therefore does not matter so much that Rousseau's passions temporarily distort his judgment because his conscience always reasserts itself in the long run, and the rule is for the long run. In the long run, then, Rousseau is as hard on himself as God is.

What then is this rule? Rousseau resolves to judge by intention and not by consequences; this is what moral worth consists in. Yet, since this makes it all but impossible to judge others at all, Rousseau can only be concerned here with judging his own lies. Only he can know his own intent. However, he can know his intent is not to harm only when there is a certainty that the error engendered in others can harm neither them nor others. Does this not simply throw Rousseau back on consequences as criteria for actions and so for lies? Perhaps not quite. Rousseau is not concerned with actual consequences so much as his own subjective certainty that he thought no bad consequences would follow. He may turn out to have been wrong. The criteria used to evaluate lies are not results but imagined results. If you can imagine harmful consequences and nevertheless go ahead with your deception, then you have lied.

> This lie, which was a great crime in itself, must have been a still greater one through its effects, of which I have always been ignorant but which remorse makes me suppose were as cruel as possible. (IV.2)

Rousseau sees two things: Intent is the location of moral worth, and intent is invisible without what it intends—consequences. One cannot identify the intent to take a walk apart from the activity of walking that would be the consequence of the intention.[8] Rousseau concludes that the criterion for judging intent is the imagined result. Once having imagined the results, does it seem to the one speaking that what he will say will harm another? Now, we have a name for this imagining of possible results of possible actions—fiction. Fiction is Rousseau's answer to the question of a rule for utility. It is lodged somewhere between the general rule, which does not consider consequences, and specific cases, which are infinite in number and which are too late to consider once they have come to be at issue. For this reason Rousseau turns in what follows to a minute analysis of the morality of fiction.

Rousseau quickly passes over fables as wrapping useful truths in pleasing forms. However, it is striking that he does not ask why it should be useful to do this. Fables are not really lies because they are so evidently meant only as packaging. They are not indifferent to the truth, and yet they are not the truth. Still, why should the truth have to be packaged? This question leads to Rousseau's reflection on a *roman*, *Le Temple de Gnide*, and to his attack on its anonymous author. While it was generally known that Montesquieu wrote the story, Rousseau respects his anonymity and never mentions him by name; he would therefore seem to be an accomplice after the fact in Montesquieu's crime. At first Rousseau seems to use *Le Temple de Gnide* as an example of the sort of fiction that is a "true lie." Unlike one who tells a fable and admits it to be a fable, Montesquieu pretends to have found a Greek manuscript. But this is simply what all authors of fiction do when their writing is not transparently fabular. Fiction presents its characters as real; Montesquieu merely pushed this process to its final end by removing his authorship from view entirely. The Fourth Walk seems to pivot on Rousseau's disagreement with Montesquieu. The *Reveries* is a book in which it is the author's purpose to reveal himself as fully as possible. *Le Temple de Gnide* is a book in which the author's purpose seems to be to conceal himself as fully as possible. Montesquieu might justify himself by claiming that telling the truth requires suppressing one's authorship—the goal being to say something that would be true no matter who uttered it. Accordingly, like all writing, *Le Temple de Gnide* must stand on its own merits. It does not matter whether an anonymous Greek wrote it or Montesquieu or another man by the same name. When Rousseau objects that Montesquieu does not reveal his authorship, he thus objects to this understanding of truth. There is no measuring the work independent of the author, for the truth of a writing depends on its intent. Rozier's words were literally true—Rousseau does consecrate his life to truth—but, as his intent was false, his words were false.

When Rousseau criticizes Montesquieu for hiding his authorship, we see that any lie is really two lies.[9] To lie means to say something that is not true, but it also means to present oneself as true when one is not. Fiction always lies in its content; it deceives us about the existence of the people, places, and situations it describes, although it need not deceive us about the relations among them. If the content of Montesquieu's novel is a lie with regard to these relations, it would be a lie of fiction. But regardless, it is a lie about the origin of a fiction. By concealing his authorship Montesquieu ensures that he will not be held accountable for the "truths" present in *Le Temple de Gnide*—the truths about the relationships within his fiction. By giving them a false antiquity, Montesquieu grants these relations an authority independent of what they could claim for themselves. He creates an instant classic. When this is coupled with the falseness of the content of the novel, Rousseau feels justified in condemning Montesquieu. But Rousseau does not seem to acknowledge that Montesquieu could well be commenting on the classics by way of this lie that everyone knows to be a lie. By presenting a modern writing as ancient, one indicates either that there could have been moderns among the ancients or that there can be ancients among the moderns. Why could Montesquieu not be making the same point that Rousseau makes in criticizing those who think of themselves as true because they take care "to cite faithfully places, times, persons" (IV.22)? Is it not possible to insist on a lie that one knows will not be believed to make a point based on its not being believed? In his concern over the fact that Montesquieu intended to lie, Rousseau seems peculiarly unconcerned with the intention behind Montesquieu's lie.[10]

Rousseau's argument with Montesquieu is about a book—a place where the word gets an existence apart from the one who uttered it. But Rousseau is more concerned with men of good faith than with these abstract truths; he is more concerned with the true man than the true sentence.

> Whether or not these distinctions are found in books, they happen nonetheless in the heart of every man of good faith with himself, who wants to permit himself nothing for which his conscience could reproach him. For to say something false to his own advantage is no less to lie than if one said it to the prejudice of another, although the lie be less criminal. To give advantage to one who ought not to have

it is to disturb order and justice; to attribute falsely to himself or to another an act from which might result praise or blame, inculpation or disculpation, is to do an unjust thing. But anything contrary to truth that hurts justice in any way whatsoever is a lie. There is the exact limit: but everything contrary to truth that does not concern justice in any way is only fiction, and I confess that whoever reproaches himself for a pure fiction as though for a lie has a more delicate conscience than I. (IV.20)

The notion of justice here is rather abstract. To be able to imagine the result of a lie as unduly to someone's advantage or disadvantage is to harm justice and lie. The injustice of Montesquieu is to want to avoid responsibility for what he has said.[11] By not considering the possibility that he might be wrong, Montesquieu ensures that only if his book is useful (i.e., only if he is not wrong) will he be just and not have lied. However, Rousseau suggests another possibility (IV.20). Would it not be possible for truths sometimes to upset the order of justice? Giving each his due does not always mean telling each the truth. In some cases is it not just to conceal the truth and even lie in matters of *utilité*? One can, or presumably one must, lie for the good of others so long as one is willing to bear the responsibility for one's lie. This is to be no less true than one who utters a truth.

Fiction is unconcerned with justice only in the sense that reality is not at issue. Fictions are concerned with the moral issues arising within their stories. In fact, fiction amounts to figuring out what to do on the basis of hypothetical situations and so harming no one in particular but in a way still benefiting (and so potentially harming) many. Fiction does not deal with what is immediately useful—it does not profit us to know that Anna Karenina was an adulteress. Nevertheless, this detachment from the useful is useful to us in thinking through what is and is not useful.[12]

So that we may understand what he means by a man who is true, Rousseau juxtaposes his true man to the man considered true by the world.

I have seen some of these people that are called true in the world. All their truthfulness exhausts itself in idle conversations in faithfully citing places, times, persons, in not permitting any fiction, in not embroidering any circumstance, in exaggerating nothing. In everything that does

not touch their interest at all they are of the most inviolable fidelity in
their narrations. But if it concerns treating some affair regarding them,
narrating some deed that touches closely, all the colors are employed
to present things in the light that is most advantageous to them. And
if the lie is useful to them and they abstain from telling it themselves,
they promote it with skill and find a way for it to be adopted without
its being able to be imputed to them. Thus prudence wills it: goodbye
truthfulness. (IV.22)

The true "true man," however, is indifferent to things where nothing is
at stake. He utters falsehoods easily when doing so is of no benefit or
harm to another, living or dead.

> But every discourse that produces for someone any profit or hurt,
> esteem or contempt, praise or blame contrary to justice and truth is a
> lie which will never approach his heart or his mouth or his pen. He is
> solidly *true*, even against his interest. . . . The difference therefore that
> exists between my true man and the other is that the one of the world
> is very rigorously faithful to every truth that costs him nothing but
> not beyond that, whereas mine never serves her so faithfully as when
> it is necessary to immolate himself for her. (IV.23)

Now, we have already seen that it is not the content of a sentence that
makes a man true but his motive in the context. Since no specific action
or utterance can reveal this motive, the true man can only be understood
as though he were a character in a fiction. This becomes apparent in
Rousseau's account of how the true man shows himself. He is never so
faithful to the truth as when it requires self-immolation, for only when
he seems to act contrary to his own interest will his true motive become
manifest. Otherwise the difference between him and the world's true
man is invisible. Of course, if one has an obligation to make morality
visible, one would have a corresponding obligation to seek out situations
of this sort or at the very least to paint oneself as self-sacrificing.

Rousseau's true man is unconcerned for trivial truth because it has
nothing to do with justice. His love of truth is only an emanation of his
love of justice.

> Justice and truth are in his mind two synonymous words that he takes
> indifferently one for the other. The holy truth that his heart adores

does not at all consist in indifferent facts and in useless names but in faithfully rendering to each what is his due in things that are truly his, in good or bad imputations, in retributions of honor or of blame, in praise and disapprobrium. (IV.24)

The true man is thus indifferent to the difference between truth and justice. The truth that justice and truth are one is thus established not because it is true but because it is just. It is therefore no surprise that Rousseau should go on to make clear how jealous the true man is of his self-esteem. He relishes situations where he can show his real worth. But his relish may threaten to lead him astray. Because the true man's holy truth does not consist of indifferent facts, he can be indifferent to the distinction between truth and justice. He can lie about the difference because it is unimportant. Of course, this means that there is a difference. The true man is unconcerned with it because his real concern is showing forth his own soul. He is therefore willing to lie if that is what is necessary to show the purity of his intentions—the only things of any moral worth. As one of the things about which he is indifferent is the difference between truth and justice, such a man may not know that he is lying. In this he is to be distinguished from Rousseau, who is about to tell us about his *Confessions*, a book in which he had to lie to tell the truth about himself.

After the true man, Rousseau returns to himself. In saying that "such were my rules of conscience on lying and truth" (IV.25), he suggests that they may not still be his rules. In any case, he moves from the effects of lying on others to its effect on him. Rousseau can do this because by generalizing from his shame at the lie he told about Marion, he has been cured of telling the kind of lie that harms others. This generalization is, of course, the result of what Rousseau imagined to have happened to Marion as the result of his lie. Rousseau generalizes his shame at an example that he imagined, and from this generalization he shames himself into not lying. He turns his *amour-propre* on itself. However, he has not been so successful with lies that harm himself. He gets into situations in which he must say something. As much as he can, he invents fables or apologues, but sometimes he cannot think quickly enough. Then, because he wants others to know that he is not really so dull as he seems, he lies. Lying is therefore presented as Rousseau's attempt to make his true nature visible.

Still, he seems rather generous to himself in his explanation.

> I swear to heaven that if the instant after I could retract the lie that
> excuses me and say the truth that lays a charge against me without by
> my retraction affronting myself anew, I would do it with all my heart.
> But the shame of myself catching myself at fault still restrains me, and
> I repent very sincerely of my fault without nevertheless daring to cor-
> rect it. (IV.28)

While this looks at first like an outrageous argument, it is in a way true.
Rousseau's shame at having been ashamed at having been inadequate is
what prevents him from owning up to his lies after they have mechanically escaped his mouth. Retracting them would make the original desire
not to shame himself seem ridiculous. This would shame him even
more, and so he succumbs to shame a second time.

What motivates these lies is really a sense of justice, as becomes clear
in the particular example he offers. On an outing with a group of people,
Rousseau is asked by a young pregnant woman whether he has had any
children. He blushes and says that he has not. Convinced that this is a
reference to his admission in the *Confessions* that he had forced Therese
to give their children up to foundling homes, and an attempt to embar-
rass him, Rousseau wishes that he had said, "That is hardly a discreet
question on the part of a young woman to a man who has grown old as
a bachelor" (IV.30).[13] Rousseau first tells us what happened and then
what he wishes had happened—what ought to have been. The latter is
what he might have written up had he been writing a novel. Indeed, he
suggests he did something of the sort in the writing of his *Confessions*
(IV.32). The reply he invents after the fact would have been perfectly
just and in that sense most true. Poetic justice means saying what will
preserve the moral order. While this example shows that justice is what
motivates Rousseau and not petty revenge, it also shows that such justice
is only possible in the imagination. But the situation is still more complicated. We know of the existence of Rousseau's children from what he
says in the *Confessions*, but in the *Reveries* he tells us that he frequently
lied in the *Confessions* to make himself look frank.[14] So on the basis of
what may well be a fiction, Rousseau tells another fiction in which he
uses a fictional embarrassment about a fictional fault to tell a truth about
fiction or lying. Can we be sure of all of this? Perhaps not, but it is

worth noting that Rousseau identifies the woman whose daughter was supposed to have insulted him as Mme Vacassin. In fact, her name seems to have been Vaucassin.[15] Every time Rousseau misspells a name, we might wonder about the status of the character he is describing.

Rousseau has written a fiction to reveal the difference between fiction and reality, but for what purpose? Rousseau is unhappy because he cannot show his true inside—his soul. Now, in every example of the Fourth Walk the souls of those with whom Rousseau converses are similarly hidden; their motives are never altogether manifest. Yet if Rousseau's stories are to serve any purpose, motives must be attached to the characters' actions. Accordingly, they must become characters in books. But then the moral order exists primarily in imaginary situations. Now, this is not to say that morality is imaginary. These imaginary situations are crucial because they make one's inside known to oneself. This seems to be the purpose of the Fourth Walk as a whole—to show how difficult self-knowledge is. Morality exists always in a conditional form. Only if someone intended something is he to be praised or blamed, and we can never be sure of the intentions of another. Similarly, we can praise and blame ourselves only insofar as we know our true motives. Such knowledge comes from inspecting our behavior toward others supposing them to have had certain motives.

That this is the issue of the Fourth Walk is clear from Rousseau's reflection on his *Confessions* (IV.31–38). His goal in that book was to show his good faith, veracity, and frankness. However, to do this he had to do more than simply tell what had happened to him. He had to make a fable or a fiction—a whole—of his life. This meant putting in appropriate (*juste*) details that might not have been altogether accurate (*juste*). More important, it required that he reveal the unexpected so that people would believe him. Rousseau had to prove his frankness by lying. This is what is necessary to make the true man manifest and so to give a picture of human virtue.

Accordingly, Rousseau now reveals two stories from his youth that he did not include in the *Confessions* because they would have made him look too good and would, therefore, have made the book less believable. But why does he reveal them now? Both seem to be paradigms for what he was doing in the *Confessions* as a whole; they are metastories. In both cases Rousseau reveals that he was physically injured by friends—one through carelessness and the other willfully. In both cases, struck by the genuine distress of those who hurt him, Rousseau takes it as a sign of regret. He is so moved that he forgets the reason for their regret and does not get angry. In the first case, the young Fazy begs him not to tell; in the second case, in which Pleince hit him in the head with a mallet, perhaps perfect justice would have required that he tell, but Rousseau decides on his own to keep quiet.

The importance of these stories becomes clearer in light of the quotation at the end of the first from Tasso's *Jerusalem Delivered*.

> Magnanimous lie! Now when is the truth
> So beautiful that it can be preferred to thee?

Rousseau had translated this section of *Jerusalem Delivered* previously and omitted these two lines.[16] He therefore restores not only the two events he had omitted from the *Confessions* but also the two lines he had previously omitted. Both restorations are meant to shock us into believing him (only an honest man would tell us so frankly that he has lied), just as their omissions had previously been meant to shock us into believing him (only an honest man would say so many bad things about himself). This is a variation on Rousseau's shame at the question of his children. Here he uses the shame of admitting to a lie as a way to smuggle in good things about himself; earlier he had used the bad or shameful things about himself to make himself look good. *Jerusalem Delivered* is an epic poem about Godfrey's recovery of the Holy Land from the infidels. The second book of the poem begins with a lapsed Christian, Ismeno, suggesting to the tyrant Aladine that a picture of the Virgin Mary be taken out of the Christian church and put in the temple of Macon. Ismeno says that he will cast a spell so that the city of Jerusalem cannot be captured as long as the picture is in the temple. This is done, but the icon disappears. In his wrath, Aladine intends to kill all the Christians, but Sophronia (whose name derives from *sophrōn*, the Greek word for "moderate" or "sane"), the beautiful young virgin, claims that she stole the icon and burned it. While the Christians are saved by her confession, it is not the truth. Her martyrdom consists in her lie. This is the context of the quotation in the Fourth Walk.

In both stories and in the *Confessions* Rousseau lies in order to sacrifice himself for others. He sacrifices truth for justice. While this may look wonderfully selfless, Rousseau indicates that he does it out of self-esteem. It is not possible to show one's dedication to benefiting others without arranging things so that the act of benefiting is a sacrifice. The purity of the will shows only in confronting adversity. Both these examples, from his childhood, the quotation from *Jerusalem Delivered*, the act of keeping the stories out of the *Confessions*, and the *Reveries* are lies told to benefit others. All therefore necessarily exaggerate the suffering of the liar in order to make their point. In doing so, they represent the necessity of a certain kind of lie or fiction for the existence of truth.

The Fourth Walk seems to move toward a subordination of truth to justice; there is to be no general prohibition against lying. It therefore comes as something of a surprise at the end of the walk when Rousseau asserts his special obligation always to tell the truth (IV.39–42). This need for this change was hinted at earlier in the walk.

> I saw that the solution of this problem [Rousseau's lack of remorse for having told many lies] depended on the accuracy [*justesse*] of the judgment that I had to make about myself on this point. . . . (IV.5)

Rousseau's motive is to determine the accuracy of his judgment about himself. This is not solely his concern, for "if it is necessary to be just for others, it is necessary to be true for oneself; it is an homage that the honest man must render to his own dignity" (IV.40). For oneself, then, *justesse* is prior to *justice*. Rousseau needs to establish his justice to prove the accuracy/*justesse* of his self-understanding.

But why is this so necessary? What is the difference between what Rousseau owes to himself and what he owes to others, between the obligation to *moi* and the obligation to *eux*? Rousseau's principle is by this time fairly clear.

> It follows from all these reflections that the profession of truthfulness that I have made has its foundation more on sentiments of rightness and equity than on the reality of things, and that in practice I have followed the moral directions of my conscience more than abstract notions of true and false. (IV.39)

And yet, how does one get these feelings about what one tells oneself? The very notion of lying for the benefit of others implies a prior distinction between the true and the false—a distinction not dependent on justice. We can tell others noble lies, but we cannot tell them to ourselves.[17] To take it upon ourselves to judge when to lie for the benefit of others means we must understand ourselves to be perfectly honest with ourselves. If, like Sophronia, we are to bear the inappropriate truth that we deny to others, we must recognize a truth independent of appropriateness—of justice. At the very least we would have to say that for ourselves *justesse* and *justice* are one.

Rousseau has articulated a notion of truth that is relative to situations, contexts, and people. But the very activity of choosing what and what not to say entails another notion of truth not relative to situations, contexts, and people. Given the importance Rousseau attributes in the Fourth Walk to utility and justice, how is it possible to articulate a notion of truth independent of interest? How is it possible to do what Rousseau claims to be doing when he tries to learn about himself? How can one resolve to take a long hard look at oneself and determine that long hard looks are always governed by self-interest? The model for Rousseau in the Fourth Walk is to look at himself as an enemy would, but of course this means an imagined enemy—Rosier, not Rozier. Ultimately this means using his imagination to look at himself as other, since "other" is what "enemy" ended up meaning in the First and Second Walks. This means looking at oneself from the outside, doing what Solon says we cannot really do until we are dead. Rousseau's substitute for death is fiction. Fiction is an interest—we enjoy it—but a sort of interest at a distance. This power to feel and yet be detached is not unlike the morality of the Third Walk—a power to be detached and yet feel. It is very close as well to what Rousseau will call reverie in the Fifth Walk. Like fiction, reverie will allow us to experience our experiencing more than what we are experiencing. It is a purer version of what every human being must to some degree experience by virtue of being human—a sentiment of oneself.

The whole point of the Fourth Walk is that Solon's maxim is necessary for one to be "wise, true, modest, and to presume less of oneself" (IV.42). That we are always learning prevents us from taking ourselves for granted. It gives us a motive to detach ourselves from ourselves, to test ourselves by way of fictions. Ironically, this self-detachment is the meaning of self-knowledge.

NOTES

1. This pairing is remarkably similar to the pairing of parts 2 and 3 in Descartes's *Discourse on Method*. Descartes begins part 2 and ends part 3 with refer-

ences to the Thirty Years War. Part 2, of course, concerns the question of knowledge; the subject of part 3 is morality. Rousseau has coupled the same two issues, but he has reversed the order of treatment.

2. Consider Rousseau's distinction between goodness and virtue in the *Second Discourse* (*Oeuvres complètes,* vol. 2, 223–24) and its connection to the difference between awareness and self-awareness.

3. See *Confessions, Oeuvres complètes,* vol. 1, 122.

4. See Plutarch, *Moralia* (New York: Loeb Classical Library, 1928) vol. 2, 24. The translation is my own.

5. Rousseau had used the motto for his *Letter to M. d'Alembert* and his *Letters Written from the Mountain* (*Oeuvres complètes,* vol. 3, 400).

6. See *Confessions, Oeuvres complètes,* vol. 1, 121.

7. See *Oeuvres complètes,* vol. 1, 151–53.

8. Compare Thomas Hobbes, *Leviathan* (Oxford: Blackwell, 1957), first part, chapter 6, 38.

9. See Victor Gourevitch's "Rousseau on Lying: A Provisional Reading of the Fourth *Rêverie,*" *Berkshire Review* 15 (1980): 93–107.

10. *Le Temple de Gnide* is a story about lovers set in a sanctuary to the goddess Venus and contains an account of both the satisfactions and the dangers of erotic love. That Montesquieu presents it in such an indirect way—as the product of an anonymous author—is surely no more accidental than the layered and indirect way in which Plato presents his account of love in the *Symposium* (172a–174a). Somehow one is not surprised that there should be a connection between erotic love, on the one hand, and secrecy, deception, lies and the imagination, on the other. Consider, in addition, the conclusion of Diana Schaub's interpretation of *Le Temple de Gnide* ("The Education of the Sentiments in Montesquieu's *Temple of Gnide,*" paper presented at the 1994 Annual Meeting of the American Political Science Association, 34).

> There [in the postscript], the god of love is found alone in a garden, temporarily deserted by his disciples. To contain his power over men, he is persecuted and buried. Assisted by a divine parent, he rises and ascends into heaven, "whence he reigns over all nature," with power to judge and punish. Stripped to its essential lines, the story appears as a comic and highly sacrilegious retelling of the death and resurrection of Christ. Montesquieu terrestrializes the religion of love.

Surely the author of the "Profession of Faith of a Savoyard Vicar" would recognize here another reason for practicing deception.

11. Rousseau's autobiographical writings are, of course, especially concerned with the fact that Rousseau was brutally held responsible for what he claims not to have said. Given how difficult it has proved to know an author's—indeed, anyone's—intentions, perhaps the motive for Montesquieu's attempt to avoid responsibility needs further reflection.

12. This is the principle behind Rousseau's introduction of books, specifically *Robinson Crusoe*, into Emile's education in *Emile*, book 3 (*Oeuvres complètes,* vol. 3, 129–36).

13. See *Confessions* in *Oeuvres complètes,* vol. 1, 252–53 and 282.

14. For related arguments, see Sebastien Mercier, *De J. J. Rousseau considéré comme l'un des premiers auteurs de la révolution* (Paris: Buisson, 1791), 262, as well as Christopher Kelley, *Rousseau's Exemplary Life: The* Confessions *as Political Philosophy* (Ithaca, N.Y.: Cornell University Press, 1987), 13–19.

15. See Charles Butterworth, *The Reveries of the Solitary Walker* (New York: Harper & Row, 1979), 60.

16. See Gourevitch, "Rousseau on Lying," 106.

17. This is the reason that "What one ought to do depends very much on what one ought to believe" is a truth that cannot be said of oneself.

9

THE ISLAND OF THE BLESSED

The Fourth Walk poses a problem. How it is possible to know that justice is prior to truth? What makes this perspective *juste* (accurate), and, if it is true, how could one ever know it to be so? Is its truth a moral issue? Is it something on which the possibility of behaving in a way that is *juste* (just) depends? This question is connected to another. Rousseau differs from other men in holding himself to a stricter standard of truth telling; he recognizes that in one's dealings with oneself the two meanings of *juste* coincide. If one lies to oneself, one cannot reasonably determine when it is *juste* (just) to say what is not altogether *juste* (accurate) to others. One has to know what one is concealing in order to conceal it, even for the best of reasons. That Rousseau would extend this level of honesty to his dealings with others means that he knows that it is the measure of all truth telling. What distinguishes him from others is that he embodies in his behavior what is implicit in them. In this way, the *Reveries* is a description of both "them" and "me" but in such a way that what operates in all men, and may even be their defining feature, is much more powerfully manifest in Rousseau. What is special about Rousseau is what is common to us all. This is especially true of the description of reverie in the Fifth Walk, which divides roughly into three parts: a description of St. Peter's Island where Rousseau spent a few months in 1765 after having been forced to leave Motier (paragraphs 1–5), an account of why Rousseau was so happy there (paragraphs 6–11), and an account of the nature of reverie (paragraphs 12–17).

Rousseau begins by identifying the one place he has lived that has made him truly happy. We who have just finished the Fourth Walk will naturally be unsure of precisely what Rousseau means by *true* happiness. We are put on our guard as well by several other peculiarities. The

169

name, St. Peter's Island, is suggestive, as is that of the lake in which the island is found, Lake Bienne, a pun on *bien* (good). Rousseau contrasts it to solid ground (*terre ferme*; V.4) and claims that during his time there

> Delivered from all the earthly passions that the tumult of social life engenders, my soul frequently would thrust itself above this atmosphere and commune in advance with the celestial intelligences of which it hopes in a little time to go to augment the number. (V.17)

The island seems to be heaven. Still, there is some question about the accuracy of Rousseau's description. He says that the island was ideally situated for a man who likes to be enclosed, but the verb he uses, *se circonscrire*, literally means "to circumscribe oneself"—"to draw a circle around oneself." That Rousseau has drawn such a circle is clear from the second paragraph where he says that the basin of Lake Bienne is "almost round." A glance at a map indicates that Lake Bienne is shaped like an isosceles triangle with its legs about three times the length of its base.[1] The Lake Bienne and St. Peter's Island of the *Reveries* are idealized versions of their real counterparts; accordingly, the *justesse* (although perhaps not the *justice*) of Rousseau's account is questionable.[2]

Furthermore, at the end of the second paragraph Rousseau describes the relation between the two islands in Lake Bienne. Earth from the smaller is regularly taken to repair the erosion of the larger. Rousseau concludes by saying, "It is thus that the substance of the weak is always used to the profit of the powerful." This allegorizing of the relation between the two islands invites us to wonder whether Rousseau does not mean the whole walk to be understood allegorically. And, of course, we know from the Fourth Walk, that "fictions that have a moral object are called apologues or fables," and "he who only peddles a fable as a fable does not in any way lie" (IV.17).

Not only is the fictionalized heavenly St. Peter's Island located within a fictionalized perfectly formed lake, it is also almost a perfect model of the whole—a microcosm. It contains large varieties of terrain, plants, and animals. At the same time, the island is so removed from the day to day traffic of the world and so filled with refuges (*asiles*; V.2) that

> it is interesting for solitary contemplatives who love to become intoxicated at leisure in the charms of nature and to collect themselves in a

silence that is troubled by no noise other than the cry of eagles, the sporadic singing of some birds and the rumbling of torrents as they fall from the mountain. (V.2)

St. Peter's Island is both the whole of nature and a refuge (*asile*) in which to collect oneself; it is the world and provides a respite *from* the world. In the *Confessions* St. Peter's is presented in a complicated way. Comparing himself to Linnaeus, Rousseau says the following:

> This great observer is to my mind, with Ludwig, the only one until now who had seen botany as would a naturalist and a philosopher; but he studied it too much in herbariums and gardens and not enough in nature herself. For me, who took the entire island as his garden, as soon as I needed to make or verify any observation, I would run into the woods or into the meadows, my book under my arm. There I would lie down on the ground near the plant in question in order to examine it on the spot, completely at my ease. This method was of much service to me in recognizing vegetation in its natural state, before it had been cultivated and denatured by the hand of men. It is said that Fagon, first doctor of Louis XIV, who would name and recognize perfectly all the plants in the royal garden, was so ignorant in the country that he no longer recognized anything there. I am precisely the opposite. I know something of the work of nature but nothing of that of the gardener.[3]

The island is wild, and so not a garden, and yet it serves the purpose of a garden; it is an artificial wild. St. Peter's is a preserve, a park. It is rather like an artificial nature and, as such, akin to Rousseau's state while he lives there. Reverie will prove to be something like an artificial state of nature. Of course, parks are for weekends, for recreation not for living, and so people come to St. Peter's during the harvest season for Sunday dances (V.3). Rousseau takes refuge on the island after having been stoned in Motier. He uses St. Peter's Island, which is owned by the Bern Hospital, for recovery. While reverie may appear to be a condition in which one is indifferent to everything and so equally interested in everything, this indifference is curative—it has its purpose.

Rousseau's paradise is disturbed by one worry; he is afraid that he will not be allowed to remain on the island (V.4). His only problem, then, is the impermanence of his situation. Accordingly, he wishes that they would make St. Peter's his permanent prison. With this finality, Rousseau's life would be perfect; he would have no problems. However, we cannot fail to notice that this completion of happiness would be its destruction. Were his condition permanent, Rousseau would have to unpack his books and make plans; yet, "[o]ne of my greatest delights of all was always leaving my books well packed and not having any writing desk" (V.7). The charm of his stay on St. Peter's Island is inextricable from its impermanence, which forces Rousseau to live in the present and not view his life as a whole. It would be foolish to make plans when at any moment he might be whisked off to England regardless of what he wills. Accordingly, Rousseau gives himself up to the pleasure of the present moment. It is, then, precisely because he has not been made a permanent prisoner on St. Peter's Island that Rousseau can forget the world and avoid troubling presentiments and so make it possible to have sentiments (V.4).

The whole of the Fifth Walk, in which St. Peter's Island serves as an image of a complete self-sufficiency in some way outside of space and time, is meant as an image of the possibility of self-forgetting (V.5). And yet, while the island is itself a refuge (*asile*; V.4), there are also refuges (*asiles*; V.9) on the island. There is thus a regress—a self-forgetting within self-forgetting. This leads us to wonder about the status of Rousseau's self-awareness during his stay. Did he know then (1765) what he knows now (1776–78)—that is, that these two months living on the island were the happiest of his life? Like the rounding of the basin of Lake Bienne—his self-circumscribing—Rousseau's depiction of life on St. Peter's Island is idealized with a view to drawing a parallel between it and reverie. Yet reverie is supposed to be precisely the sort of situation in which one does not reflect on one's life as a whole. This puzzle is deepened by the end of the Fifth Walk where Rousseau indicates that remembering even augments the pleasure of the initial experience of reverie.

> In dreaming that I am there [St. Peter's Island] do I not do the same thing? I do even more: to the attraction of an abstract and monotonous reverie I join charming images which enliven it. (V.17)

Rousseau knows full well that the power of the experience he has called reverie only seems to consist in its belonging totally to the present. When we experience nostalgia from hearing again the songs that were popular in our youth, we need to catch ourselves and ask whether we actually once liked these songs that now seem to mean so much to us, or whether it is rather the experience of *rehearing* them that is so resonant. Often what meant little to us at the time takes on such significance only in retrospect. It has a kind of fullness for us precisely because it is an image, a fiction, and *not* real.

The second section of the Fifth Walk deals with why Rousseau was so happy on St. Peter's Island.

> What then was this happiness, and in what did its enjoyment consist? I would leave it to be divined by all the men of this century from the description of the life that I led there. The precious *far niente* was the first and principal enjoyment that I wanted to savor in all its sweetness, and all that I did during my stay was in effect only the delectable and necessary occupation of a man who devoted himself to idleness. (V.6)

Rousseau must show what happiness consists in because it is not possible to give the essence of "doing nothing." In fact, no one really does nothing; for human beings, doing nothing means doing something that approximates idleness. It is not possible to see "doing nothing," for it amounts to not doing other things. How is it possible to observe someone not unpack books?

The seventh paragraph of the Fifth Walk is a long and complex depiction of reverie that divides in three. The first part deals with the preconditions for reverie. Rousseau wants to be left on the island where his enemies can see that he never does anything—that is, of course, nothing visible. By imagining that they might leave him there forever, he imagines that his time is unlimited. This prevents him from arranging his affairs, for the thought that he has an unlimited amount of time to do everything leads him to do nothing. The closest thing to an experience of eternity seems to be living in the now, for the difference is not easy to discern between not unpacking because one has an unlimited time to do so and not unpacking because there is no time to do so. In both cases one would not be forced to arrange one's life according to priorities. This amounts to freedom. That Rousseau's greatest delight comes from not unpacking means that it is the release from having to arrange things that lets one feel free.

Yet Rousseau clearly must do something, and, to the extent that he does so systematically, he does it in a rather peculiar way. This emerges in his account of his botanical studies in the second part of paragraph 7.

> I undertook to do a *Flora petrinsularis* and to describe all the plants of the island, without omitting a single one of them, in sufficient detail to occupy myself for the remainder of my days. It is said that a German did a book on a lemon peel; I would have done one of them on each lawn-grass of the meadows, on each moss of the woods, on each lichen that carpets the rocks. Finally, I did not want to leave a blade of grass, not a plant particle that was not amply described. As a result of this beautiful project, every morning after breakfast, which we all had together, a magnifying glass in hand and my *Systema naturae* under my arm, I went off to visit a district of the island, which I had for this purpose divided into small squares with the intention of going through [*parcourir*] them one after another during each season. (V.7)

Now, if St. Peter's is a microcosm, then Rousseau's *Flora petrinsularis* would be like a minute botanical description of the entire world. And, because he will examine every plant, his activity calls for no *arrangement*—he need set no priorities. The study of the whole is in some sense indifferent to the particularity of the parts. One might do a book on a lemon peel (or the brain of the leech) not because it is particularly important but because any part is as worthy of study as any other. Any part will do at any time for Rousseau because he has no purpose in mind in describing the whole other than to describe it. For Rousseau, *justice* has become *justesse*.

If there are threats to the microcosmic character of Rousseau's enterprise, his two tools are meant to ameliorate them. His magnifying glass enables Rousseau to be indifferent to distinctions of size. As the very small becomes available to him, so, too, do the most distinctive features of individual plants. And using Linnaeus's *Systema Natura*, a book on identifying and classifying plants, Rousseau may make observations that extend far beyond St. Peter's Island and, hence, neutralize the apparent particularity of his location. His two tools make the small big and the big small.

Rousseau colorfully describes the happiness resulting from his botanical excursions.

> Nothing is more singular than the ravishments, the ecstasies that I experienced with each observation that I made on vegetal structure

and organization and on the role of the sexual parts in fructification, the system of which was then completely new for me. The differentiation of general types, of which I had not previously the least idea, enchanted me, verifying them on the common species until one of the rarer ones offered itself to me. The forking of the two long stamens of the self-heal, the spring of those of the nettle and the pellitory, the explosion of the fruit of the balsam and of the pod of the boxwood, a thousand little games of fructification that I observed for the first time filled me with joy, and I went around asking all if they had seen the horns of the self-heal as La Fontaine asked if all had read Habakkuk. (V.7)

Rousseau certainly knows that three of these plants are medicinal, but it is not this sort of cure with which he is concerned. When he coupled ravishments and ecstasies previously, it was in connection with contemplating himself (II.3). Here it seems to have to do with the curative power for the self of losing the self in the contemplation of something else. The strangest part of Rousseau's account is his reference to La Fontaine. In his memoires, Louis Racine, the son of the great playwright, tells the full story. La Fontaine was filled with admiration for Plato and Homer. In an attempt to woo him from his attraction to this pagan beauty and replace it with Christian religiosity, Jean Racine took him to church. When La Fontaine became bored by the ceremony, Racine gave him a volume of the Bible containing the lesser prophets. La Fontaine came upon the prayer for the Jews in Baruch and went around asking everyone whether they had read Baruch and proclaiming him a genius.[4] In the version of the Fifth Walk, Rousseau substitutes Habakkuk for Baruch—that is, a nonapocryphal for an apocryphal book of the Bible. The book he substitutes, Habakkuk, divides in five. In the first part (1.1–4), Habakkuk complains to the Lord about unpunished sins in Judea. In the second (1.5–11), the Lord tells him that punishment will come at the hands of the Chaldeans. Habakkuk then complains that the Chaldeans are also wicked (1.12–2.1), and the Lord replies that they, too, will be judged (2.2–20). The final section (3.1–19) is Habakkuk's prayer about the final judgment. Part of this prayer is of particular interest.

2. O Lord, I have heard thy speech, and was afraid; O Lord, revive thy work in the midst of the years, in the midst of the years make known; in wrath remember mercy.

3. God came from Teman and the Holy One from Mount Paran. Selah. His glory covered the heavens, and the earth was full of his praise.

4. And his brightness was as the light; he had horns coming out of his hand; and there was the hiding of his power.[5]

Maimonides cites Habakkuk 3.3 as one of the passages where what is at stake is the crucial issue of the oneness of God.[6] He is explicitly concerned with the split between God's glory and his praise, but one might as easily be concerned with the split between God and the Holy One. Maimonides' resolving of the problem of the unity of God involves various ways in which God's multiplicity must be read metaphorically. If any of this is on Rousseau's mind, it is no doubt of interest that it all should follow directly upon his own reflection on his reaction to having learned about the fork in the stamen of the self-heal plant, which he calls here the horns of the self-heal. This splitting has echoes in the discovery of the dualism of fructification. Rousseau's text thus suggests the following series of "forks." First there is an implied split between the acceptable (or good) Habakkuk and the unacceptable (or bad) Baruch. Within Habakkuk there is a split between the Chaldeans and the Judeans; the former, while not good, as punishers of the Judeans, are instruments for the good. Finally, in the third chapter there is a split between God and the Holy One of the horned hands. While the connections here are not as clear as one might wish, the joy expressed by Rousseau seems to have to do with the discovery of the necessity of the bad for the good. In the context of the Fifth Walk, this calls our attention once again to the fact that for Rousseau to enjoy heaven, he must be aware that he is under the threat of expulsion. Awareness of one's mortality seems the necessary condition for understanding immortality as a good.

Beginning with the third part of the seventh paragraph, Rousseau turns explicitly to reverie. Having spent his morning examining plant life in all its detail, he turns in the afternoon to a more general appreciation of nature. This reprises the movement of the Second Walk (II.5–6), where, beginning with the identification of particular plants, Rousseau had been moved to reflections about the whole of nature and his place within it. Here in the Fifth Walk there are three examples of this sort of reverie. The first occurs when

I would slip off and go throw myself alone into a boat that I guided to the middle of the lake when the water was calm, and there, stretching myself out my full length in the boat, eyes turned toward heaven, I let myself go and drift slowly at the pleasure of the water [*au gré de l'eau*], sometimes for several hours, plunged into a thousand confused but delectable reveries, which, without having any well determined or constant object were nevertheless to my mind [*à mon gré*] a hundred times preferable to any of the sweeter ones I had found among what are called the pleasures of life. Often, warned by the setting of the sun that it was the hour of retreat, I found myself so far from the island that I was forced to labor with all my might to arrive before nightfall. (V.7)

Looking at the sky is, of course, something like looking at nothing. Rousseau fills his visual field without really placing anything particular in his visual field. That reverie so easily leads to a violent struggle to avoid the darkness is clearly meant to remind us that this state of *far niente* comes perilously close to death.[7] Describing a second example of reverie, Rousseau says

Other times, instead of straying into open water, I found pleasure in coasting along the verdant banks of the island where the limpid waters and fresh shadows often persuaded me to bathe. (V.7)

He describes a third case in which he boats to the smaller island and takes "very circumscribed walks" during which his plant identification leads him to conclude that the vegetation would easily support rabbits. This leads him to hatch a plan for creating a rabbit colony.

Now in all three of these cases idle and purposeless activity comes to an end as a result of purposive action of some sort. Discovering how late it has become, Rousseau rushes back to shore; becoming enchanted by the shoreline, he decides to bathe; losing himself in reflection on the plants of the little island, he decides to import rabbits. Reverie apparently allows one to get so caught up in one's idle thoughts that these thoughts lead to the death of reverie. In the Second Walk, Rousseau's musing makes him so inattentive that he is run over by a Great Dane. The enormous pleasure in the disorder and purposelessness of thought always threatens to disappear as the result of purposes that occur to one willy-nilly as soon as one drops one's guard—one's purpose. This is especially clear given the sequel to the last of Rousseau's three examples. Having determined that rabbits would thrive on the smaller island, Rousseau suggests a project.

> I presented this idea to the tax collector who had male and female rabbits brought from Neuchâtel, and, in great pomp, his wife, one of his sisters, Therese and I went to establish them on the little island, where they began to multiply before my departure and where they will without doubt have prospered if they have been able to bear the rigor of the winters. The founding of this little colony was a festival. The pilot of the Argonauts was not more proud than I, leading the company and the rabbits in triumph from the big island to the small, and I noticed with pride that the wife of the tax collector, who dreaded water excessively and always felt ill on it, embarked under my guidance with confidence and showed no fear during the crossing. (V.7)

The language and the hyperbole here suggest that the rabbit colony is meant as an image of political life.[8] When an idea comes to Rousseau, he cannot resist pursuing it even when (as in this case) it threatens to destroy the conditions for thinking it. As the rabbits multiply on the little island (and as rabbits will, they have started to do so almost before Rousseau deposits them there) and with no natural predators to control their numbers, they will certainly destroy the vegetation that gave rise to Rousseau's idle reverie, which, in turn, gave rise to his idea for colonizing the island. The rabbit colony is like civil society; although it begins in a desire to preserve the sweetness of life, it ends by generating a kind of frenzy destructive of that very sweetness. It has been aptly characterized as the "joyless quest for joy."[9] That Rousseau has this problem in mind is clear from his description. He and three women engage in an activity in which he wants to impress them. He wants to be esteemed; his *amour-propre* has been aroused.

And yet the situation is meant to be comical and a little unbelievable. It seems unlikely that a woman who lives on an island would be terrified of boats, and, even if she were, she would form part of an unlikely group of "heroes." Founding a rabbit colony seems scarcely to justify a comparison to the Argonauts. Only because of the comic tone is this event not obviously at odds with the spirit of reverie that is the subject matter of the Fifth Walk. Does Rousseau mean to suggest that a kind of reverie remains possible in political life as long as one does not take oneself too seriously? Or is the project itself simply part of an absurd daydream? That is, is there a kind of ordinary activity that is not simply at odds with the detachment characteristic of reverie? Rousseau's description of reverie in the sequel as something like a combination of motion and rest, engagement and detachment, suggests as much.

When there is too much agitation, too much movement, on the lake, Rousseau spends the afternoon either going about (*parcourir*) the island looking for plants or, after climbing to high ground, letting his eyes peruse (*parcourir*) the view (V.8). This same ambiguity in the meaning of *parcourir* had figured prominently in the first account of reverie in the Second Walk (II.5–6). In both cases an actual movement is replaced by a metaphorical movement. At the approach of evening Rousseau descends from the *cimes* to some refuge (*asile*) near the shore. As the word *cime* may mean either "height" or "cyme"—a cluster or swell of flowers—the sentence describes indifferently Rousseau's movement away from either of his previous activities. His reverie is equally a release from walking and contemplating, and from his contemplation of a part and his contemplation of the whole.

> There, the noise of the waves and the agitation of the water, riveting [*fixant*] my senses and chasing from my soul every other agitation, plunged it into a delectable reverie where night often surprised me without my having perceived it. The ebb and flow [*flux et reflux*] of this water, its noise, continual but swollen at intervals, striking my ear and my eyes without pause, supplanted the internal movements that reverie extinguished in me and was sufficient to make me sense my existence with pleasure, without taking pains to think. From time to time some weak and short reflection arose on the instability of the things of this world of which the surface of the water offered me an image; but soon these light impressions were worn away in the uniformity of the continual movement which lulled me, and which, without any active cooperation from my soul, did not allow me to detach myself, so that, called by the hour and by the agreed upon signal, I was unable to pull myself away from there without effort. (V.9)

Reverie requires that one's senses be occupied but not so occupied that one's attention is completely given over to their objects. Only in this way does it become possible to feel oneself feeling and so experience the sentiment of one's own existence. As in the previous examples, here, too, the rhythm of the waves so lulls Rousseau that it makes him lose sight of the oncoming night, which, as we know, he fears. One sort of experience of movement in time is thus sufficiently regular as to imitate no movement in time and thus make us lose sight of our ordinary temporal existence. This ordinary temporal experience is marked by internal movements—the pains of thinking. Fear of the approach of night is a discrete experience that requires our full attention. In reverie such things are supplanted by the regular ebb and flow of an external movement that is not only uniform and continual but also affects each of our senses in something like the same way. Rousseau perceives the waves with his eyes and with his ear, but the rhythm of the dance of the waves is the same as the rhythm of their music. There is no discrepancy within or between the experiences, and so Rousseau has experience (he is alive) but of an almost indeterminate kind. At most, his experience calls forth a weak impression of the transience of things temporal. Thus, insofar as reverie leads to thought, it leads to the sort of thought that applies equally to everything in the world. On the one hand, the experience that gives rise to reverie is sufficiently indeterminate to make it possible for us to experience our own experience; we have a sentiment of our own existence. On the other hand, because of this indeterminacy, our experience is not really of anything in particular and might have anything as its object; this was hinted at when Rousseau collapsed his viewing of whole and part in the word *cime*. Accordingly, what we experience in reverie is nothing in particular but rather being as such. In reverie being and thinking are one; we sense ourselves in sensing the world and sense the world in sensing ourselves. As the movement of our souls is not at odds with the movement of the world, we are not able to detach ourselves—we are not apart from or alienated from the world. At the same time, we have not simply gone back into the world—we are alive and not dead. This experience of what cannot ever change drives out any longing for novelty: "and finally one would go to bed content with one's day and desiring only a similar one for the morrow" (V.10).

But what is it about reverie that causes it to so stimulate desire? This is the question for the remainder of the Fifth Walk.

> That one might tell me now what there is there sufficiently attractive
> to excite in my heart regrets so vivid, so lasting and so tender that at

the end of fifteen years it is impossible for me to muse over this cherished abode without every time feeling myself transported there by rushes of desire. (V.11)

What is it that makes idleness or purposelessness seem the ultimate purpose of human life?

Having just depicted in his examples of reverie certain brief periods of extreme contentment, Rousseau now makes a surprising claim.

> In the vicissitudes of a long life I have remarked that the times of the sweetest enjoyment and of the most vivid pleasures are yet not those of which the memory most attracts and touches me. These short moments of delirium and passion, as vivid as they may be, are, however, even in their vivacity, only very scattered points on the path of life. They are too rare and too quick to constitute a state, and the happiness that my heart regrets is not at all made up of fleeting instants but is a permanent and simple state that has nothing vivid in it, but of which the duration augments its charm to the point where one finally finds supreme felicity in it. (V.12)

Clearly a few hours in a boat are not enough on which to build a life of supreme felicity. And yet, if "all is in continual flux on the earth" (V.13), and if Rousseau's extended example of reverie was built on experience of the *flux et reflux* (V.9) of the waves on the lake, then the realization that everything is in flux ought to mean that any experience is raw material for reverie.

But where does the conclusion that everything on earth is in flux originate? In a different context (VIII.1), Rousseau provides a hint.

> In meditating on the dispositions of my soul in all the situations of my life I am extremely struck to see so little proportion between the various contrivances of my destiny and the habitual sentiments of well or ill being by which they affected me. The various intervals of my short prosperity have left me nearly no agreeable memory of the intimate and permanent way in which they have affected me, and conversely, in all the miseries of my life I felt myself constantly full of tender, touching and delectable sentiments, which, pouring a salutary balm on the wounds of my broken heart seemed to convert its sadness to voluptuousness, and of which the amiable memory alone comes back to me detached from that of the ills I experienced at the same time. It

seems to me that I have tasted the sweetness of existence more, that I have really lived more, when my sentiments, constricted, so to speak, around my heart by my destiny, did not become giddy over all the objects of men's esteem, which themselves merit it so little and which are the single concern of people that one believes happy.

If reverie is the experience of experiencing, unhappiness is more likely to induce it, for there is a bond between the two original meanings of suffering or *pathos*. We suffer when we are in pain, but we also suffer or allow something to happen. To suffer something is what it means to experience it. To experience the sentiment of one's own existence is to feel that one is alive, but this, in turn, means to be aware that something not under our control is pressing in on us from without. To be self-aware thus means to be aware of the vulnerability of our condition—its imperfection. We can experience this lack, and with it ourselves, only when we have particular sentiments. Unchanging felicity would thus require a steady diet of change, of contingency, even if the experience of the steadiness is finally more important than the experience of the change. This is the reality to which the image of the waves on the lake corresponds. All experience is accompanied by a sentiment of one's own existence, which, in turn, is only possible if one's experience is of flux. Accordingly,

> [e]verything is in continual flux on the earth; nothing there keeps a constant and settled form, and our affections which are attached to external things pass and necessarily change as they do. Always before or behind us, they recall the past, which is no longer, or anticipate the future, which often is not at all to be; there is nothing solid there to which the heart may attach itself. Also, here below, one has scarcely any pleasure but that which passes; as for happiness that endures, I doubt that it may be known here. There is hardly in our most vivid enjoyments an instant where the heart may truly tell us: *I would that this instant endure always*; and how can one call happiness a fleeting state that still leaves us a heart worried and empty, which makes us regret something before or desire yet something after? (V.13)

Our pleasures are necessarily transitory because things change and we change. What thing, then, and what feeling could remain constant? Only a feeling that was feeling in general and an object that was indifferently any object whatsoever.[10] Reverie seems at first to be a particular experience of the universal character of all experience as necessarily particular.

Given the way Rousseau has idealized St. Peter's Island from the outset of the Fifth Walk, we have reason to be suspicious of the reality of reverie as such an experience. There are additional reasons.

> But if there is a state where the soul finds a sufficiently solid seat [*assiette*] to rest on it entirely and there assemble [*rassembler*] all its being, needing neither to recall the past nor encroach upon the future; where time is nothing for it, where the present endures always without nonetheless marking its duration and without any trace of succession, without any sentiment of deprivation or enjoyment, of pleasure or pain, of desire or fear other than that of our existence alone, and that this sentiment alone could fill it entirely; while this state endures the one who finds himself in it can call himself happy, not with an imperfect happiness, poor and relative such as that which one finds in the pleasures of life but with a happiness sufficient, perfect and full that does not allow the soul any emptiness that it might sense the need to fill [*remplir*]. Such is the state where I often found myself at St. Peter's Island in my solitary reveries, be it asleep in my boat that I allowed to stray at the pleasure [*au gré*] of the water, be it seated on the shores of the agitated lake, be it elsewhere on the bank of a beautiful river or of a stream murmuring over gravel. (V.14)

Although seeming to slide away from it, Rousseau begins the description conditionally—*if* there is such a state, this is what it would be. As there are no rivers or streams on St. Peter's Island, it is clear that either Rousseau means to include other unmentioned locations of his reveries, or he has once again strayed into fiction. This calls attention to the ambiguity of the final sentence of the paragraph: "Such is the state where I often found myself at St. Peter's Island in my solitary reveries. . . ." Now, this may mean that these reveries took place on St. Peter's Island, or it may mean that Rousseau finds himself at the island when he falls into reverie. What exactly does reverie consist in? Rousseau describes it as a place where the soul can assemble all its being. The verb he uses is *rassembler*, which certainly means "to assemble" but also bears the alternative meaning and the etymological significance of "to reassemble."[11] As in the Second Walk, here, too, reverie seems to be an experience necessarily reassembled—a retrospective reconstruction. This is especially striking given the manifest impossibility that "the one who finds himself in [this state] could call himself happy."

Reverie at first seems to make available to us a pure sentiment of our own existence, which a second look proves merely to be a version of the human longing to be god.

> What does one enjoy in such a situation? Nothing external to oneself, nothing if not oneself and one's own existence, as long as this state endures one suffices to oneself, like God. The sentiment of existence stripped of every other affection is by itself a precious sentiment of contentment and of peace, which alone would suffice to render this existence dear and sweet to whoever could detach from himself all the sensual and earthly impressions that come ceaselessly to distract us from it and trouble its sweetness here below. (V.15)

Granted, however, that we might wish to be as self-sufficient as God, is such a state possible for us "here below"? Rousseau goes on to suggest that were most men to strive for such purity, it is likely that they would fall into disgust with their everyday activities, which now would seem to them duties. For them, the conditions of the best life seem to be at odds with the conditions for life. But for Rousseau, the case is different. Being, however unwillingly, cut off from all human society, he claims to have been able to experience the sentiment of existence not only "imperfectly lasting a few instants" and as an "obscure and confused idea" (V.15), but in its purity. This is what differentiates him from others. All human beings share the possibility of experiencing the sentiment of their own existence, but Rousseau's awareness of this fact differentiates him and makes the experience available to him in a qualitatively different manner. The fact that all human beings experience life temporally becomes for him a temporal experience that blots out the destructive character of time. This possibility, not able "to be sensed by all souls or in all situations" (V.16), is available to Rousseau because his isolation, by removing him from ordinary human concerns, has placed him at peace and without any passion to trouble his calm. At the same time, some inner movement must remain, for

> what is necessary is neither absolute rest nor too much agitation but a uniform and moderate movement that has neither shocks nor gaps.

Without movement life is only a lethargy. If the movement is uneven or too strong, it awakens one; in recalling us to surrounding objects, it destroys the charm of reverie, and wrests us from within ourselves so as in an instant once again to place us under the yoke of fortune and of men and to return us to the sentiment of our misfortune. An absolute silence leads to sadness. It offers an image of death. Then the succor of a cheerful imagination is necessary and presents itself naturally enough to those whom heaven has favored. Movement that does not come from without then comes to be within us. Rest diminishes, it is true, but it is also more agreeable when light and sweet ideas, without agitating the depth of the soul, so to speak, are made only to skim the surface. Only so many are necessary as suffice to remind one of oneself while forgetting all one's troubles. This species of reverie may be enjoyed especially where one can be tranquil, and I have often thought that in the Bastille, and even in a dungeon where no object struck my sight, I would still be able to dream agreeably. (V.16)

Reverie requires experience, but not so intense as to draw us out of ourselves. What Rousseau likens to God's experience (V.15) in our case requires the intervention of a "cheerful imagination." Our attitude toward the movement that skims across the surface of our souls without shock or gap is rather like our attitude toward the events of fiction, which engage us without engaging us so deeply as reality. Reverie involves the pleasure of living off the pleasure of watching oneself live and is, for Rousseau, deeper than the intense pleasures of life lived firsthand. It is an activity even capable of redeeming suffering. Its indifference to the priorities embedded within ordinary experience makes it strangely objective. But reverie is not really dispassionate; it is rather much more like what possessed La Fontaine when he went about telling everyone about Baruch. In reverie our passions are engaged equally about everything; it is the pure sentiment of pure existence. Accordingly, although for reasons that still need to be explained, reverie is more apt to be inspired by idyllic natural settings, it can in principle occur anywhere at any time. As we are always experiencing something, the cheerful imagination may always work its magic. Calm and lulling experiences simply make it easier for "a dreamer knowing how to nourish himself on agreeable chimeras in the middle of the most unpleasant objects" to "satisfy himself at his ease by making come together in them everything that really struck his senses" (V.17) The imagination constructs a wholeness that is never really experienced; it is like a chimera. This fiction makes it possible to stand back from the whole so as to see it at some distance, and so to experience oneself experiencing.

By the end of the Fifth Walk this relation between reverie and fiction has become explicit.

> In coming to from a long and gentle reverie, in seeing myself surrounded by greenery, flowers, birds and letting my eyes wander in the distance on the romantic shores that bordered a vast extent of clear and crystalline water, I assimilated all these amiable objects to my fictions and, finding myself finally returned by degrees to myself and to what surrounded me, I could no longer mark the point of separation between fictions and realities. (V.17)

Indeed, the walk concludes by indicating that it has itself been a fiction.

> Men will take care, I know it, not to return me to so gentle a refuge [*asile*] where they did not want to leave me. But at least they will not prevent me from transporting myself there each day on the wings of the imagination, and from tasting there for a few hours the same pleasure as if I lived there yet. The sweetest thing I would do would be to dream there at my ease. In dreaming that I am there, do I not do the same thing? I do even more: to the attraction of an abstract and monotonous reverie, I join charming images which enliven it. In my ecstasies, their objects often escaped my senses, and now the more profound my reverie is, the more vividly it paints them. I am often more in the middle of them, and more agreeably still than when I was really there. The misfortune is that to the degree that my imagination cools, this happens with greater pains and does not last as long. Alas, it is when one begins to leave his skin that one is most prevented from seeing. (V.17)

Rousseau finally makes explicit that the memory of St. Peter's Island, and so the Fifth Walk as a whole, is not even meant to be accurate. The memory of the island and of being ejected from it has made the whole event even sweeter. And as it becomes less immediately real, it becomes itself an occasion for Rousseau to experience himself. St. Peter's Island is heaven insofar as the sentiment of existence is pure contentment. The problem, however, is the last sentence of the walk. Imagination makes a bridge possible between what is experienced and the one who experiences. But, imagination is always of particulars. Really leaving one's skin would mean losing the possibility of the sentiment of existence. This amounts to an admission that pure experience, and with it the pure sentiment of one's own existence, is not really possible; there is no heaven.

But if the isle of the blessed is only a useful fiction, what is its use? It remains for Rousseau to give an account of what approximates for human beings the idealized version of pure contentment he has sketched so powerfully in the Fifth Walk. He has suggested two possibilities and will return to both in subsequent walks. Within the story Rousseau tells about his stay on St. Peter's Island, his occupation is botany of a special sort. While not forcing him to consider any particular thing, this occupation does permit him to experience delight in the particular. This is akin to the function of fiction, which while celebrating the particular, prevents us from losing ourselves in it. That and how Rousseau's two occupations, botany and dreaming, are really one are in some sense the subject of the remainder of *The Reveries of the Solitary Walker.*

NOTES

1. Lake Bienne is the present-day Bieler See. In the *Confessions* (*Oeuvres complètes*, vol. 1, 367) Rousseau himself indicates that it is a "nearly regular oval." See also Charles Butterworth, *The Reveries of the Solitary Walker* (New York: Harper & Row, 1979), 195–200, for a useful account of the differences between the account in the *Confessions* of Rousseau's stay on St. Peter's Island and the account in the Fifth Walk.

2. This is no doubt connected to the fact, generally accepted (see, e.g., Butterworth, *The Reveries*, 189), that the Fifth Walk is the most beautiful of the ten walks of the *Reveries*. See also Plato, *Republic*, 505d.

3. *Oeuvres complètes*, vol. 1, 369–70.

4. The passage from Louis Racine's memoires is quoted at length in Butterworth, *The Reveries*, 73.

5. Habakkuk 3.2–4, King James version of the Bible.

6. *The Guide of the Perplexed*, trans. Shlomo Pines (Chicago: University of Chicago Press, 1969), 173.

7. Again, this reminds us of the Second Walk (II.13–14).

8. See Butterworth, *The Reveries*, 193.

9. Leo Strauss, *Natural Right and History* (Chicago: University of Chicago Press, 1968), 251.

10. Aristotle would have called the object of this experience "being as being" and the experience itself "first philosophy." Avoiding such terms, Rousseau instead emphasizes the feeling or sentiment involved. Still, his description is such that the object of the experience and the experience itself are hard to separate. See chapter 3.

11. In his *Second Discourse* and *Social Contract*, Rousseau uses *assembler* and *rassembler*, as well as *unir* and *réunir*, very carefully to indicate the various ways in which the explicit origin of political life always presupposes a prior implicit presence of political life. See, for a few of the many examples, *Oeuvres complètes*, vol. 2, 222, 230, 239, 242, 523, 536, and 563.

10

AUTHORITY

The Fifth Walk seems to claim that a kind of detachment is possible in reverie that is at once passionate and disinterested. Reverie is an experience of myself experiencing—the sentiment of my own existence—and is somehow akin both to the experience of fictions and to Rousseau's kind of botany. Yet while the passion that attaches to reverie derives from particular everyday passions, without which there can be no sentiment of existence, it remains unclear how ordinary passion can be sustained once one recognizes the sentiment of existence as the true object of one's longing. Accordingly, the perspective of disinterested passion that the Fifth Walk seems to describe is radically dependent on interested passion. To take "pleasure" in the death of Anna Karenina requires that one have some experience of real death and of the grief that attends it.

If the first two walks of the *Reveries* articulate the necessary doubleness of the human soul, the three walks that follow mean to suggest ways of addressing the alienation that accompanies this doubleness. They give accounts of our experience of our being as a whole. In the Third Walk, morality is understood as purity of intention; the particular content of justice matters less than the feeling of justice in general. In the Fourth Walk, "being true" is the truth of truth telling and consists less in the content of what is said than, once again, in purity of intention. Finally, in the Fifth Walk, happiness is not a matter of the content of one's feelings but rather consists in the feeling of feeling—the sentiment of one's existence. The three walks share a difficulty; in each case what human beings really want is not the particular, but in each case what they want is available only through the particular.[1] At the same time, there is also a tension between justice as pure intention or will and the

purely passive experience that characterizes the sentiment of existence.
It is easy to see how Rousseau could love both; each in its way is an
experience of freedom. Still, the two are not obviously compatible.
Rousseau turns to this tension in the Sixth Walk.

Because the Sixth Walk has a double intention, its overall structure
seems less clear than that of the previous walks. Rousseau begins
(VI.1–2) with an example of his own sense of the freedom of spontaneous and purposeless activity, which in the end proves to have an unacknowledged motive. This connects the Sixth Walk to the Fifth and suggests that the one may be meant to correct the other. The next eight
paragraphs (VI.3–10) present an argument designed on one level to establish that in society the freedom of spontaneous acts of goodness must
always give way to the constraint of duty but on a deeper level to call
into question the very possibility of such freedom. It may be true that
"to do good is the truest happiness that the human heart can taste"
(VI.3), but such true happiness may nevertheless be unavailable to us.
The concluding argument of the Sixth Walk (VI.11–21) is also ambiguous. On the one hand, it is a reflection on the peculiarity of Rousseau's
situation meant to justify his decision to refrain from performing acts of
goodness to others. On the other hand, it is an account of such freedom
as is really possible for him, and, since Rousseau's situation has throughout the *Reveries* been meant as paradigm for the human situation generally (he is at great pains to distinguish himself not only from social beings
but also from gods), the argument is an account of such freedom as is
possible for human beings.

Rousseau begins by setting the stage for a discovery about himself.

> We have scarcely any mechanical movement of which we would not
> be able to find the cause in our heart, if we knew well enough how
> to look for it. Yesterday, passing over the new boulevard to go look
> for plants along the Bièvre from the Gentilly side, I made a turn to
> the right in approaching the gateway of Enfer [Hell], and, turning
> aside into the country, I went by the Fontainbleau road to gain the
> heights that border this little river. This path was very much a matter
> of indifference in itself, but, in reminding me that I had several times
> mechanically made the same detour, I sought the cause of it in myself,
> and I could not prevent myself from laughing when I came to unravel
> it. (VI.1)

The word *heart* occurs eighteen times in the Sixth Walk.[2] Here it seems to mean the cause of whatever we do—or, rather, almost always the cause. Later Rousseau will call it his "most secret inside" (VI.4). The causes of what we do are thus secret within us. Accordingly, activity that seems utterly aimless and purposeless, and so free, is really governed by hidden purposes and not free at all. How, though, is it possible to know this? Rousseau seems to think that you can discover the secret cause if you only know how to look; indeed, he will seem to offer a cause for his detour in the second paragraph. But we do not really know what movement Rousseau has it in mind to seek the cause of. The first paragraph presents two movements—the first, going out to look for plants initially and the second, turning off in an unexpected direction. Do both movements have hidden causes? If so, is *herboriser*—looking for plants— not the innocent, purposeless activity it seems in the Fifth Walk? Rousseau detours to the right to avoid the gateway of Enfer. Is this habitual turning aside, which "was very much a matter of indifference," really for the sake of avoiding hell? And is hell to be understood as the punishment for not doing good when one might have? This would mean that the hidden purpose of the "mechanical movement" of Rousseau's example is negative in character. Rousseau's underlying purpose will prove to be to avoid a duty for which his previous actions have made him responsible. The detour is, thus, necessary to avoid the consequences of a previous action; Rousseau understands the existence of such necessary consequences to be hell. But why does he laugh? Is he amused at his own presumption in thinking any action to be a matter of indifference? Is it because a small child could have such power over him? Or does Rousseau laugh because, having realized that his detour, while seemingly spontaneous and free, was secretly caused, he also realizes that the same must apply to his original action? If the freedom of one is illusory, why should that of the other not be? Are small and unnoticed things secreted in our hearts always the cause of the freedom we so value?

We get to the heart of some of these questions in the second paragraph.

> In the summer at a corner of the boulevard at the exit of the Enfer gateway, a woman who sells fruit, tisane and rolls sets up shop every-day. This woman has a little boy, very pretty but lame, who, limping with his crutches, goes about with quite good grace asking alms from

those passing. I had made a kind of acquaintance with this good little fellow; he did not fail each time that I passed to come to me to pay his little compliment, always followed by my little offering. The first few times I was charmed to see him and gave to him with a very good heart, and I continued for some time to do so with the same pleasure, even most often adding to it that of prompting and listening to his little chatter, which I found agreeable. This pleasure, having become by degrees habit, was, I know not how, transformed into a kind of duty, of which I soon sensed the constraint, especially because of the preliminary harangue to which it was necessary to listen and in which he never failed often to call me M. Rousseau to show that he was well acquainted with me, which taught me, quite to the contrary, that he was no more acquainted with me than those who had instructed him. From then on, I passed by there less willingly, and finally by habit I took most often to making a detour when I approached this crossing. (VI.2)

Rousseau is annoyed because the boy seems now to demand what was previously freely offered. Yet this is scarcely presumptuous. The situation has not changed. The boy is still pretty, charming, and asks graciously. If it was right to receive alms before, it ought to be right now so long as M. Rousseau has remained the same as he was. Now, if the boy really is well acquainted with M. Rousseau, the implication would be that what feels spontaneous and free to Rousseau is really done out of a constant disposition—let us say it is done from his heart. But then is it freely done? The problem is that Rousseau made a "kind of acquaintance," and his gift was "transformed into a kind of duty," which suggests that Rousseau himself is a kind of man and thus predictable and not a unique and free individual. This is what Rousseau resents. Becoming aware of his fixed nature, he wants not to conform to this nature. Rousseau resents that the boy has come to think of him as an object and uses him accordingly, not treating him as though he had any freedom whatsoever. He takes this resentment up later.

> As for me, let them see me if they can, so much the better, but that is impossible; they would never see in my place anything but the J.-J. that they have themselves made and that they have made according to their heart to hate at their ease. (VI.20)

Others, apparently, mechanically produce a Rousseau—an object the cause of which is in their hearts. Rousseau transforms them into objects in his resentment of them for treating him as an object.

At this point the question of the Sixth Walk seems to shift.[3] From having concluded that "the true and first motives of most of my actions are not as clear to me myself as I had long imagined," Rousseau draws the further conclusion that "the only good that is henceforth in my power is to abstain from acting out of fear of doing ill without wishing it and without knowing it" (VI.3). Still, the two are connected. Rousseau's inability to see motives—now even his own motives—paralyzes him. If "to do good is the truest happiness that the human heart can taste" (VI.3), why do human beings not always do good? It could only be that they cannot, for otherwise selfishness itself would enjoin doing good. That they cannot seems to have to do with not knowing their own motives.

It is surely not obvious, however, that we do not know our own motives. Rousseau thinks back to "happier times when, following the movements of my heart, I was sometimes able to render another heart content" (VI.4). He finds the sweetest pleasure in doing something for another, for such an act—totally for its own sake and not performed out of need—is an expression of one's freedom. It is generous in the etymological sense. Nevertheless, Rousseau's experience with the lame boy was not atypical. What begins as an act of supreme generosity soon engenders expectations; thereafter it becomes a duty. Now, since no act can ever be severed from the chain of effects it begins (Rousseau claims to have learned this from his accusation of Marion), no act can ever simply be for the sake of itself. So, for example, if one has to scale a height, one may at first be grateful for the loan of a ladder, but will one ever be able to climb without a ladder again without regretting or even resenting its lack? Today's benefits are understood tomorrow as rights. Rousseau claims not to have been much bothered by all of this in practice until he became famous—that is, until he became a writer. The loss of his innocent freedom is coincident with his having become a public man. The movement of his own life is thus presented as following the movement traced in the *Second Discourse* from the state of nature to the state of civil society. Every natural impulse—even the impulse to do good—gets corrupted when, for example, the one to whom the good is given comes to think not about what is given in particular but about the situation in general. Reason coupled with impulses leads inevitably to corruption—to *amour-propre.* Rousseau has traced his troubles to his public life, and his public life to his writing. His writing seems almost a paradigm for the sort of good that can be given without calculation or expectation of return—a spontaneous, gratuitous gift. But publishing and the celebrity that comes with it bring a throng of "friends" who claim various benefactions as their right. One cannot help wondering whether Rousseau could not have avoided all of this trouble had he followed Montesquieu in keeping his person and his name separate so that no one could claim to be well acquainted with M. Rousseau.

For all of the pains they have caused him, however, Rousseau does not regret these experiences

> since, through reflection, they have procured for me new insights on the knowledge of myself and on the true motives of my conduct in a thousand circumstances over which I have so often deluded myself. I saw that to do good with pleasure it was necessary that I act freely, without constraint, and that, in order to sever from me all the sweetness of a good act, it sufficed that it become a duty for me. From then on the weight of the obligation makes for me a burden of the sweetest enjoyments, and, as I have said in *Emile,* or so I believe, I would have been a bad husband among the Turks at the hour when the public cry calls them to fulfill the duties of their state. (VI.6)

If self-knowledge is the goal, even an experience of something bad can be a good experience. Only because doing good becomes tedious to him when it is a duty, does Rousseau come to know that what he really longs for is freedom. His example, fulfilling one's sexual obligations among the Turks, is chosen with some care. It involves making what seems quintessentially private and particular—sex—public. Furthermore, the double entendre of *état* (as political and as state of marriage) playfully indicates the deep connection between duty and civil society; the state of civil society is an internal as well as an external phenomenon. Rousseau seems to misremember the original location of his remark about the Turks, which appears not in *Emile* but in book 5 of the *Confessions.*[4] Yet, as his parenthetical "or so I believe" suggests, perhaps he does not simply err. By referring to the *Emile,* Rousseau brings to mind the principal feature of the "education according to nature" that it contains.

To avoid encouraging slavishness, Rousseau arranges Emile's education so that nothing should be perceived as imposed on him by his teacher. As is the case with any education, the student must be manipulated, but in such a way that he comes to what he learns "freely," which is to say in such a way that what he decides to do agrees with what his teacher wants him to do. In this way he will accept an authoritative view—for example, that the shortest distance between two points is a straight line—without deferring to authority.[5] If authority does not remain invisible in this way, a teacher cannot avoid the problem of all legislating—that in engendering obedience to the law, it may also engender a desire to be in the position of the lawgiver, and so resentment of the law. The overall problem, then, is society—"man is born free but everywhere he is in chains."[6] What troubles Rousseau, and indeed civilized man generally, is that when duty, or obedience, replaces freedom, the pleasure of freedom is lost.

Rousseau's remark about Turkish marriage practices in the *Confessions* is prompted by recalling two attempts to seduce him by mothers of his music students. He reported one attempt to Mme de Warens, with whom he lived and whom he called *Maman*: she learned on her own of the second seduction, a more sinister affair involving one of her enemies. In the wake of these discoveries, Mme de Warens offered to take Rousseau on as her second lover—the point being to avoid not only these seductions but also all the other obvious temptations for a man as yet inexperienced sexually of teaching so many young women. In this context Rousseau says that Mme de Warens made the mistake of offering herself to him on certain conditions, but, because the goal was so desirable to him, he never even considered the meaning of these conditions. He likens this to the mistake of teachers and even of himself in *Emile*.[7] Now, since Rousseau assiduously attempts to avoid this error in teaching Emile, he seems to mean that his own error had to do with placing a too desirable goal before those whom he was teaching in *Emile*—namely, his readers. The goal he sets out for us, his readers, is freedom. Does he mean that in *Emile* he did not sufficiently call attention to the conditions that accompany this goal? Rousseau begins the Sixth Walk with an extended example that suggests that all motion with a goal is tarnished, that it is motion born of need and so too governed by that need to be other than slavish. Still, without a goal, there will be no motion at all. How, then, is it possible to act freely if action means being dazzled by what one wants, and freedom requires indifference. A conditional freedom is possible, it seems, by replacing a first-order desire—say, sexual longing—by a second-order desire—duty. This is what the Turks do, presumably because acting as one ought is not acting slavishly; it means overcoming one's "needs." But the conditions accompanying this freedom are very severe; for Rousseau, at least, such duty undermines the pleasure and charm of what is desired. The cost of freedom understood as duty, once one reads the fine print, is happiness. If there is another sort of freedom, it would seem to require rejecting "motion" altogether. This rejection, itself a sort of motion, would be the only genuinely free act and would be the justification for the word *scarcely* in the first sentence of the Sixth Walk.

But is even duty a manifestation of freedom? At first Rousseau seems to indicate that, while others may, he cannot act contrary to his inclinations.

> There is what very much modifies the opinion that I long had of my own virtue; because there is none at all in following one's inclinations and in giving oneself, when they lead us to it, the pleasure of doing good. But it consists in vanquishing them when duty commands in order to do what it prescribes for us, and there is what I have known less how [less been able] to do than any man in the world. Born sensitive and good, carrying pity to the point of weakness, and feeling my soul exalted by everything connected to generosity, I was humane, beneficent and helpful by taste, by passion even, as long as one only engaged my heart. (VI.7)

At first this seems a description only of Rousseau's weakness, but of course it comes very close to descriptions elsewhere in his writings of the distinction between goodness and virtue—the one natural and the other conventional.[8] Rousseau's idiosyncratic nature is in fact human nature, and what he says of himself is in some way true of men generally:

> [B]ut to act against my inclination was for me always impossible. Whether it be men, duty or even necessity that commands, when my heart is silent, my will remains deaf, and I cannot [do not know how to] obey. (VI.7)

Because all human actions have their sources in the heart, the principle of which is pleasure ("what I do not do with pleasure is soon impossible for me to do"; VI.7), no one can really act contrary to inclination. Rousseau is different only in knowing that this is the case.

What is possible is to resist inclination: "when my duty and my heart were at odds, the first was rarely the victor, unless it was only necessary for me to abstain" (VI.7). Freedom apparently consists in the ability to say no; it is the ability not to act.[9] Rousseau introduces this new psychology in order to indicate the connection between action and need, weakness, or lack of power. He claims that if he had been the most powerful of beings he would also have been the best, most merciful, and least vengeful. Because the desire for revenge is born from feeling vulnerable, the power to avenge destroys the need to. Rousseau seems to mean that insofar as he is M. Rousseau with a fixed nature or "heart," he is ruled by his peculiar wants and pleasures against which he is powerless to act. But freedom consists in being able not to do what he wants to do. Thus, those who *do* things out of duty and do not simply refrain from acting—the virtuous—at heart are doing them out of a kind of pleasure.

Obligation not only deprives a good deed of pleasure; it makes it painful, for it makes it a law to do what was previously done freely (VI.8). If to obey the law is always painful, then society is unnatural for human beings. It is no surprise, then, that having moved from obligation to law, Rousseau edges his way toward the problem of the social contract. The movement of Rousseau's life parallels the movement of the human race from happiness to misery in the *Second Discourse*. As freedom gives way to duty, innocent goodness gives way to virtue—what is expected of one. But, even at its best, doing what one ought means not being content with what one is; it means alienation. Insofar as this tension admits of resolution, it would seem to come from taking innocent pleasure in doing what is expected. In the social contract that originates civil life, this pleasure in being virtuous takes the form of willing the general will. But this will not work for Rousseau because it is a pleasure that can only be habitual and not natural, and, where habit is involved, there is no freedom. Accordingly, the deepest of human pleasures will be absent.

Civil life requires regular standards of behavior, but, in laying down laws, it undermines the natural sense of goodness that initially motivates us. Once the law exists, whether we conform to it from a sense of justice, from duty, or from fear of punishment, we no longer act simply out of goodness. The problem of civil society is thus embedded in the example with which the Sixth Walk begins—the lame boy.

> I know that there is a kind of contract, and even the most sacred of all, between the benefactor and one under an obligation. It is a sort of society that they form one with the other, narrower than that which unites men in general, and if one under an obligation tacitly pledges himself to gratitude [recognition], the benefactor likewise pledges himself to maintain with the other, so long as he does not make himself unworthy of it, the same good will he just showed him and to renew its acts for him whenever he is able and whenever it is required of him. (VI.9)

One who has no right to complain if refused an act of spontaneous generosity has indeed been injured if, having once granted such generosity, someone "in a *similar* case refuses to the *same* person the *same* favor" (VI.9, italics added). Not the original motive but the implied contract is binding. What is most sacred is the agreement; naturally, this could not have any force unless the original event were repeatable. Like all law, this contract involves a species analysis according to which there are certain kinds of cases, kinds of people, and kinds of goods, and according to which what is common takes precedence over what is peculiar to individual events and people. Yet, since every event and person we experience in nature is particular, this species emphasis means the destruction of the experience of natural goodness.

This might be taken to be a simple rejection of reason, which can only function by identifying kinds, were not Rousseau's treatment of the difficulty itself an analysis of "a kind of contract." That it is not so easy to avoid the tendency of law to obscure by generalizing is borne out in the sequel in Rousseau's list of faithless friends whom he once benefited (VI.10). The list is meant as evidence against the possibility of lasting friendship; just as natural goodness decays into habitual goodness, friendship declines because of the loss of the feeling that initiated it. One begins by being attracted to a person and ends by being obligated to the fact that one was once attracted. Put differently, the same friendship is necessarily not the same. Once having given alms to the little lame boy, Rousseau could never again reproduce the experience, for now the boy will always be different from what he was initially. The boy to whom

Rousseau felt an impulse to give alms will be "the boy to whom I give alms." Similarly, someone who is my friend is not someone whom it can be said that I befriend. Rousseau and his friends thus change without changing at all.

Rousseau traces the change in the affection of his "friends" for him to the change in his fortunes from celebrity to infamy. He takes to task for their inconstancy especially the Count of Charmettes, Father Palais, Father Binis, and Moultou. This is a curious selection. Rousseau gives an account in the *Confessions* of how he met the Count of Charmettes when both were young men and adds in a marginal note how much he has since changed, his attitude toward Rousseau having presumably been affected by the machinations of the Duke of Choiseul.[10] The count originally sought Rousseau out in order to learn music. They developed a friendship based on a mutual interest in philosophy and letters. Commenting that it was a good thing for him that the count had little musical ability, Rousseau alludes to how little musical education he himself had; at the time he was passing himself off as a music teacher, picking up along the way what learning he needed to supplement his genuine love of music. So Rousseau, who complains bitterly of the inconstancy of the friendship of the Count of Charmettes, acknowledges in passing that at the outset of this friendship he misrepresented himself. Furthermore, although Rousseau describes himself here in the *Reveries* as the benefactor of Father Palais, in the *Confessions* he describes the little gatherings in which this man was made the butt of his humor.[11] Father Binis may well have been the beneficiary of Rousseau (we are unaware of the details), but Rousseau's own testimony makes it clear that Binis was certainly his benefactor, for when Rousseau was secretary to the French ambassador in Venice, Binis warned him of a plan to have him arrested.[12] Finally, although these examples are supposed to be concerned with how "friendship" wanes with a change in fortune, in the *Confessions* Rousseau makes it clear that he always loved Moultou, "although his conduct with regard to me had often been equivocal."[13] Of Rousseau's four examples of inconstancy, then, the first suggests that he himself may have been inconstant, the second that he may not have been the best of friends, the third that he may have underestimated his own indebtedness and the last that the friendship really did not change but was from the outset a relationship of considerable ambiguity. None, of course, show what he claims they show—that others have been regularly faithless to him.

All of this prepares us for the special irony of Rousseau's final denunciation of his four "friends": "Hah! How could I keep the same sentiments for those in whom I find the contrary of what made them come to birth" (VI.10). This demand that others remain as constant as their names sounds strange from one who was so irked by the fact that a small boy took the liberty of counting on the constancy of M. Rousseau. The constancy required of friendship is merely another version of the constancy of all contracts and the attendant replacement of pleasure by duty. If the latter inhibit freedom, so must the former. Rousseau tacitly acknowledges the difficulty of his position by admitting that he too may have changed. At first he seems to mean only that someone experiencing a life as difficult as his would of course change. If "they" are always watching, then every possibility to do something good by which Rousseau is tempted may be only a new trap by which "they" conceal something bad for him. He must choose whether to act on the good intentions that are characteristic of his heart or to resist them because his certainty that he is only a dupe of others injures his self-esteem and deprives these acts of pleasure. But the choice is not as consequential as it seems, for Rousseau will have changed no matter which course he chooses. Either he resists change and so, given the effort that such resistance requires, changes himself, or he does not resist change and so changes. One need not do anything to lose one's innocence. Repetition will soon give way to habit, which, in turn, will give way to duty and loss of freedom. Attempting to break the habit of giving alms to the little boy, Rousseau found himself making a detour "by habit" (VI.2).

Rousseau is no longer tempted to do good since

> certain that I am not allowed to see things as they are, I abstain from judging on the basis of the appearances that they are given, and, of any lure with which motives are covered, it suffices that these motives be left within my reach in order that I be sure that they are deceitful. (VI.12)

Although it first seems that once again his persecutors are the source of this deceit, we soon learn that this cannot be, for the problem began in Rousseau's youth well before he believes the plot to have existed. In his "natural state" Rousseau was unaware of the prevalence of deception; he traces his loss of innocence to his discovery of the nature of men in general. The serious "plot" against him as the result of a "universal agreement" has more at its root than the will of a few enemies.

> Once convinced that that there were only lying and falseness in the dissembling demonstrations that were wasted on me, I passed rapidly to the other extreme; because when one has once let go of one's nature, there is no longer any limit that restrains us. From that time, I was disgusted with men, and my will, agreeing with theirs in this regard, holds me yet more apart from them than do all their devices. (VI.13)

That Rousseau's will is in agreement with that of others means, of course, that he must claim to be able to know their wills, but if it is possible to know the will of another, then the universality of Rousseau's isolation is in question, and, with it, his decision to abstain from judging, and so doing, good deeds. Yet this is a curious knowledge of others since it leads one to doubt whatever initial instinct one has about them in any particular situation. In the aftermath of this doubt one has no firm ground on which to judge them; all one knows is that one can never know. This universal suspicion might lead to hatred for all men but

> I myself love myself too much to be able to hate whoever it may be. This would be to constrict, to compress, my existence, and I would rather extend it over the whole universe. (VI.14)

Hatred involves too much experience and not enough experience of experience. When overcome by a particular experience, our selves are restricted; they become solely whatever this experience calls forth. To extend ourselves over the whole universe, we must take care not to lose sight of the relative insignificance of each part by itself.[14] Rousseau can pity men rather than hate them because he understands his kind (*sorte*—VI.12) of adversity as his lot (*sort*—VI.13).

This confirms our earlier conclusions about the way fiction serves as a model for Rousseau in achieving the detachment necessary for contentment.

> I prefer to flee them [men] than to hate them. Their appearance strikes my senses and through them my heart with impressions that a thou-

sand cruel looks render painful to me; but the uneasiness ceases as soon as the object that causes it has disappeared. I am concerned for them, even despite myself, because of their presence, but never by the memory of them. When I see them no longer, they are for me as if they did not exist at all.

They are a matter of indifference for me only in what relates to me; because in their relations among themselves, they can still interest me and move me as would the characters in a drama that I might see represented. My moral being would have to be annihilated in order that justice become a matter of indifference for me. (VI.15–16)

Rousseau is more able to be just the less he has to do with men. As a "spectator" one's heart is not engaged so that, for example, one's own little vanities and embarrassments do not get in the way of treating another fairly. Thus, one could be more just, love men more, and, if one could act without being perceived as acting, do more good as a spectator of the human drama than as an actor in it.

If my face and my features were as perfectly unknown to men as are my character and my nature, I would yet live without pains amidst them. Even their society could please me as long as I were perfectly a stranger to them. Delivered over without constraint to my natural inclinations, I would still love them if they never concerned themselves with me. I would exercise toward them a universal and perfectly disinterested benevolence. (VI.17)

He would be, in short, rather like a god in the midst of men or an author in relation to his characters.[15]

It is in this context that Rousseau invokes a story told by Glaucon in the second book of Plato's *Republic*.[16] Dissatisfied with Socrates' defense of justice against the attack of Thrasymachus, Glaucon tells of an ancestor of the Lydian Gyges who discovers a ring that makes him invisible. Glaucon introduces the story to argue that anyone who could would take advantage of invisibility to practice perfect injustice. Rousseau argues here that this sort of power would rather do away altogether with the need for injustice, which is rooted not in pleasures themselves but rather in the need to violate the law in order to show that one is not ruled by it.[17] Injustice understood in this way has more to do with a longing for freedom than with a desire for sex, food, or riches. But demonstrating one's freedom would require that one be *recognized* as unjust. As it would not involve escaping unnoticed, the power of a Gyges' ring to render one invisible would be superfluous. If it is freedom that men want most of all, and if this is behind Glaucon's rebellion at the beginning of *Republic*, book 2, then, if men were strong and free, they would have no reason to do anything but good.

> If I had remained free, obscure, isolated, as I was made to be, I would have done only good, for I do not have in my heart the seed of any harmful passion. If I had been invisible and all powerful like God, I would have been beneficent and good like him. It is strength and freedom that make excellent men. Weakness and slavery have ever made only wicked ones. (VI.18)

So long as they are weak, human beings will deceive others and be deceived about themselves. The heart, the hidden core inside me with which the Sixth Walk begins and has been so preoccupied, is identical to my idiosyncratic collection of imperfections. What I want or desire depends on the various ways in which I am wanting or lacking. The fully open being, the being for whom there is no hidden core and for whom accordingly everything is on the surface, is both perfect and superficial.

Could such perfection be approximated without superficiality? How might it be possible for men to be invisible without being tempted to do injustice? An author of a book takes an interest in his characters without seeking to get the better of them. Rousseau has indicated this. Plato knew it as well; Socrates' response to the challenge of Glaucon's original story is to involve him as an interested party in the creation of an imaginary city. Because the citizens of their "city in speech" are no longer potential competitors, they can become beneficiaries. Glaucon discovers justice through a fiction. Still, why does one bother? If our own motives are as unknown to ourselves as are those of others (and this is certainly the suggestion with which the Sixth Walk begins), then to make one's heart visible to oneself would mean to see what one would look like if one suddenly possessed the ring of Gyges. Where there is no reason to dissemble, we will show ourselves as we really are. Rousseau had specified that it was not while talking to the little lame boy that he realized his true motive for taking the detours; it was only possible to do so when reflecting afterward.

> I am concerned for them [men], even despite myself, because of their presence, but never by the memory of them. When I see them no longer, they are for me as if they did not exist at all. (VI.15)

From the outset of the Sixth Walk, the problem has been self-knowledge. The concluding paragraphs of the walk demonstrate a movement toward that end. After imagining the ring that would give him the sort of freedom that belongs to a god or an author, Rousseau gives a long account of how just and merciful he would be under these circumstances (VI.18). Of course, that he does not have such power means that it is his nature to be lacking, and so, in a certain sense, if Rousseau had such power he would no longer be Rousseau—he would no longer be a man. This emerges when he admits that there is one temptation he might not be able to resist. One is tempted to conclude that he is talking about sexual desire since Rousseau once before mentioned a fault in a similarly imprecise way only to let it be known indirectly that he was referring to sexual desire.[18] And, of course, sexuality figures prominently in the Gyges stories of both Plato and Herodotus. Sex is also the desire that perhaps most characterizes the imperfection of our humanity, and so our separateness from God. We are each male and female but not both, and yet "God created man in his own image, in the image of God created he him, male and female created he them."[19] This temptation ought and ought not to be resisted. On the one hand, in speaking of his one weakness, Rousseau surely means to call our attention to the antinomian quality of sexuality. On the other hand, it is just as important that Rousseau leaves his weakness unspecified, for he intends to show that the fiction of the ring of Gyges is a means to disclose to us our hearts, whatever their idiosyncratic content. We learn of our natures in assuming something—perfect strength and freedom—that is really incompatible with our natures. Because "the one whose power places him above man ought to be above the weakness of humanity" (VI.19), "all things considered, I believe that I will prefer to throw away my magic ring before it has made me do something foolish" (VI.20). Having used the fiction of being a god to disclose his heart to himself so as presumably to gain some control over it, Rousseau recognizes that he must discard its reality.

Rousseau concludes the Sixth Walk by describing how he in particular is not really suited for civil society, yet his reasons seem to apply to human beings generally. For all of us our "independent nature" is at odds with "limitation, obligation and duty" (VI.21). Human freedom presents a problem. We cannot do what we want, for to do so is a sign of imperfection and lack; this means our ultimate motives are hidden from us, and thus we cannot be sure of doing what we want. All that remains for us is to refrain from doing what we do not want.

> I abstain from acting, for all my weakness is regarding action, all my strength is negative, and all my sins are of omission, rarely of commission. I have never believed that the freedom of man consists in doing what he wants, but rather in never doing what he does not want. . . . (VI.21)

Having announced this principle regarding human freedom, Rousseau protests that others have been too quick to regard him as pernicious. Those who "omit [doing] nothing servile in order to command" (VI.21) are those who cannot afford to admit their ignorance of their own motives. For them Rousseau's principle of negative freedom would be a hard lesson. Rousseau's protest, then, is somewhat disingenuous.

> Their wrong, therefore, has not been to separate me from society as a useless member, but to proscribe me from it as a pernicious member, for I have done very little good, I admit it, but as for evil, it has not entered into my will in my life, and I doubt that there is any man in the world who has really done less of it than I. (VI.21)

The man who once said that "every useless citizen can be regarded as a pernicious man"[20] knows full well that his call to idleness will be perceived as a threat to civil life, which requires that motives be ascertainable and that men be treated as responsible for their actions and so as free.

But is Rousseau really a useless citizen and so a pernicious man? The Sixth Walk is an extended justification for not doing any positive good, but is it itself not part of a positive action? We must still explain the status of *The Reveries*. Had he not written, Rousseau might simply be a man who in a rather melancholy way understands the limits of what is possible for human beings. But he apparently believes it will do some good to make the limits of our humanity known. The act of writing somehow transforms negative freedom into a positive good. Rousseau gives us something that pretends to be private so as to make it impossible for it to be the ground of claims upon him—we are not to assume the role of little lame beggars. At the same time he makes it public. *The Reveries of the Solitary Walker* is the paradigm both for what it means to be a book and for such freedom as is available to human beings.

The problem of the Sixth Walk is freedom. On the one hand, it means doing what we want; on the other, that we want means we are not free—the causes of our movements are hidden in our hearts. The first, and ordinary, understanding of freedom as doing what we want assumes that we know what we want, but our motives for apparently free and aimless actions are complex. Rousseau's detour was such an action, but, as we saw, so was his initial act of giving alms to the boy. At the very least, then, true freedom would require self-knowledge; we would have to know what really motivates us. This, in turn, would require that we know exactly how our motives are more complex than they at first seem.

For Rousseau, freedom really has two problems. The apparently more fundamental one is that a being defined by its desires may take pleasure in their satisfaction but cannot take pleasure in the fact of their satisfaction; it is not free to desire anything but what it desires, and so, because not really responsible for its own being, it cannot take pleasure in its own being. Apparently less fundamental is that seemingly spontaneous action is caused by concealed motives. There is a sequence to this concealment. We first want to do something—we are moved by some good. Having done it, we derive the pleasure of "acting freely." Now, when placed in a similar situation, we will once again "want" to do the same thing, and so spontaneity yields to habit. Recognizing this activity as something "we do" habitually amounts to giving a law to ourselves; this is what we mean by duty. With this step the original spontaneity is finally left behind, and with it the original pleasure. Of course, if no action is genuinely spontaneous, this history of the origin of duty is something of a fiction. Habit is simply the manifestation in time of what it means that each of us has a fixed structure of desire.

Morality and political life follow remarkably similar paths. Civil society requires a regularity of behavior and so requires shared standards, which are either implicit, like habits, or explicit, like laws.[21] The latter are felt as commands and so as limitations of our freedom; the former seem to be "second nature" and, while limiting us similarly, are not felt as such. Habit conceals nonspontaneous activity behind apparent spontaneity. Still, however effortless, habitual actions are not free. The man who wishes to be free will thus necessarily be at odds with civil society, which cannot help insulating us from nature and so from our own natures. Civil society wants to engender the habit of doing good and ultimately wants to substitute doing good out of duty for doing good out of natural pleasure. To the extent that it succeeds, it must destroy natural pleasure, which provides a reason for acting beyond the law and thus in a way potentially contrary to the law. Ironically, this intent to make us altogether law-abiding unwittingly undermines support for the law. In the face of these obligations, we could simply rebel—Rousseau stopped traveling to the Enfer gateway—but this simply gets us in deeper. Since Rousseau's real motive for the detour is to avoid the boy to whom he gave alms, in choosing a different path, he is controlled negatively by the habitual activity he originally wished to avoid. As his activity is defined by "not going to the gates of hell," Rousseau is ruled by the thought of hell. Realizing this, he wants to devise a way to avoid men without hating them.

In light of this limitation on human freedom, Rousseau defends himself for no longer doing good; the defense has two parts. First, because he is so thoroughly deceived, he no longer knows what is good and, accordingly, cannot do it. Second, as he is unable to do what gives him no pleasure, and knowing that he acts without freedom deprives him of pleasure, he cannot do anything simply for the sake of duty. These two are connected insofar as Rousseau sees that if he relies on his "instincts" as he would have to as a participant in the human drama, he would inevitably have to fall back on second nature—habit or virtue. Although he now knows that this is not really doing good, and so must find a way of acting without habit, still he has no other inclination to replace those that are now discredited. The question Rousseau poses in the Sixth Walk is this: How is the life without habit possible?[22] His answer is tantalizing, but as yet not sufficiently clear.

> I have never believed that the freedom of man consisted in doing what he wants, but rather in never doing what he does not want, and it is this that I have always claimed [*réclamée*], often preserved, and by which I have been most a scandal to my contemporaries. (VI.21)

This freedom justifies the qualification of the mechanistic claim of the first sentence of the Sixth Walk: there is "scarcely" any mechanical movement of which we are unable to find the cause in our hearts. Apparently, we can say no and by so doing tacitly call into question the habit, duty, or law urging us to act. This negation seems the only way to recover the "original" impulse that motivates every habit. In moving from apparent spontaneity to hidden cause to negation, we have moved from "me" to "them" to "me."

As we have seen, this movement is possible only if one does not reject duty in anger or from a desire to replace it with something else. Not anger but flight or withdrawal is Rousseau's solution. His goal is to become like the spectator of a drama, who, because not interested in the outcome of the action in the sense of feeling compelled to act on his own behalf, can engage in the sort of questioning of law and habit that leads to the discovery of the origin of habit—to the discovery of the heart. Yet Rousseau's apparent denial that this goal is possible for one acting out of need seems finally to deny its possibility for anyone. He therefore presents equally impossible alternatives: the positive freedom of a god and the negative freedom to "resist" duty and so come to understand what is good. The model for this second sort of detachment is the book; Rousseau's nonaction manifests itself in books that are in a way his good deeds.

The account of the Sixth Walk threatens to be so negative as to be tragic; we want what we can in principle never have. No possible human action satisfies our demand for freedom. Rousseau's justification for doing nothing comes perilously close to inducing paralysis. In the Seventh Walk Rousseau will return to what he in fact does with his life. His occupation is botany, and the question of the Seventh Walk will be why. In the Sixth Walk Rousseau was troubled by the fact that he had a nature; the Seventh Walk will be an account of the goodness of nature.

NOTES

1. The word *Dasein*, no less than the inextricable link between the *tode ti* and *ti esti*, suggests that "the problem inherent in the surface of things and only in the surface of things is the heart of things" (Leo Strauss, *Thoughts on Machiavelli* [Seattle: University of Washington Press, 1958], 13).

2. VI.1, VI.2, VI.3, VI.4 (thrice), VI.7 (thrice), VI.8 (in a compound—*contrecoeur*), VI.9, VI.11, VI.15, VI.18 (thrice), and VI.20. See also chapter 7, note 6.

3. See Charles Butterworth, *The Reveries of the Solitary Walker* (New York: Harper & Row, 1979), 200–1.

4. See *Oeuvres complètes*, vol. 1, 525 (note 64) and 193–94, as well as Butterworth, *The Reveries*, 84 (note 3).

5. See *Oeuvres complètes*, vol. 3, 97–99.

6. *Oeuvres complètes*, vol. 2, 518.

7. *Oeuvres complètes*, vol. 1, 195.

8. See, for example, *Emile* (*Oeuvres complètes*, vol. 3, 19–21), *Second Discourse* (*Oeuvres complètes*, vol. 2, 223–24), and *Social Contract* (*Oeuvres complètes*, vol. 2, 524).

9. Compare Rousseau's account of the relation between illness and freedom in the *Second Discourse* (*Oeuvres complètes*, vol. 2, 218).

10. See *Oeuvres complètes*, vol. 1, 202–3.

11. See *Oeuvres complètes*, vol. 1, 191–92.

12. See *Oeuvres complètes*, vol. 1, 241.

13. *Oeuvres complètes*, vol. 1, 274.

14. See *Second Discourse*, note i (*Oeuvres complètes*, vol. 2, 251–54) and chapter 6.

15. Consider the first sentence of *Emile* (*Oeuvres complètes*, vol. 3, 19).

16. See *Republic*, 357a–361d; an earlier story in which Gyges figures prominently and which is also concerned with the question of justice and visibility is to be found in Herodotus, *Inquiries*, I.8–14. Revealing interpretations of the two stories appear in Seth Benardete's *Socrates' Second Sailing* (Chicago: University of Chicago Press, 1989), 35–40, and *Herodotean Inquiries* (The Hague: Martinus Nijhoff, 1969), 11–15 and 25–26.

17. This seems to be Plato's view as well; it is Glaucon's characteristic mistake to think that he longs for the objects of his desire when he really longs for the satisfaction of having achieved them. See, for example, *Republic*, 372c–e with Benardete, *Socrates' Second Sailing*, 51–52.

18. See the account of the Savoyard Vicar in *Emile* (*Oeuvres complètes*, vol. 3, 183–84).

19. *The Holy Bible*, King James version, Genesis I:27.

20. *Oeuvres complètes*, vol. 2, 58.

21. This is the same doubleness already present in the Greek word *nomos*—law or convention.

22. This is, of course, a Socratic formula for philosophy. See *Phaedo*, 77a–84b.

11

BEAUTY

The overall structure of the Seventh Walk divides in three. In the first section (VII.1–4), Rousseau asks why botany of all things is appropriate for him. The second section (VII.5–24) answers this question in four parts. Rousseau first treats botany as a substitute for reverie (VII.5–11). He then asks why others do not understand it as he does but instead confuse it with pharmacology; the problem of this section is natural teleology (VII.12–16). Next he compares botany with the other natural sciences that treat nature as a whole, minerals, animals, and the stars (VII.17–21). Finally, he returns to the question of teleology in a discussion of botany understood as idle curiosity (VII.22–24). The third and final section of the Seventh Walk (VII.25–30) is a series of anecdotes in which Rousseau muses first about a walk in which he unexpectedly discovers a stocking mill (VII.25–27), then about discovering a bookseller in the midst of rural Switzerland (VII.27), and finally about an episode that turns on some "poison" berries (VII.28). These anecdotes are followed by a brief conclusion in which botany emerges as the key to memory. Anecdotes, one might say, turn out to be the hidden purpose—the heart—of botany.

The Sixth Walk ought to have taught us to reserve judgment about Rousseau's stated motives—whatever they might be. Here botany is presented as a substitute for reverie.

> The collection of my long dreams has hardly [*à peine*] begun, and already I feel that it reaches its end. Another amusement succeeds it, absorbs me and even takes from me the time to dream. I give myself over to it with an infatuation that touches on extravagance and that makes me laugh at myself when I reflect on it; but I nonetheless give

211

myself over to it because, in the situation where I am, I have no longer any other rule of conduct than that of following without restraint my inclination in everything. (VII.1)

If we read the passage perhaps overly literally, Rousseau begins the Seventh Walk by coupling the claim that collecting dreams (*rêves*) now causes him pain with the claim that this activity is close to its *fin*—its end, but perhaps also its goal or purpose. Rousseau will thus present botany as the *fin* of reverie. How far are we to take the parallel? Is collecting dreams in some way akin to collecting plants, making the *Reveries* a sort of herbarium? Rousseau's enthusiasm for botany moves him to laughter.[1] He seems not to have believed he would ever again be so devoted to something external to him (see I.6–7). Previously, Rousseau found no food for his heart on earth and therefore accustomed himself "to nourish it on its own substance and to seek all its fodder within [himself]" (II.2). Now, in pursuing botany, he is once again an exophage and playfully makes grass his nourishment. Wisdom itself counsels Rousseau to follow his inclinations with no limit but his strength and imagination; these inclinations lead him back to the world and specifically to plants. Yet for Rousseau, who is taking up botany *again*, the pleasure of his "new" activity comes as much from rediscovery as from discovery. His botanical activity, like reverie, thus has a certain doubleness to it, and his pleasure derives as much from remembering, and so reflecting on his own pleasure, as it does from experiencing plants. Had Rousseau really given up reverie for botany, we would not have the Seventh Walk—he would have been too immersed in the garden of the world to think it, let alone record it. Granted that this walk quickly leaves behind *me voilà* (VII.1) for *voilà toujours une plante de plus* (VII.2), the two are not simply different, for Rousseau's reproduction of nature is at the same time a reproduction of his earlier life.

Rousseau pursues his new pastime with considerable ardor given the difficulties he faces.

All of a sudden at more than sixty-five, deprived of the little memory that I had and of the strength that remains to me to traverse the countryside, without guide, without books, without a garden, without a herbarium, here am I taken again by this folly, but with still more ardor than I had in giving myself over to it the first time; here am I occupied with the wise project of learning by heart all of Murray's *Regnum vegetabile* and with recognizing all the plants known on the earth. (VII.2)

His plan of action is extravagant, for if we take Rousseau seriously, he aims to get the whole world by heart—"all the plants of the sea and of the Alps and all the trees of the Indies" (VII.2). He goes out of his way to make his new love seem preposterous in another way as well. Calling it a fantasy not only wise but also virtuous, Rousseau identifies botany as *the* means available to keep him from longing for revenge. And yet, in keeping him from revenge, botany is Rousseau's revenge, for

> it is the means of not allowing to germinate in my heart any leaven of vengeance or of hate. . . . This is how I avenge myself on my persecutors in my way; I do not know how to punish them more cruelly than to be happy in spite of them. (VII.3)

Botany, itself an activity, cannot be merely a means to keep Rousseau from an active life. Its apparent aimlessness, thus, has a deeper goal.

At first glance botany appears a strange occupation to guarantee Rousseau's peace of mind and serve as punishment for his enemies, especially given how ill suited he seems to be for it. Still, Rousseau thinks that if he can explain its attraction for him he will understand himself better. While reason may prescribe in general that the heart should lose itself in something, it cannot explain why certain things attract us and certain things do not. For Rousseau to understand himself is to attend to the particular things that attract him. The Seventh Walk therefore begins with the following movement. First, botany replaces reverie as the activity of Rousseau's leisure. Then reflection or meditation on botany replaces botany. All three activities are in the service of self-knowledge, and so there is an end or goal of botany just as there was an end or goal of reverie. At the same time, each of these activities has been and will continue to be described as idle, aimless, and without purpose. They are the activities of *promener* rather than *marcher*. By nevertheless making botany the end of reverie, reflection the end of botany, and self-knowledge the end of reflection, Rousseau suggests the possibility of an activity that combines purposiveness and aimlessness—a reflection that cannot finally be understood to have an aim apart from itself.

It is not, however, an activity that comes easily, as Rousseau makes clear in the second part of the Seventh Walk, when in asking why botany leads to reflection, he reflects on the relation between reverie and thought, reflection, or meditation.

> I have sometimes thought profoundly enough, but rarely with plea-
> sure, almost always against my will [*gré*] and by force: Reverie re-
> freshes me and amuses me, reflection fatigues me and saddens me; to
> think was for me always an occupation painful and without charm.
> Sometimes my reveries end through meditation, but more often my
> meditations end through reverie, and during these strayings, my soul
> wanders and soars in the universe on the wings of the imagination and
> of ecstasies that exceed all other enjoyment. (VII.5)

Unlike reverie, thought is goal directed. It tires Rousseau because, having its own necessities, it forces him in a certain direction, and as we know from the Sixth Walk, to be aware of being compelled is painful. Still, thinking is a requirement of our survival in the world. Life is an ongoing series of problems that demand resolution; we must, for example, eat. Our need to think guarantees that reverie will diminish.

Purposive and nonpurposive mental activity are naturally at odds. Rousseau pinpoints the time in his own life when the one begins to drive out the other. For fifty years reverie substituted for "fortune and glory" and made Rousseau "in idleness, the happiest of mortals" (VII.6). But all of this ended when he was "thrown into a literary career by foreign impulsions" (VII.6). Now, as Rousseau was born in 1712, the pressures of the literary life seem to have begun for him in 1762. Before this time the purposelessness of reverie still prevailed. And yet, the *First Discourse, Second Discourse, Social Contract, Emile, Julie,* and *Letter to D'A-lembert*—in short, virtually all of Rousseau's nonautobiographical works—were composed before 1762. Rousseau's *"carrière littéraire"* thus seems rather a reference to the difficulties resulting from the reputation he earned for publishing, especially for publishing *Emile,* than to the activity of writing itself. Since Rousseau's writings after 1762 are primarily autobiographical, reverie seems to stand in relation to thinking as nonautobiographical writing stands in relation to autobiography. It is not so much thinking that is painful but thinking about oneself.

Even reverie, however, can turn painful. Left to itself, one's imagination turns willy nilly to oneself. Rousseau is afraid lest "the continual sentiment of my hardships [*peines*] constricting my heart by degrees finally crush me from its weight" (VII.7). Because happiness seems to require that one's thoughts or imagination be directed toward what is other than oneself, Rousseau's instinct is to shut down his imagination and look at what surrounds him—nature. The turn to botany is thus presented as a cure for his melancholy, in which the world, not as a whole but in its details, is to serve as a substitute for the imagination.

At first it seems that this overall movement—from reverie to thoughts about oneself to a consideration of the details of nature—is the movement of Rousseau's life. However, Rousseau makes it clear that he did not really discover nature at the age of fifty. Plants are like the clothing of the earth—like its wedding dress (VII.8). Rousseau had always tended to lose himself in nature and to see himself as one with it so that reverie is almost defined here as the perception of oneself by way of perception of the whole.[2] Yet, in his attempt to preserve the "heat" of his heart from "the dejection into which it was by degrees falling" (VII.10), Rousseau did not knowingly turn to nature. Rather, he turned away from himself and discovered the variety of nature almost by chance.

> I wandered heedlessly in the woods and in the mountains not daring to think for fear of stirring up my sufferings. My imagination, which rejects objects of pain, let my senses give themselves over to the light but sweet impressions of the surrounding objects. My eyes wandered [*se promenaient*] without cease from one to the other, and it was not possible that in so great a variety something would not be found which would fix them more and stay them longer. (VII.10)

Rousseau did not seek nature as a cure but happened upon it naturally and, just as naturally, developed "a taste for this recreation of the eyes" (VII.11). That his pleasure is of the eyes and not of the heart clarifies his earlier use of clothing as an image for plants. This pleasure is an alternative to the sort of pleasure, especially sexual pleasure, that always promises more than is initially seen. If Rousseau had looked to nature as a cure for what ails him, he would have been trying to find something in it that was not immediately obvious. To happen upon nature as a cure, however, is possible only because one is moved by what one does see.

It would be wrong, then, to say that nature is not purposive. Rather, to seek nature's purposes is what prevents one from finding them. Nature is presented here as something like a reverie made real. It at first appears to be characterized by randomness, but in this very randomness it reveals its purpose. Beauty seems to consist in this "rational randomness of the natural."

The obstacle to this view of nature is represented by pharmacology—"the habit of seeking in plants only drugs and remedies" (VII.12).

> But thanks to a certain Dioscorides, a great compiler of recipes, and to his commentators, medicine has so seized control of plants transformed into simples that one sees in them only what one does not see in them at all, to wit, the pretended virtues it pleases all the world to attribute to them. (VII.12)

Now, by bringing up recipes, Rousseau reminds us that we have no choice but to think of hidden properties. Nature is for eating as well as for beholding; we would not be able to live in a world where we did not value the properties of living things insofar as they nourish us. But, as these properties are not always manifest—some things that look nourishing may in fact kill us (see VII.28)—at a very rudimentary level, we are compelled to seek to know the hidden powers of nature. Rousseau calls these hidden properties "pretended virtues"; the phrase perfectly fits his previous account of virtue as taking one's bearings by what ought to be and so by what is not.[3] This pharmacological way of treating nature thus has something to do with lying—saying the thing that is not—and with attending to the authority of men. There is, of course, a connection between lying and having hidden purposes. Civil life molds us so that we rely on what is said to the exclusion of what is seen. It is an experience of a world of hidden purposes made manifest rather than an experience of the world as manifest. And these hidden purposes articulated in what is said are always rooted in some need. Still, lest we jump too easily out of this cave of ordinary human experience into the light of the sun, we ought to notice that, while Rousseau begins the Seventh Walk by claiming that in his present situation "it is a great wisdom and even great virtue" (VII.3) to pursue botany, nevertheless the reason that commands him to do so does not teach him why botany attracts him so, and "it is an oddity that I would like to explain to myself" (VII.4). In wanting to

know the hidden power of botany, is not Rousseau behaving pharmaco-
logically?

On the most obvious level, Rousseau is recommending something
like the activity of Adam in Eden prior to the Fall—a naming that exists
for its own sake with no view to its utility. As we have seen, he can do
that only if he maintains a distinction between drugs and food, between
pharmacology and economics or household management. But what precisely is the difference between nature as a "storehouse of foods"
(VII.14) and nature as a storehouse of drugs? Rousseau refers to tisane
here as a drug (VII.14), but earlier it was the source of a tea sold along
with rolls by the little lame boy's mother at the gates of Enfer (VI.2)—it
was understood to be food. Rousseau seems to suggest one clear distinction between drugs and food.

> But it has never entered my mind to seek drugs and remedies there
> [in nature]. I see nothing in her various products that indicates such a
> use to me, and she would have shown us the choice had she had
> prescribed it to us, as she has done for what is edible. (VII.14)

Yet, even ignoring the fact that the Seventh Walk ends with an anecdote
that at the very least makes nature's intention unclear with regard to the
nutritional value of certain berries, it is certainly not the case that one
always delights in the contemplation of nature when one eats. If hunger
is an infirmity, then awareness of it would have to poison the pleasure
of botany. We may suffer from curable ills, but we nevertheless, by nature, suffer from ills.[4] This becomes clear when Rousseau generalizes the
problem of pharmacology to include any turn of mind concerned with
material gain or interest, and then goes on to make clear that such a
concern is required by virtue of the fact that we have bodies (VII.15).
We therefore have two modes of interest in nature. One is born of
sickness, need, or imperfection and leads to a teleological understanding
of nature. The other is born of satisfaction and calm and leads to a nonte-
leological understanding of nature. Rousseau suggests that the former is
necessarily self-oriented; any teleology conceals a desire to structure the
world so that it is of benefit to the perceiver—it is a species of wishful
thinking. Accordingly, one looks for laws of nature and unwittingly finds
oneself.

> From all this sad tiring toil much less knowledge than pride ordinarily results, and where is the most mediocre chemist who does not believe he has penetrated all the great operations of nature by having found perhaps by chance some little concoctions of art. (VII.19)

That this fate is not so easy to avoid becomes clear when one attempts to separate all elements of body from one's understanding of self, person, or soul. Rousseau, therefore, must ask why botany proves more successful than other pursuits in overcoming our natural interestedness in the world. He turns to this question in the next section of the Seventh Walk (VII.17–21).

Rousseau wants to avoid unwittingly attributing to nature purposes that are really his own. He has been forced outside of himself so as not to dwell on his misfortunes; it would be sad were he simply to let this self-preoccupation return through a back door. At the same time, since Rousseau's age restricts the range of his extension outside of himself, he is able to contemplate only the nature that is within his reach. There seem to be three possibilities for him; nature divides into minerals, animals, and plants.

> Minerals are not suitable objects of contemplation first because they are not by themselves lovable or attractive. Furthermore one must labor excessively to get at them, and this labor involves the unpleasantness of digging under the earth out of the light. In addition to profit in the study of minerals, it is necessary to be a chemist and a physicist to do troublesome [*pénibles*] and costly experiments, to work in laboratories, to spend much money and time amidst charcoal, melting pots, furnaces, retorts, in the suffocating smoke and vapors, always at risk to one's life and often at the expense of one's health. (VII.19)

Minerals themselves have no visible structure; on the phenomenal level they are not wholes but masses. Accordingly, to get at what is genuinely interesting about them, one must transform them by way of experiments. What is seen is to this extent an artifact and not the nature of the thing by itself. Thus, life in this cave involves feeding off other men and what they say. It can never be a direct study of nature.

Animals are wholes in a way that minerals are not. Part of their study, anatomy, would involve the unpleasant business of dissection; in this regard one can only learn what it means for them to be alive by way of performing an autopsy on them once they are dead. Even if one wished only to study them in terms of their behavior, animals have purposes or wills of their own. To study them, one has to catch them and cage them. In both of these cases, the study of animals requires that one subordinate their purposes to one's own in studying them. But this is to deform what is most worthy of study in them.

The optimal object of study for Rousseau would strike a mean between minerals, in which too little purpose is manifest, and animals, in which too much purpose is manifest. Otherwise it will prove necessary to transform the object of study in order to study it, and this would mean looking for what is not manifest. Because the studies of animals and of minerals force us to look beneath the surface, both are ugly. One would therefore have to want to study them before coming to them. One could not happen upon them; they would have to be born of some need. They therefore fail to meet Rousseau's standards for the study of nature.

> Attracted by the cheerful objects that surround me, I consider them, I contemplate them, I compare them, I learn finally to classify them, and here I am suddenly as much botanist as one has need of being who wants only to study nature in order ceaselessly to find new reasons for loving it. (VII.21)

Rousseau wishes to be active in a way that combines purposiveness and aimlessness. For this he requires an object of study that is manifestly purposive but in such a way that does not require him to thwart its purposes to contemplate them. It is the charm of botany to fulfill both of these requirements. Botany is the model for Rousseauan observation generally. The goal is always to classify with a view to seeing how plants (and other things) work. Rousseau observes the purposes of the parts of a complex system, a whole, in order to take pleasure in the working of the system. But to do this, one cannot have a stake in the system. Here, Rousseau means any system, including *the* whole—the cosmos.

> Plants seem to have been sown with profusion on the earth like the stars in the sky in order to invite man through the attraction of pleasure and curiosity to the study of nature. (VII.23)

Rousseau would therefore like to be able to observe men as he observes plants, but because he is a man he can never quite do it. Theophrastus, the philosopher whom he calls "the only botanist of antiquity" (VII.12), was also the author of the *Moral Characters*, a book in which a variety of human types are described. In the Seventh Walk Rousseau refers to the object of the study of animals as their habits (*moeurs*) and characters (VII.20). Of plants he says that

> there is neither cost nor trouble for me in wandering heedlessly from plant to plant to examine them, to compare their divers characters, to mark their relations and their differences, finally to observe vegetable organization so as to follow the course and the play of these living machines, to find sometimes with success their general laws, the reason and the end of their structures, and to give myself up to the charm of grateful admiration for the hand which made me enjoy all of this. (VII.22)

In describing the fate of botany gone wrong, Rousseau even goes so far as to compare it to a plant. "In denaturing this amiable study, they transplant it into the midst of cities and academies where it wilts no less than exotic plants in the gardens of the inquisitive" (VII.23).

Noticing this comparison between the way Rousseau investigates plants and the way he suggests other things need to be investigated, one first thinks to object that most of the argument of the Seventh Walk has been devoted to showing why it is only plants that can be investigated in this way. On the other hand, this sort of investigation, with its combination of aimlessness and purposiveness, is not so clearly possible even in the case of plants, for

> as soon as one mixes with it a motive of interest or of vanity, be it to fill positions or to make books, as soon as one only wants to learn in order to instruct, as soon as one searches for plants only to become an author or professor, all this sweet charm vanishes; one sees in plants no longer anything but the instruments of our passions, one finds no longer any true pleasure in their study, one wants no longer to know but to show that one knows, and in the woods one is only on the stage of the world, occupied with the concern for making oneself admired. (VII.23)

All this, of course, from the author of the Seventh Walk.

What, then, is Rousseau really concerned to study? He wants to understand the spontaneous products of the earth "not forced by men" (VII.24)—that is, prior to human intervention. Rousseau wants to study what is really real independent of human interference. Finally, however, this includes, as it did for Theophrastus, the study of human beings as they really are. The study of untouched nature prepares the way for the study of man. The Seventh Walk ends with a series of anecdotes because this is what it has been from the outset building toward.

The first of these anecdotes follows a pattern already established by Rousseau in the Second and Fifth Walks—the walks most explicitly devoted to giving an account of reverie. It shows how botany leads to reverie, which in turn is brought to a sudden end by vanity. Out walking in a mountain wood owned by a doctor, Rousseau comes upon

> a retreat so hidden that I have not in my life seen a sight more savage. . . . Some gaps that led beyond this somber enclosure opened up only to sheer rock faces and horrible precipices that I dared look upon only by lying down on my stomach. (VII.25)

Rousseau recognizes birds, large and small, rare and common, and explicitly identifies five species of plants and remembers identifying still more. Nevertheless, he finds his surroundings uncanny.

> But insensibly dominated by the strong impression of objects, I forgot botany and plants and I sat down on pillows of *lycopodium* and mosses and began to dream, more at my ease because thinking that there I was in a refuge unknown by the whole universe where persecutors would not unearth me. A movement of pride soon inserted itself into this reverie. I compared myself to those great voyagers who discovered a desert island, and I said to myself complacently: "Without doubt I am the first mortal who has penetrated as far as this; I look upon myself almost as another Columbus." (VII.25)

Rousseau so loses himself in the contemplation of his surroundings that he becomes vulnerable to seeing them in terms of his own situation. His very selflessness is what gives way to self-absorption, as vanity, always just around the corner, brings him back to himself and to his own self-interest. Rousseau falls out of his state of nature and back into civil society.

> While I preened myself with this idea, I heard not far from me a certain clicking that I believed I recognized; I listened—the same noise was repeated and multiplied. Surprised and curious, I got up, broke through a thicket of bushes on the side from which the noise was coming and, in a dale twenty paces from the same place where I believed myself the first to have arrived, I perceived a stocking [*bas*] factory. (VII.25)

Rousseau, who loses himself in nature only to begin daydreaming about himself, is rudely brought back to himself by discovering that his solitude, his refuge, is not a stone's throw from a place where something is produced, *bas*, that is a homonym for the base. Rousseau is quick to point out how illusory his refuge was, since he was quite sure that he recognized men in the factory who were part of the plot against him. We, of course, are just as quick to recognize this as a case of vanity working overtime. And yet in the end vanity does not win out. "I hastened to set aside this sad idea, and I ended by laughing to myself both at my puerile vanity and at the comic manner in which I had been punished" (VII.26). Apparently Rousseau has learned to treat himself as an interesting species.

This becomes yet clearer from the way Rousseau uses his own experience, born of reverie, born of botany, to reflect on Switzerland as an image of the human condition. Switzerland provides a queer mixture of the savage and human industry. It is like a city divided by long streets between which one finds the appearance of untrammeled nature. What seems natural is bounded by civilization; when we most think we are alone, we are thoroughly social. Rousseau is reminded of another vignette. While he was in the country looking for plants, a solitary house was pointed out to him. He was asked and was unable to guess the occupation of the inhabitant, who was a bookseller.

In the final anecdote of the Seventh Walk Rousseau comes closest to dropping the pretense that he is telling stories about *herborisation*. He recalls taking a walk with M. Bovier near Grenoble. As Rousseau twice identifies Bovier as a lawyer, he seems to mean to call attention to him as somehow the opposite of a naturalist. Bovier was a man who "neither loved nor knew botany" (VII.28). For reasons Rousseau does not give, Bovier made himself his personal guard.[5] While the two were walking together, Rousseau sampled some berries. A third person warned him that they were poisonous. When Rousseau asked Bovier why he did not tell him of this, he replied in a respectful tone, "I did not dare to take this liberty" (VII.29). Rousseau found this very funny and laughed aloud. Rousseau laughed at the incident at the stocking factory not only because he was so vain as to think that he was the first to have seen this part of the wood but also because he was so vain as to have been sure that there were conspirators in the plot against him working at the factory. He laughed at himself. Here he first laughs at Bovier, not, we are pleased to discover, because he suspects that Bovier is trying to kill him but rather because the law—convention—looms so powerful for us that this man could not behave impolitely even in order to fulfill his vow to protect Rousseau's life. It is no accident that this anecdote is set in France, which is for Rousseau always the example of social life, law, and custom pushed to the point of absurdity; it is the most denatured of civil societies. Rousseau laughs at men in general because the power of opinion is so great in us that a whole society can believe that the berry of the *hippophae* is poisonous apparently with no evidence whatsoever. At the same time, Rousseau laughs at himself. He is the man who is so sure that nature provides its own indication of what is good and bad for us that nothing that tastes sweet can be harmful. Yet, in this instance he lacked sufficient courage in this conviction to keep from worrying about his safety for the rest of the afternoon. This, too, is funny, for Rousseau cannot escape the fact that the opinions of others influence him even though he is most famous for having called this power others have over us into question. *Amour-propre* is easier to identify than it is to overcome.

That Rousseau means to use botany as both an excuse and a model for understanding whole settings is clear from the way the Seventh Walk concludes. In reflecting on his various botanical expeditions, Rousseau comments that he need only look at the specimens he collected in order to be transported back to the places where he collected them. They serve as reminders of whole situations—presumably the *hippophae* of M. Bovier and the *lycopodium* of the stocking factory. His herbarium is thus a journal of his experiences and is therefore like the *Reveries,* which is also a compilation of his reveries.

> It is the chain of accessory ideas that attaches me to botany. It assembles [*rassemble*] and recalls to my imagination all the ideas that flatter it more. The meadows, the waters, the woods, the solitude, especially

the peace and the repose that one finds in the middle of all that are retraced by it necessarily in my memory. It makes me forget the persecutions of men, their hatreds, their contempt, their outrages, and all the ills with which they have repaid my tender and sincere attachment for them. It transports me to peaceful habitats among simple and good people, such as those with whom I formerly lived. It recalls to me both my youth and my innocent pleasures; it makes me enjoy them anew and renders me happy often enough still in the midst of the saddest lot a mortal has ever suffered. (VII.30)

In the Seventh Walk the accessory ideas that attach Rousseau to botany are revealed by anecdotes, and, as we have seen, all seem to return to the issue of vanity and self-interest. This is certainly clear from the last lines of the walk quoted above. Yet Rousseau seems to think that botany, which can study "systems" without being a part of a system is the model for how to understand the human system of which one is a part. For Rousseau, botany is a means of getting into the habit of having no habits—of not being, like Bovier, a creature of custom. That this project is still more complicated than it at first seems becomes clear once one asks a simple question of Rousseau: Where does the herbarium of which he speaks in the last two paragraphs of the Seventh Walk come from? In the first paragraph he tells us that he sold it. If he now has a new one, then it must contain new plants. These recently acquired plants, which no doubt have the same character as the earlier ones, apparently are sufficient to generate the memories and anecdotes of the Seventh Walk. The memories are thus not attached to the original plants but to others of the same species. One wonders, then, if this is true of the anecdotes as well. That Rousseau possesses an herbarium at the end of the Seventh Walk means that he is redoing what he did before. The herbarium is not the same; it has the same species but different individual plants. Rousseau remembers events in his life by attaching them to the picking not of a plant but of a species. In the same way, his scrapbook of anecdotes is a collection of the species characteristics of men. It is Theophrastus's *Characters* posing as an autobiography.

NOTES

1. Rousseau laughs a great deal in the Seventh Walk. See VII.26–27.
2. "A sweet and profound reverie takes possession then of his senses, and he

loses himself with a delightful drunkenness in the immensity of this beautiful system with which he senses himself identified" (VII.9).

3. See VI.6–9 and chapter 10.

4. See *Emile, Oeuvres complètes*, vol. 3, 16.

5. See Charles Butterworth, *The Reveries of the Solitary Walker* (New York: Harper & Row, 1979), 108–9.

12

THE END OF SUFFERING

The problem of the Sixth Walk was the tension between free actions and the same actions once they have become habitual and then lawful. If we are born free, how do our actions become so habitual that we come to be everywhere in chains? The sequence Rousseau sketches moves from a particular action (in this case, giving alms to the lame boy) to the repetition of the action to the discovery of this repetition. Rousseau, of course, does not confirm his action but instead only discovers that it has come to be a habit for him because of his subconscious decision not to do it. His detour in order to avoid the boy represents a decision to break the law he has unwittingly laid down for himself. When we discover that an action has become habitual, we say to ourselves "this is what we do" or "this is our way." Yet this avowal has a certain ambiguity, for it is at once a statement of fact and a way of implying that we do not do what we say we do. A nursery school teacher says "We don't throw blocks here" as a response to block throwing. As soon as we affirm that we do something habitually, we have at once tacitly made doing it a law and introduced the possibility, even the desire, not to do it. But then when exactly is it habitual? Can a habit be a habit before we are in some sense aware of it as a repetition? Until then it makes some sense to understand each occurrence as "spontaneous." Yet to be aware of the repetition is simply to say to ourselves that we do this thing. This, in turn, is like laying down a law for ourselves, which, accordingly, makes the thing that we do already questionable and so not simply habitual. "We do it this way" involves an awareness that there is another way. Habitual action thus seems illusory. Before it is articulated it is indistinguishable from spontaneity—each time may as well be the first time; after it is articulated, it has become a law and so questionable.

227

This status of habit as impossibly lodged between spontaneity and law is akin to the status of natural man as between animal and civil man. Understanding how ephemeral it is will help us to narrow considerably the distance between Rousseau and civil men, between *moi* and *eux*. Habit is the ground of civil society, but since when habit shows itself it is already in decline, already law, civil society necessarily contains within it the possibility of questioning itself. The possibility of saying no—of freedom—is suggested by civil society itself. Habit is a creation of law in the same way that the state of nature is a creation of civil society.

The Seventh Walk, too, is about the relation between civil society and nature insofar as civil society is connected to a teleological understanding of nature. Social men are characterized by looking for the hidden "virtues" of things and of men. In seeking what something is for, they seek not what it is but what it is not. At some level, social man is more concerned with what is said about things than with the reality of things. This, obviously true of designer jeans, is no less true of atomic theory. Accordingly, the connection between civil society and teleological science is that both involve being alienated from things by laws, which invariably tell us as much about ourselves as they do about the phenomena they are designed to describe. Rousseau's alternative to this sort of science is neither dumb, inarticulate nature worship nor even articulate nature worship. He does not, for example, regard the heavenly bodies in their orderly movement and turn them into gods. Instead, Rousseau takes as a paradigm botany, a science recognizing purposes but not mistaking our purposes for those of what it studies. Because the knowledge of human beings requires that one must flee them in order to avoid getting caught up in their purposes, Rousseau's solitude is a blessing. Yet the final paragraph of the Seventh Walk indicates that Rousseau's solitude is not altogether successful. Because he does, after all, take pleasure in his botanical studies, they do serve a purpose, perhaps *the* human purpose. Rousseau's problem is thus revealed by that moment when he thought himself a "new Columbus" in the midst of a wilderness and then discovered a nearby stocking mill. Any purposive activity involves satisfaction not only from *what* I am doing but additionally and perhaps even primarily from what *I* am doing. Rousseau's comeuppance did not require a stocking mill; it was present as soon as he so delighted in himself. His problem is not unanticipated factories but *amour-propre*. How happy or content it is possible for any human being to be will depend on the extent to which this *amour-propre* can be overcome. Accordingly, it is the issue to which Rousseau turns in the Eighth Walk.

The Eighth Walk divides in four. The first part (VIII.1–4) is concerned with the necessity of adversity for the possibility of happiness. In the second (VIII.5–8), Rousseau describes his own sadnesses or adversities and then turns in the third (VIII.9–13) to a discussion of how to transform these adversities into happiness—i.e., to treat them as necessary and not intentional. Finally, in the fourth part (VIII.14–23), Rousseau identifies the obstacle to this strategy as *amour-propre* and describes how to overcome it.

We know there is something new in the Eighth Walk because of its beginning.

> In meditating on the dispositions of my soul in all the situations of my life, I am extremely struck to see so little proportion between the divers schemes of my destiny and the habitual sentiments of well- or ill-being by which they have affected me. The diverse intervals of my brief prosperity have left me nearly no agreeable memory of the intimate and permanent manner in which they have affected me, and, on the contrary, in all the miseries of my life I sensed myself constantly full of tender, touching and delectable sentiments, which, pouring a salutary balm on the wounds of my broken heart seemed to convert its sadness into sensual pleasure [*volupté*], and of which the amiable memory alone comes back to me detached from that of the evils that I experienced at the same time. It seems to me that I have tasted the sweetness of existence more, that I have really lived more, when my sentiments, constricted so to speak around my heart by my destiny, did not exhaust themselves on men's objects of esteem, which merit it so little in themselves and which are the unique occupation of the people one believes to be happy. (VIII.1)

The Eighth Walk is to be a meditation, but meditation (as we know from the Seventh Walk), because it is purposive and so at odds with the aimlessness of reverie, is rarely pleasant (VII.5). Unlike reverie, which involves a sentiment of existence induced by an external movement so gentle as to call scarcely any attention to itself (V.16) and which is "by itself a precious sentiment of contentment and of peace which alone would suffice to render this existence dear and sweet" (V.15), meditation is painful. In reverie, the soul expands and fills with its light existence all the objects that it perceives (II.10); like man in the state of nature, although unknown to itself, the soul is master of all it surveys. Meditation, on the other hand, constricts the soul and turns it back on itself; only the man who is not master of all he surveys and feels constrained by what surrounds him can recognize what such mastery means. Nevertheless, here Rousseau claims to be struck by the split between what he has suffered or experienced and the *habitual* sentiments of well- and ill-being by which they affected him. That is, he claims that he has sensed the sweetness of existence more in reflecting on his former misery than he ever did when he was happy. Happiness takes one out of oneself; the sentiment of existence now seems to require self-awareness.[1] In misery, Rousseau is moved to sense himself. Thus, the memory of misery transforms suffering into *volupté*. And, since this is when he feels most alive, Rousseau needs suffering, or, rather, he needs "to have suffered." Only suffering turns the self back on the self.

Happiness means being unself-aware—shallow.[2]

> When all was in order around me, when I was content with everything that surrounded me and with the sphere in which I had to live, I filled it with my affections/affects [*affections*]. My expansive soul extended itself over other objects and ceaselessly drawn out of myself by a thousand species of taste, by loving attachments which ceaselessly occupied my heart, in some fashion, I myself forgot myself; I was entirely with what was alien to me, and I experienced in the continual agitation of my heart all the vicissitudes of the human things. This stormy life allowed me neither peace within nor repose without. (VIII.2)

Ironically, complete order leaves Rousseau with the sense that something is lacking.[3] A completely ordered world, one in which everything fits perfectly, is so smooth that its smoothness resists being noticed. In a world where all is effortless one could not feel any resistance. When one pushes, one needs to feel the world pushing back in order to feel oneself. We want to be like natural man—ruler of the world—but we want also to know that we rule. Since knowing requires that we feel some resistance from the world, it also requires that our rule be incomplete. Accordingly, to know that we are happy means to cease to be altogether happy. All of this, implicit in the *Second Discourse*, is explicit in the Eighth

Walk. "Happy in appearance, I had no sentiment that could sustain the trial [*l'épreuve*] of reflection and in which I could truly delight" (VIII.2). Natural man only seems happy, for happiness requires self-awareness and effortless activity is unself-aware. For a human being, then, perfect contentment would have to be the combination of peace, or reverie, and self-awareness, or meditation, and yet the one threatens the other. Rousseau thus describes his earlier life as lacking nothing in content but nevertheless not satisfactory.

> I saw no one in any state whose fate seemed preferable to mine. What, therefore, did I lack in order to be happy? I am unaware of it; but I know that I was not it. (VIII.2)

Apparently when the content of his life is right, the form is wrong, and when the form is right, the content is off.

This tension between meditation and reverie is, as Rousseau reminds us, a version of the relation between the young and the old Rousseau. Once again, the old Rousseau is nourished from his own substance by way of memories of his youth. In the present, of course, our happiness is best served by reverie. But we are so little present to ourselves in reverie that it ill serves us for the future, which, to nourish meditation, will require that there have been present suffering. It is surely not accidental that so many of the formulations Rousseau used in previous walks to describe his misery should return in the Eighth Walk, which is explicitly called a meditation.[4]

Having once again just emphasized what distinguishes him from other men—what makes him "the most unfortunate of mortals" (VIII.3), Rousseau concludes the first section of the Eighth Walk by calling attention to what he shares with others.

> It is to this return to ourselves that adversity forces us, and it is perhaps this that makes it insupportable to the greater part of men. As for me, who finds only faults for which to reproach myself, I blame my weakness for them and I console myself; for never did a premeditated evil approach my heart. (VIII.4)

Adversity is good because it forces *us* to return to ourselves. Most men are unaware of this fact, but this self-opacity, too, is good, for, were they aware of the goodness of adversity, they would not experience adversity as bad, and that, of course, is what is necessary for it to be good. It is not easy at first to see how the two sentences of this paragraph are related. Rousseau seems to indicate that mistakes are necessary—this is what adversity means. But how then are we to avoid the guilt that follows upon such faults and infects future reflection with unhappiness? Only if these faults, while necessary, are not intentional and so not evil can remembering them be the source of *volupté*. That our errors are involuntary means that virtue is the key to making the sweet sense of ourselves possible as a reflection on our defectiveness.

Having made the general case for the necessity of adversity, Rousseau turns to his own particular *douleurs*. In general, we must detach ourselves from ourselves if we are to contemplate our own sadness without becoming sad once again. He must see himself "almost with indifference" (VIII.5). But something gets in the way.

> Infamy and treason surprised me unawares. What honest soul is prepared for pains of such a sort? It would be necessary to deserve it in order to foresee it. (VIII.6)

To anticipate betrayal it is necessary to hedge on one's own trust and so to betray others in advance of their having betrayed you. Had Rousseau been less trusting, he would have been less a dupe, but then he would have been like those who betrayed him. He is therefore left to respond after the fact, and his response is fury. He loses his bearings in anger. In discovering the impossibility of truly knowing others from the inside, he discovers solitude,

> and in the horrible darkness where they did not cease to hold me submerged, I no longer perceived either light to guide myself or support or grip where I could hold myself firm and resist the despair that swept me away. (VIII.6)

As in the Second Walk, what drives Rousseau to despair is darkness.

> How to live happy and tranquil in this frightful state? I am nevertheless still in it and more sunk in it than ever; in it I have found calm and peace, in it I live happy and tranquil and in it I laugh at the unbelievable torments that my persecutors give themselves in vain while I remain at peace, occupied with flowers, with stamens and with childishness so that I do not even dream of them. (VIII.7)

One is struck by the obvious contradiction of Rousseau's claim. Far from not dreaming of them, even if only laughing at them, he seems to think of his enemies constantly and to exaggerate their enmity.

Rousseau sees himself "suddenly travestied as a frightful monster such as never existed." Struggling to explain himself, with each attempt he seems to become more enmeshed in the false image of him. He hopes to find "a man of sense" and "a just soul" who will understand him as he truly is, but he concludes that there are no such men, that the "league is universal, without exception, irreversible" (VIII.8). Rousseau thus discovers the impossibility of knowing the intentions of others by seeing what an impossible monster they have made of him. As in the First Walk, the universal character of the plot against him is a sign of the universality of the problem he confronts.

It is striking that Rousseau claims to undergo this transformation from total preoccupation with the misrepresentations of his enemies to peace and calm "naturally, imperceptibly and without pain" (VIII.8). Its first step was the discovery of the possibility of betrayal. But this is simultaneously the discovery of hidden intentions and of the impossibility of ever getting at these intentions. This, in turn, has consequences for Rousseau's understanding of the general position of men with respect to one another.

> After having tormented myself for a long time without success, it was necessary to take a deep breath. However, I always hoped; I said to myself, "A blindness so stupid, a presumption so absurd could not win over the whole human race. There are men of sense who do not share this delerium; there are just souls who detest deceit and traitors. Let us seek. I will perhaps finally find a man. If I find him, they are confounded." I sought in vain; I found him not at all. (VIII.8)

Rousseau goes further than not being able to find a just man. He cannot find any man; it is impossible to do so, for it is the natural condition of human beings that they cannot be found.

Having made it clear that it is impossible ever to be sure of the intentions of another, for the sake of transforming his suffering into happiness, Rousseau is nevertheless bent upon understanding the plot against him as intentional to the highest degree. This is somehow to be the means whereby his suffering is transformed into happiness.

> It is in this deplorable state that after prolonged anguish, instead of the
> despair, which seemed bound finally to be my part, I found again
> serenity, tranquility, peace, even happiness, since each day of my life
> recalls to me with pleasure that of the day before [wakefulness—*la
> veille*] and because I desire nothing other at all for the following day.
> (VIII.9)

Of course, if this were really to come to pass, then tomorrow Rousseau's
experience would consist solely in reflecting on what he does today—
namely, reflecting on yesterday. Ultimately this reduces to reflection on
reflection—pure thought thinking thought. Is it really possible that life
can consist altogether of reflection with no first-order experience at all
so that true wakefulness (*la veille*) is always today's experience of the day
before?

What makes this movement from sorrows to serenity possible?

> From where does this difference come? From one thing alone. It is
> because I learned to bear the yoke of necessity without murmur. It is
> because I was forcing myself still to hold on to a thousand things, and
> because all these having successfully escaped my grasp, reduced to
> myself alone, I finally found my place (*assiette*) once again. Pressed on
> all sides, I dwell in equilibrium because, attaching myself no longer to
> anything, I rely only on myself. (VIII.10)

Rousseau discovers that for human beings, freedom is acknowledging
that one ought not to try to alter what it is beyond the human will to
alter; it is the recognition of necessity.[5] Granted that to attempt the impossible is to guarantee misery, how does one learn this? Rousseau discovered that our opinions are governed by necessity, first in the ordinary
sense of originating in our passions (so that even when they are correct
our opinions are only so by chance) but also in another sense true even
of Rousseau's own attack on opinion. It is not possible to honor others,
or even oneself, for what they are because opinion cuts one off from
genuine sentiment. We can never quite know why we do what we do.
Do we refrain from doing what is bad because we perceive it to be bad
or because we perceive that it is thought to be bad? This is not the
relatively minor problem of the distortion of judgment by particular
passions so that, for example, we do not always think fairly when we are
angry. Rather, the problem is that once we can name something, how is

it possible to know that it is the thing and not the name that we are concerned with? At the same time, Rousseau knows that prior to naming things there is really no contact with them as they are in themselves. The underlying problem is therefore alienation. Rousseau sees that opinion (for the Greeks it was *doxa*—seeming) connects us to the world while at the same time blinding us to the world to which it connects us.

Rousseau uses his situation as a paradigm for such alienation.

> I began to see myself alone on the earth, and I understood that my contemporaries were in relation to me only mechanical beings who acted only by impulse and whose action I could only calculate by the laws of motion. Any intention, any passion that I might have supposed in their souls, these would never have explained their conduct with respect to me in a fashion that I might understand. It is thus that their internal dispositions ceased to be anything for me. I no longer saw in them anything but variously moved masses, deprived of all morality with respect to me. (VIII.12)

To be alone means to understand one's contemporaries as not really men but as beings whose actions are so unreasonable as to seem utterly automatic, and therefore governed by laws external to them. To be governed totally by impulses—to be mechanical—is to have no inside. These "men," governed by the laws of motion, are thus not moral. Morality means precisely not being governed by such laws—being able to say no. Accordingly, Rousseau solves the problem of his alienation. To avoid hating men one need only say that there are none. The sign of alienation is thus the invisibility of intention.[6]

> Material sadness is what one feels least in the blows of fortune, and when the unfortunate do not know upon whom to lay the blame for their ill fortune, they lay it upon destiny, which they personify and to which they attribute eyes and an intelligence for tormenting them by design. It is thus that a gambler vexed by his losses puts himself in a fury without knowing against whom. He imagines a fate that is implacable against him by design in order to torment him, and finding nourishment for his anger, he animates himself and inflames himself against the enemy he has created himself. (VIII.13)

What, then, can be done to avoid this mistake?

> The wise man, who sees only the blows of blind necessity in all the ill
> fortune that happens to him, has none of this senseless agitation; he
> cries out in his sadness, but without getting carried away, without
> anger, he senses only the material blow of the ill to which he is prey,
> and the blows that he receives in vain wound his person, for not one
> arrives at his heart. (VIII.13)

The wise thus substitute necessity for intention and, by doing so, disarm
anger.

Still, it does not seem really to work in Rousseau's case. He does
still rail against his fate, sounding considerably more like the gambler
than the wise man. Accordingly, even though he hates men less, and so
suffers less, Rousseau still personifies his enemy out of anger and so
becomes enraged at the enemy he has created. Given that he is surely
aware of this, does his awareness alter the situation? Rousseau recognizes
necessity, but he does so to avenge himself on his enemies; the Eighth
Walk ends with the words *en dépit d'eux*—"in spite of them." That
Rousseau's reconciliation to necessity is in its own way purposive is clear
from the next section of the Eighth Walk, where he claims not that men
are automata and machines but rather that he must *say* that there are no
men once he realizes that their intentions are forever closed to him.
Rousseau must therefore regard his destiny *as if* it were governed by
pure fatality.

> My reason showing me only absurdities in all the explanations that I
> sought to give to what happens to me, I understood that the causes,
> the instruments, the means of all that—being unknown and inexplica-
> ble to me—ought to be nothing for me—that I ought to regard all the
> details of my destiny as so many acts of a pure fatality of which I ought
> not suppose either direction or intention or moral cause. (VIII.14)

In effect, Rousseau turns his *amour-propre* against itself. He creates an
opinion that will neutralize the effect of opinion on him.

Reason tells Rousseau not to see the intentions of his enemies but
rather to see only automata, but reason does this for a reason—it has its
intentions. So Rousseau sees that he is really the problem.

> It is much to have come to this point, but it is not everything if we
> stop there. It is well to have cut out the evil, but it is to have left the

root. For this root is not in the beings who are strangers to us; it is in ourselves, and it is there that it is necessary to work in order to extract it completely. (VIII.14)

Accordingly, Rousseau's *amour-propre* ceases to be indignant with his enemies and now becomes indignant with reason. Reason makes the self rather unlovable and passive. It diminishes Rousseau just as his enemies had. The original problem seems simply to have been reinstated on a higher level. Still, *amour-propre* is not altogether wrong here; reason does have its ulterior motives.

Amour-propre ordinarily causes us to mistake "pride in one's little person" for a "pure love of justice." Its combination of simple, unobjectionable love of oneself with reason results in inventive rationalizing that allows us to disguise our preference for ourselves behind a universal principle. But since "esteeming oneself is the greatest motive of proud souls" (VIII.15), when we are brought face to face with this deception, our *amour-propre*, embarrassed by the spectacle of its own pettiness, dries itself up. Its skewing of the facts is an insult to self-esteem, and it reacts accordingly.

> I never had much of a penchant for *amour-propre*, but this factitious passion was magnified in me in the world and especially when I was an author. I had perhaps still less of it than another, but I had it prodigiously. The terrible lessons that I received soon confined it within its first limits; it began by revolting against injustice but ended by disdaining it. By falling back on my soul and cutting it off from the external relations which render it exacting, in renouncing comparisons and preferences, it was content that I be good for myself; then becoming again love of myself [*amour de moi-même*], it returned into the order of nature and delivered me from the yoke of opinion. (VIII.16)

Rousseau has introduced a new term into the argument. We are familiar with *amour-propre* and *amour de soi-même*. Now he speaks of *amour de moi-même*. The question is how *amour de soi-même* becomes *amour de moi-même* without becoming *amour-propre*. *Propre* somehow seems to cancel the difference between *moi* and *soi*; it means treating oneself as another. Rousseau thus needs to describe how it is possible for me to be aware of myself and at the same time remain innocent enough so that it *is* myself of whom I am aware.

He does not seem to think himself altogether successful.

> From that time I rediscovered peace of soul and almost felicity. In whatever situation that one finds oneself, it is only because of it that one is constantly unhappy. When it is quiet so that reason speaks, it [reason] consoles us finally for all the ills that it was not up to us to avoid. (VIII.17)

Rousseau is only "almost" happy. He does not simply rid himself of *amour-propre*, for "whatever may happen, it is all a matter of indifference to me, and this indifference is not the work of my wisdom; it is that of my enemies" (VIII.17). It is not reason that annihilates the ills that afflict us, not Rousseau's wisdom, but his enemies; his depiction to himself of the plot against him is what makes his indifference possible. Accordingly, Rousseau seems to need his enemies, and so his tendency to attribute intentions to others (his *amour-propre*) in order to free himself of the tendency to see everything in terms of intentions (his *amour-propre*) and thus make indifference possible. One needs a notion of suffereing other than bad luck in order to be more than pathetic, to experience oneself as in some way having significance.

The problem can be put somewhat differently. Rousseau connects *amour-propre* especially to the question of authorship because to be an author means to compose, to fit things together in such a way as to ascribe purposes to them. This is why the Eighth Walk is a progressive clarification of the passionate character of reason.[7] Because *amour-propre* is present, and necessarily so, whenever one desires to know, Rousseau finds thinking painful. At first it seems as though Rousseau means to supply the lack that he feels by virtue of his flight from men with his own creations. When he is actually in the presence of others he cannot ignore them. But

> all the rest of the time, delivered up by my inclinations to the affections that attract me, my heart nourishes itself still on the sentiments for which it was born, and I enjoy them with the imaginary beings who produce them and who share them as if these beings really existed. They exist for me who have created them, and I fear neither that they betray me nor that they abandon me. They will endure to the extent of my misfortunes themselves and will suffice to make me forget them. (VIII.18)

And yet it is precisely the safe or mechanical character of these imaginary beings that makes this solution impossible. Rousseau can only really attribute intentions to those who are as closed to him as he is to them, those who will, in turn, necessarily misunderstand him by taking him to be a dupe—a character in their fictions.

There seem, then, to be two possibilities for the quieting of Rousseau's *amour-propre*. Either the occasional meetings with others, which raise Rousseau's passions only while he is in their presence, are a torment to him but remain the necessary condition for his reflection on his own state, and thus for his relative happiness (and so Rousseau would take pleasure not so much in being in the country but in slipping away to the country; VIII.21), or it is not the particular ills he suffers that lead to self-reflection but rather his awareness of the necessity of *amour-propre* even for the sake of undermining *amour-propre* that makes him regard himself as in some way governed by necessity from within.

The latter possibility needs some explanation. Having essentially destroyed all of his enemies, the problem is that Rousseau is not simply content (VIII.17). He therefore reverts to *the* enemy—the universal plot against him—and ends by saying that he laughs at their intrigues and enjoys himself *en dépit d'eux*—in spite of them. He seems to need this imagined enemy to rid himself of real enemies, to make himself indifferent. What this means seems clear from VIII.9:

> It is in this deplorable state that after prolonged anguish, instead of the despair which seemed bound finally to be my part, I found again serenity, tranquility, peace, even happiness, since each day of my life recalls to me with pleasure that of the day before [wakefulness—*la veille*] and because I desire nothing other at all for the following day.

We have already seen that if this were really true, Rousseau would never have anything to think about. Where, then, does the content of his suffering come from?

> This action of my senses on my heart constitutes the sole torment of my life. The days when I see no one I think no longer about my destiny, I sense it no longer, I suffer no longer; I am happy and content without diversion, without obstacle. But I rarely escape from any sensible blow, and, when I am thinking least about it, a gesture, a sinister look that I perceive, a venomous word that I hear, someone malevo-

> lent whom I encounter suffices to upset me. All that I am capable of
> in such a case is to forget very quickly and to flee. The trouble in my
> heart disappears with the object that caused it, and I return to calm as
> soon as I am alone. Or if something does worry me, it is the fear of
> enountering along my way the subject [*sujet*] of some new sadness.
> (VIII.21)

Rousseau's sole pain is his inability to ignore the slights of real people;
he cannot help attributing purposes to them. Earlier in the Eighth Walk,
Rousseau claims to have rid himself of the tendency "still to hold on to
a thousand things" (VIII.13); this was the sign of his attempt to spread
himself over the whole world. And yet as late as VIII.21 he is still doing
it.

> In leaving my home I sigh after the country and solitude, but it is
> necessary to go so far to seek it that before being able to breathe easily
> I find in my way a thousand objects that constrict my heart, and half
> the day passes in anguish before I may attain the asylum that I went to
> seek.

This "constriction" of the heart is, of course, precisely what at the outset
of the argument (VIII.1) Rousseau claimed to be necessary for feeling
oneself and so for real happiness. The constant danger faced by Rousseau's project to attain a state of indifference is, therefore, success. Accordingly, it is actually a blessing in disguise that "convinced of the impossibility of containing these first involuntary movements, I ceased all
my efforts with regard to it" (VIII.23). The impossibility seems owing
to a quite natural movement from sensation to reflection. On a still
deeper level, the "enemy" consists in the realization of this fact. Rousseau's enemy—his one source of torment—is that he needs his "enemies" to make himself feel himself.[8] He must move "from them to me."
The awareness of adversity serves a purpose, and yet, as it is still of
adversity, it prevents Rousseau from considering his condition perfect.
In the end, Rousseau can be roused to reflection not by any particular
instance of adversity but by the fact of the necessity of adversity. The
necessity of painful meditation gives him the pleasure of meditation.

NOTES

1. That this may not be Rousseau's final word on the matter is clear from
The Tenth Walk, where he describes his time with Mme de Warens as "that

unique and short time of my life where I was fully myself without admixture and without obstacle and where I can truly claim to have lived." Rousseau goes on to describe the calm and peace that gave rise to his "expansive" sentiments as opposed to the tumult and noise that "constrict" them (X.1).

2. Compare *Du Contrat social*, book 1, chapter 8 (*Oeuvres complètes*, vol. 2, 524), where Rousseau makes it clear what is lacking in the state of nature.

3. See my *Ancient Tragedy and the Origins of Modern Science* (Carbondale: Southern Illinois University Press, 1988), 115–16.

4. Compare, for example, VIII.3 with I.14, II.1, and II.2.

5. This understanding of freedom is present already in *Emile*. See, for example, *Oeuvres complètes*, vol. 3, 21–28.

6. Elsewhere Rousseau indicates that anger is the origin of our tendency to see purposes everywhere and is thus the origin of religion. See, for example, *Oeuvres complètes*, vol. 3, 24–26.

7. "And, ceasing to use my strenghth in vain resistance, I await the moment for conquering by letting my reason act because it speaks to me only when it can make itself heard. Alas, how I am speaking! My reason? I would do a great wrong by honoring it with this triumph, for it has hardly a part in it. Everything comes out the same for an inconstant temperament that an impetuous wind disturbs, but which returns to calm the instant that the wind does not blow. It is my ardent nature that disturbs me; it is my indolent nature that appeases me. I yield to all present impulses; every shock gives me a lively and short movement. As soon as there is no longer any shock, the movement ceases" (VIII.23).

8. See VIII.2–3.

13

THEM

The Eighth and Ninth Walks are at odds in a number of ways. The Eighth Walk contains no examples; the Ninth Walk is almost nothing but examples. The theme of the Eighth Walk is the necessity of adversity for happiness and therefore the priority of what Rousseau calls his *douleurs*, but the Ninth Walk is full of happy events. In the Eighth Walk Rousseau speaks of the necessity of a constricted heart if one is to experience the sentiment of one's own existence. In the Ninth Walk, his heart is always expanding as it did in reverie.[1] The crux of this tension between the two walks is that, whereas in the Eighth Walk Rousseau shows why solitude or detachment is necessary for contentment (i.e., why it is necessary to see men as automata), in the Ninth Walk he shows why this detachment is not enough. Rousseau provides an elegant indication of this problem in an anecdote. An awkward, but literal, translation is needed to make the point.

> It was in the unhappy time when, insinuated among the rich and the people of letters, I was sometimes reduced to sharing in their sad pleasures. I was at La Chevrette at the time of the name day of the master of the house; his whole family had reunited to celebrate it, and all the splendor of noisy pleasures was put to work for this end. Games, spectacles, banquets, fireworks, nothing was spared. One had no time to catch one's breath, and instead of amusing oneself, one's head was spinning. After dinner one went to take the air along the avenue; one held a sort of fair. One danced; the gentlemen deigned to dance with the peasant women, but the ladies preserved their dignity. One sold spice bread there. A young man of the company thought of buying some to throw them, one after the other, into the middle of the crowd, and one took so much pleasure in seeing all

these rustics rush headlong into one another, fight with one another and upset one another in order to have some that all wanted to give themselves the same pleasure. And spice bread flying right and left, and girls and boys running, piling up on one another and maiming one another—that appeared charming to all. I did as the others did out of self-consciousness [*mauvaise honté*] although on the inside I was not as amused as they were. But soon, wearying of emptying my pockets in order to get people crushed, I left the good company there and took a walk alone through the fair. (IX.15)

Rousseau goes on to relate another story but without the curiously formal language of this one. And even in the story about the spice breads, as soon as Rousseau is shamed into taking an interest in these peasants as real people, the indefinite pronoun *on* disappears from his account. This *on* points to the danger of the detachment advocated in the Eighth Walk; it can turn almost insensibly into an easy sense of one's own superiority—an aristocratic disdain that makes one quite miserable. When Rousseau uses the word *all* in this account, it is noteworthy that he means only all the "good people." Genuine contentment would thus seem to require something like a mixture of detachment and love, something like *amour de moi-même*. While this is the concern of the Ninth Walk, it has also been the concern of the *Reveries* as a whole, the stated purpose of which is for Rousseau to give an account of himself by moving from "them to me" (I.1). This, in turn, might be understood as an account of the relation between society and the individual. In the Ninth Walk this political issue crops up repeatedly, for example, as the question of how to distribute goods—spice bread, apples, wafers—justly. As in the First Walk, Rousseau then connects this issue to writing and authorship. Publication and politics have in common at their core the question of the relation between the isolated individual and a public.

The Ninth Walk, at first appearance a haphazard series of powerful anecdotes, nevertheless has a certain structure. It begins with a general reflection on the distinction between happiness and contentment (IX.1). Rousseau then defends his love of children (IX.2–7). Stories about M. P. and Mme Geoffrin (IX.2), the du Soussoi children (IX.3), and Rousseau's own children (IX.3) are followed by a reflection on Rousseau's observations of children (IX.5–7). After this follows a series of more extended anecdotes in which the subjects are progressively older (IX.8–

15). A story about a toddler who hugs Rousseau's knees (IX.8–9) is followed by an account of Rousseau's scheme for distributing wafers to a party of schoolgirls (IX.10–14), and then, in a briefer account, the already cited story of the spice bread gives way to the contrast of Rousseau's delight in buying apples from a girl to distribute to some Savoyard boys (IX.15). In what is the most extended argument of the Ninth Walk, Rousseau then discusses the connection between seeing others content and being content (IX.16–20). This is followed by a story about Rousseau and aged military veterans (IX.21–23) and finally a short contrast of Europe with Asia on the issue of hospitality (IX.24). The Eighth Walk forces us to ask whether one human being can ever really know another; the overall movement of the Ninth Walk encourages us to ask whether it makes a difference whether these human beings are children or adults.

Given what has just preceded it, the Ninth Walk begins strangely. The same Rousseau who claims in the Eighth Walk that after a long period of anguish he has finally regained "serenity, tranquility, peace, even happiness" (VIII.9) here makes it a universal feature of human nature that happiness is not available to us.

> Happiness is a permanent state which seems not made here below for man. Everything is, on the earth, in a constant flux which does not allow for anything to take a constant form there. Everything changes around us. We change ourselves, and nothing can assure someone that he will love tomorrow what he loves today. Thus all our projects for felicity in this life are chimeras. Let us profit from contentment of mind when it comes; let us keep from alienating it through our own fault, but let us not make projects to chain it up, for those projects are pure follies. I have seen few happy men, perhaps none at all; but I have often seen content hearts, and of all the objects which have struck me, it is this which has made me myself the most content. I believe that it is a natural consequence of the power of sensations on my internal sentiments. Happiness has no external sign; to know it would be necessary to read in the heart of the happy man; but contentment is read in the eyes, in the demeanor, in the tone, in the bearing, and seems to be transmitted to the one who perceives it. Is there a sweeter enjoyment than to see a whole people deliver itself up to joy on a holiday and every heart expand to the supreme rays of pleasure that pass rapidly but in a lively way across the clouds of life? (IX.1)

The very beginning is very ambiguous. That happiness is not made here below does not, of course, mean that it does not exist here below. It could be the sort of thing that one ought not pursue, that, like a friend or a good conversation, one acquires by pursuing something else. For example, the happiness of the Eighth Walk seems attached to a stability born of the awareness of the constant flux of everything here below. Nevertheless, the beginning remains strange. Rousseau seems to admit that the Eighth Walk was not entirely successful, that he cannot be entirely at peace and happy. The new reason is the permanence of flux or change, and what is perhaps most striking is our inclusion within this constant flux—*nous changeons nous-mêmes*. This melancholy reflection on the impossibility of happiness is a sort of preface for a series of stories about happy events.[2] The clouds provide the background for the rays, and the holiday of a whole people must be understood as a release from work.

But what does this melancholy have to do with the other theme of the Ninth Walk—childhood? Rousseau had used this language of chimeras and flux in a similar context in *Emile*.

> In order not to run after chimeras at all, let us not forget what suits our condition. Humanity has its place in the order of things; childhood has its in the order of human life. It is necessary to consider the man in the man and the child in the child. To assign each his place and to put him there, to order the human passions according to the constitution of man is all that we can do for his well being. The rest depends on alien causes which are not at all in our power.
>
> We do not know what absolute happiness or unhappiness is. Everything is mixed in this life; one tastes no pure sentiment here; one does not remain two moments in the same state. The affects of our souls as well as the modifications of our bodies are in a continual flux. Good and ill are common to all but in different measures. The most happy is he who suffers the least pain; the most miserable is he who senses the least pleasure. Always more suffering than enjoyment—that is the distinction common to all. The felicity of man here below is therefore only a negative state; one ought to measure it by the least quantity of ills that he suffers.
>
> Every feeling of pain is inseparable from the desire to be delivered from it; every idea of pleasure is inseparable from the desire to enjoy it; every desire presupposes privation, and all the privations that

one feels are painful; it is therefore in the disproportion of our desires and our faculties that our misery consists. A feeling being for whom faculties equaled desires would be an absolutely happy being.

In what therefore does human wisdom or the road to true happiness consist? It is not precisely to diminish our desires; for were they themselves beneath our power, a part of our faculties would remain idle, and we would not enjoy all our being. No more is it to extend our faculties, for were our desires at the same time extended in a greater ratio, we would only become more miserable; but it is to diminish the excess of desires over faculties and to put power and will into perfect equality. It is only then that, all forces being in action, the soul, nevertheless will remain peaceful, and that man will find himself well ordered.[3]

Plans for happiness in this life are chimeras because they put together the power of adults with the needs of children. This is why they are monstrous—they combine incompatible beings. The flux generally ruling in the world shows itself in human beings as the movement from childhood to adulthood to old age. To hold happiness constant would involve freezing this motion; growth would stop, and we would die. The conclusion of the argument of the Eighth Walk is thus justified; suffering is the necessary condition for human contentment.

Still, why the emphasis on children? Once again, it is useful to consider the argument in *Emile*.

It is thus that nature, which does everything for the best, at first constituted him [man]. She gives him immediately only the desires necessary for his preservation and the faculties sufficient for satisfying them. She put all the others as though in reserve at the bottom of his soul, to be developed at need. It is only in this primitive state that the equilibrium between power and desire is to be met with and that man is not unhappy.[4]

Rousseau thus turns to children in the Ninth Walk for the same reason that he invented natural man in the *Second Discourse*—to make the nature of human contentment visible.

One might well wonder why Rousseau should make the distinction between happiness and contentment turn on physical or visible attributes. To recognize happiness would require reading the heart of the man who is happy. Because happiness requires self-awareness, to know it in another would be to know him from the inside, and such access is never available to us. We may read someone's contentment in his external manner; it may be obvious to us that he is content but not to him. We could not in principle be observers of the happiness of another, and our own experience of the constriction of the heart that accompanies self-reflection and the expansion of the heart that accompanies contentment must make us wonder about the possibility of their combination. The relation between happiness and contentment thus seems to parallel the relation between *amour de moi-même* and *amour de soi-même*. Yet Rousseau adds another element to the argument here. Contentment is "transmitted to the one who perceives it."[5] Rousseau thus connects himself (*moi*) and them (*eux*) insofar as his contentment consists in seeing them content. Inasmuch as this is the case he seems to have a direct experience of what is otherwise available to him only indirectly. He experiences others as other, and so, owing to its sense of isolation, his heart constricts; still, in experiencing others as content, he experiences their hearts as expansive, and this proves contagious. Rousseau's heart is thus simultaneously expansive and constricted, a combination that leads to something new—*amour de moi-même*. Now, that Rousseau experiences this contentment in connection with a "whole people" suggests that "they" may not be merely indiscriminate others but civil society itself. When in the sequel (IX.2) the question of criminality (i.e., of not being civil) is connected with not loving children, perhaps we are meant to connect the theme of the Ninth Walk—Rousseau's love of children—with the question of his relation to civil society generally. The Ninth is the most political of the walks of the *Reveries*.

Children first enter the Ninth Walk by way of a story that concerns the death of Mme Geoffrin, whose salon was prominent in the intellectual life of Paris.[6] A Monsieur P. visits Rousseau with a copy of d'Alembert's eulogy of Mme Geoffrin. Monsieur P., an excitable and gossipy sort of man, begins to read the eulogy while still laughing at certain of its features. Rousseau "listened to him with a seriousness that calmed him, and seeing always that I did not imitate him at all, he finally ceased laughing" (IX.2). While saying nothing to Monsieur P. of his offensive manner, Rousseau nevertheless succeeds in calming him down; this seems to be an example of how human beings feel the responses of others. The heart of the eulogy is d'Alembert's praise of Mme Geoffrin's "good nature," for which he cites as evidence the pleasure she took in being in the company of children. Thus far, Rousseau does not object.

> But he did not stop there and firmly accused of a bad nature and of wickedness all those who had not the same taste, to the point of saying that, if one asked those one led to the gallows or to the wheel about it, all would confess that they had not loved children. (IX.2)

Rousseau does not deny that this is the case—that the guilty do not prize innocence is perhaps arguable—but rather questions d'Alembert's motive for bringing it up in the eulogy, saying that "the author, in writing it, had in his heart less friendship [*amitié*] than hatred" (IX.2). And yet, a glance at the eulogy reveals that d'Alembert did not even make the remark; he was simply quoting Mme Geoffrin.[7] Rousseau thus provides us an example of how easily something can literally be "read" but misinterpreted as a sign of what is in the heart. One might well say of Rousseau what he says of d'Alembert—that his heart is so overcome by hatred that it misreads what is in the heart of another.

Of course, the cause of this misinterpretation is *amour-propre*. Certain that d'Alembert's remark was meant to recall the fact that Rousseau abandoned his children in foundling homes, he broods and takes more offense than is warranted. Then (while on his way to a military school) he rises to his own defense. By now, none of this is unexpected; still we do learn something new from Rousseau's reaction.

> I had put my children in a foundling home. This was enough to have misrepresented me as an unnatural father, and from that, extending and caressing this idea, little by little, they had drawn the evident consequence from it that I hated children. Thinking through the chain of these gradations, I admired with what art human industry knows how to change things from white to black. (IX.3)

Because of the way people react to what they "see" (e.g., tortures and wrongdoings), they are susceptible to persuasion. Without uttering a word, Rousseau had calmed Monsieur P. with his "body language." That we can be deceived in this way is a necessary consequence of our ability to feel the feelings of others—what Rousseau elsewhere identifies with natural pity and makes the foundation of social life.

But there is a more particular reason for Rousseau's *amour-propre* in this case.

> The same day when M. P. came, an hour before his visit I had had one from the two little du Soussois, the youngest children of my landlord, of whom the elder could only be seven years old. They had come to embrace me with so good a heart, and I had returned their caresses so tenderly that despite the disparity of age they had seemed to be sincerely pleased with me. And, as for me, I was put completely at ease by seeing that my old face had not repulsed them. The younger even appeared to come back to me so voluntarily that, more child than they, I felt myself already developing a preference for him, and I saw him leave with as much regret as if he had belonged to me. (IX.3)

Rousseau was affected by the two children, as Monsieur P. had been by him. He confesses that the younger one reminds him of his own children, and so we add of their abandonment. Rousseau thus seems to have taken out his frustration on d'Alembert—attributing to the eulogy of Mme Geoffrin motives that in fact have more to do with the earlier visit to Rousseau of the du Soussoi children. This connection is easy to miss, for with much "human industry" Rousseau artfully reverses the time sequence of the two events.

Rousseau takes offense at d'Alembert's "charges" because he has been thinking about his own children; defending himself against these charges, he "unwittingly" reveals something important. It may be that "never had a man loved more than [Rousseau] to see little bambinos frolic and play together" (IX.3), but watching children play shows no concern whatsoever for what they will become. When Rousseau says of the little du Soussois that he was "more child than they," it is very clear that he does not think of them as a parent would. His pleasure comes from being able to feel with them, not from taking care of them or overseeing any change in them. He is delighted by them, wishes them well, and certainly longs to be loved by them, but he does not presume to care for them. His relation to them is, in small, the same as his relation to the children he abandoned; this relation, in turn, seems a paradigm for Rousseau's connection to the world, and his connection to the world for that of anyone. Unable to be completely responsible for what his children would become, Rousseau cut himself off from them altogether.

When he claims that "no father is as tender as I would have been for them" (IX.4), the ambiguity of "no father" is revealing. This remark follows a reference to Séide, a character in Voltaire's play *Fantatism, ou Mahomet le prophète*. Séide is a slave raised by Mohammed for the purpose of committing parricide. What distresses Rousseau is that children can kill their parents. Those supposedly closest to him and by whom he would long most to be understood are in principle no closer to him than anyone else. This is why his connection to children is expressed either in terms of observing them or in terms of playing with them, but never in terms of raising them.[8]

Is Rousseau really an outcast from society, then? He hints that he means us to consider his books his true children.

> I have recorded in my writings the proof that I occupied myself with this research too carefully not to have done it with pleasure, and it would assuredly be the most incredible thing in the world that the *Héloise* and the *Emile* were the work of a man who did not love children. (IX.5)

Héloise and *Emile* are of all Rousseau's books the only ones with proper names as titles.[9] Since the observations of children and of other things found in Rousseau's writings are meant to have effects in the world, his noncriminal or social nature seems to follow from the fact that he writes books. Through books he will "raise" others and be understood by others. Rousseau observes real children in order to understand the human heart; because children have not yet learned to conceal what is going on inside them, one can see their feelings. He then translates this—"the first and true impulses of nature of which our learned men know nothing" (IX.5)—into books so that we, his readers, can learn to read human nature. Children seem to be the beginning for Rousseau's reflection on "natural man."

Yet, even with the most generous of motives, studying children, like studying men generally, requires that one be with them, and what one learns of them is inevitably affected by the fact of one's presence. They are not like plants; what one does to learn about them changes them. This is what Mme Geoffrin did not realize; because she wanted children to amuse her, she did not allow them to amuse themselves and therewith missed her chance for a much deeper amusement. However, since, as Rousseau never tires of repeating, children do not much like the sight of old age, observing them is no longer really open to him. Now, age cannot be the real obstacle. Rousseau wrote *Emile* before he turned fifty, and the principle of Emile's education is that his tutor should manipulate him into thinking that he is free. The problem, there as here, is that unself-conscious growing is at odds with observation. Rousseau feels free to talk to the du Soussoi children only when he is not being observed by the maid—*la bonne*. The good is the problem. Only in the absence of an ulterior motive, of teleology, can Rousseau observe children in their innocence.

By devoting himself to the activity of understanding, Rousseau tries to bring together in himself the active pleasures involved with the will with the passive pleasures of reverie. But this activity, because it treats others as objects, as automata, is necessarily suspect. It does not treat others as what they are and so is not objective. Rousseau, therefore, seems to have two choices. He can isolate himself by choosing to flee, or he can attempt to conceal what he is really doing so as not to introduce a principle of uncertainty into his observations. This self-concealment is, of course, Rousseau's regular practice in his writing, as should by now be clear. Since it would be very difficult to do in the world of real people who are not characters in books, Rousseau has made writing his solution to the problem of solitude. Accordingly, they have been since the First Walk the twin themes of the *Reveries*. Writing combines private and public life; it is Rousseau's answer to the question of the proper relation of philosophy to society.

Rousseau identifies the first of his more extended anecdotes concerning children as particularly important.

> Here is one of them which in every other state I would have nearly forgotten, and of which the impression that it made on me well depicts all my misery. (IX.8)

It is somehow meant to exhibit the problem of his relation to human beings generally. Rousseau's love of children is simply the more obvious version of his love of men.

> Oh! If I still had some moments of pure caresses that come from the heart were it only from a child still in a frock, if I could still see in

some eyes the joy and contentment of being with me that I formerly
saw so often or at least of which I would be the cause, for how many
ills and pains would not these short but sweet outpourings of my heart
compensate me? Ah! I would not be obliged to seek among animals
the look of benevolence that is henceforth refused me among human
beings. (IX.8)

Formerly Rousseau got contentment from observing how contented
others were to be with him. His awareness of the love of others makes
possible a self-aware self-love in him. We need others to transform *amour
de soi-même* into *amour de moi-même*. This, in turn, has something to do
with the need to see others, and even oneself, through anecdotes. To
explain to ourselves what we mean when we say of another that he is
kind or just or easy to anger, we must resort to exemplary stories.

In this exemplary story Rousseau is walking and daydreaming when
a young child comes up to him and hugs him around the knees. He is
moved by the experience—again thinking of his own children and how
they might have done the same thing. Rousseau picks the child up,
kisses him several times, and then goes on his way. But, not able to let
the experience end, he returns, gives the child some money to buy a
treat, and begins a conversation with him. Rousseau asks where his
father is, and the child points to a man hooping barrels. Then things turn
darker, for Rousseau sees someone whispering to the father, someone
Rousseau assumes to be sent by his enemies to follow him and tell those
he meets about him. His heart constricting, Rousseau hurries away and,
although he returns periodically, never sees the child or the father again.

How is this story particularly significant? Rousseau is first moved,
as was the case with the du Soussoi children, because in his imagination
he makes the boy his own.

> I was walking, distracted and dreaming, without looking around my-
> self, when suddenly I felt my knees seized. I look and I see a little
> child of five or six years of age who was squeezing my knees with all
> his might and looking with an air so familiar and endearing that my
> insides were moved and I said to myself "It is thus that I would have
> been treated by my own." (IX.8)

When, out of a "growing need" (IX.8), Rousseau returns, he tries to
capture the moment in a more permanent way by giving the boy an

external sign of his internal contentment—money. The boy, of course, being only five or six, does not think of that, but Rousseau knows that his external reaction had not been a sufficient reflection of his internal state. At the very same time, the spy is talking to the boy's father, who proceeds to glare at Rousseau. The speech of the spy changes what would have seemed an innocent matter into something sinister. This drives away all Rousseau's pleasure, and he flees. He returns to the scene occasionally, but the memory is always a "mixture of sweetness and sadness" (IX.9).

The event is an image of Rousseau's whole condition insofar as his inability to translate his inside to the outside—his metaphysical isolation—shows itself in the misinterpretation of his actions by others. It is this fact about men that makes it impossible for them to live peaceably with one another. Rousseau's desire "to see in some eyes the joy and contentment of being with [him]" leads him to actions that are necessarily open to misinterpretation. After all, the boy's father might simply have been concerned about a strange man lifting his child up to kiss him. It is thus Rousseau's very desire to be with others fully that necessarily sets him apart from them. At the same time, Rousseau demonstrates that the difficulty works both ways, for it is certainly as likely that he misunderstood the external look of the father as it is that the father misinterpreted Rousseau's behavior with his son.

If Rousseau's innocent and uncontrived expression of good will was so subject to misinterpretation, it is not surprising that his next story should concern a benevolent action rooted in blatant deception. It seems to mark a progress in the argument—we are now to understand that the best way to make oneself known as what one is may be to consciously misrepresent oneself—although Rousseau says that this event occurred two or three years before the previous one. He sets the stage for the story with a reflection on the relation between misery and happiness.

> There is compensation for everything. If my pleasures are rare and short, I taste them so much more vividly when they come than if they had been more familiar to me. I ruminate on them so to speak by frequent memories, and, however rare they may be, if they were pure and without mixture, I would be more happy perhaps than in my prosperity. In extreme misery one finds oneself rich from little. (IX.10)

The rarer the pleasure, the deeper the memory, and yet these rare pleasures from the outside seem so ordinary that they are virtually invisible.

> One would laugh if one saw the impression in my soul that the least pleasures of this type make there, which I can conceal from the vigilance of my persecutors. (IX.10)

Returning home from dinner Rousseau and his wife come upon some twenty young schoolgirls accompanied by some sort of nun. A man approaches who sells chances to spin a wheel and win wafers or cookies.[10] Some of the girls want to play, but others have no money. So Rousseau tells the nun that he will pay for all of them. He organizes the whole thing so that they line up and take turns. He even bribes the wafer man to let all the girls win something. Therese urges those winning more to share with those less fortunate. Rousseau even succeeds in getting the nun to take a turn. When events lead to disagreements, he serves as a judge. His generosity delights him far out of proportion to its actual cost.

The story clearly has political implications. Unlike the previous tale it is not about a spontaneous outpouring of affection. Here Rousseau has a plan to give himself pleasure by allowing himself to observe pleasure. He can follow through on his plan because, as in the case of the maid and the du Soussoi children, he wins over the person in charge—in this case, *"une manière de religieuse"* (IX.11). Rousseau arranges things from the beginning as a lawgiver would, sits as judge when his rules need interpretation, and otherwise behaves as the leader of the little community he has established. Yet all of this is only possible because he lies and makes chance more beneficent than it really is.

> For the purpose of making the festival gayer still, I told the wafer man to use his ordinary skill in a contrary sense in making as many good lots fall as he could, and that I would keep tabs on it for him. (IX.12)

Rousseau's plan thus requires that he conceal the extent of his own beneficence to enjoy its results.

> By means of this foresight there were nearly one hundred wafers distributed, although the girls each took only a single turn, for about that I was inexorable, wanting neither to favor by deceit nor to show

preferences which would produce discontent. My wife suggested to those with good lots to share with their comrades, by means of which the distribution became nearly equal and the joy more general. (IX.12)

As in the previous story, Rousseau ends up expressing and explaining his contentment in terms of money, even if only to deny its importance. And in both cases he returns repeatedly to the scene of events that could only occur as spontaneous. The two stories differ in one important respect, however. In the first, Rousseau is a complete participant, and it ends badly. In the second, he is a detached manipulator, and it ends well. In the first, Rousseau's self-description notwithstanding, he was not simply taking pleasure in the pleasure of another; rather, he was taking pleasure in being acknowledged by another. His anonymity as benefactor is what assures the pleasures of the second. Lest we think that one learns life lessons from such experiences, of course, we need to remember that the second precedes the first by two to three years.

The way in which self-love interferes with beneficence, and so with its pleasures, becomes clear in Rousseau's next two examples. In the first, already cited earlier in this chapter, aristocrats throw spice bread into a crowd to watch those beneath them scramble for crumbs. It is a caricature of benevolence that looks like pure *amour-propre*. To give to those one considers scarcely human makes it impossible to take pleasure in their pleasure. Thus, not those receiving but the givers turn into depersonalized agents who are described by the impersonal pronoun *on*. The second example points to an alternative. When Rousseau buys a tray of puny apples from a girl and gives them to five or six Savoyards who have been eyeing them, the result is "one of the sweetest spectacles that can gratify a man's heart, that of seeing joy united with the innocence of age" (IX.15). The sweetness of the spectacle is the measure of the difference between Rousseau's two examples.

> For my part, when I have reflected well on the kind of sensual pleasure that I tasted on these sorts of occasions, I have found that it consists less in a sentiment of beneficence than in the pleasure of seeing contented faces. This aspect has for me a charm that, even though it penetrates as far as my heart, seems to belong uniquely to sensation. (IX.17)

The one requires that we be acknowledged, the other not, although Rousseau still says of the joy of giving the apples that "even the spectators in viewing it shared it, and I, who shared so cheaply in this joy, I had in addition that of sensing that it was my work" (IX.15).

Rousseau has described a human pleasure that is genuinely social. It can only be social, however, insofar as it does not involve one-upmanship or aristocratic disdain. Accordingly, he connects the pleasure one takes in the pleasures of others to republican government. In monarchical France it is not even common among the lower classes, but in Geneva and in Switzerland generally one finds it often.

> Well-being, brotherhood, concord there dispose hearts to expand, and often in the transports of an innocent joy strangers greet each other, embrace each other and invite each other to enjoy together the pleasures of the day. For me to enjoy these amiable festivals, I do not need to belong to them; it suffices me to see them. In seeing them, I share them. And among so many gay faces I am very sure that there is no heart gayer than mine. (IX.17)

The problem with this sensible pleasure in the pleasures of others is that it must be innocent. And this innocence is not always easy to determine; it requires that one look to the context.

> Although that may be only a pleasure of sensation, it certainly has a moral cause, and the proof of it is that this same sight instead of gratifying me or pleasing me can rend me with sadness and indignation when I know that the signs of pleasure and of joy on the faces of the wicked are only indications that their malice is satisfied. (IX.18)

We are not always able to tell whether the pleasure is innocent or the pain genuine. Imagination deceives us; knowing that we cannot be sure, we often feel the pain of others more than they do themselves. We must conclude, then, that, while contentment may be visible, justice—i.e., the worthiness to be content—is never so clear. This is why the Ninth Walk has been filled with children. In a way, a society of children is more likely to be just than is a society of adults, for children are not so adept at concealing their true motives. And, while adults sometimes preserve the honesty characteristic of innocence, it is severed from natural impulses. Soldiers are blunt, but they also wear uniforms and salute.

Rousseau ends his general reflection on the connection between seeing others content and being content oneself by returning to the issue of his solitude.

> I let myself be carried away by these external impressions often without being able to escape from them other than by flight. A sign, a gesture, a glance from a stranger suffices to trouble my pleasures or calm my pains. I am only for myself when I am alone; except for that I am the plaything of all those who surround me. (IX.19)

> Need anyone be astonished that I love solitude. I see only animosity on the faces of men; nature always laughs with me? (IX.20)

Rousseau wants to be what he is when he is alone when he is with others. This is the reason for his turn to books—seeing gives way to speech. Two difficulties remain, however. First, as the beginning of the Ninth Walk suggests, this means Rousseau must be at the mercy of middlemen like Monsieur P. to carry the reactions of the world to him and to carry his reactions to the world. Second, he will no longer be able to experience the pleasure of the sensation of the pleasures of others. Thus,

> I must confess, I nevertheless still feel pleasure from living in the midst of men as long as my face is unknown to them. But it is a pleasure that I am scarcely allowed. (IX.21)

The problem is not simply that "they" have a plot against Rousseau. An observer is never simply passive; his actions will be noticed, and, because they are as ambiguous with regard to their morality as any other action, they will frequently look suspicious. To the extent that anonymity is never perfectly possible for Rousseau, he will look rather sinister. His deepest wish is to be what he is when he is alone when he is with others. In despair of this, he reconciles himself simply to being alone. But being alone also turns out to be a mode of being with others. That Rousseau's face is unknown to them means that he is a stranger, and a stranger is only a hair's breadth from being an enemy.

In the *First Discourse*, Rousseau had suggested a connection between the martial virtue of Sparta and Rome and the innocence of the rustic (and finally, perhaps, even to the utter lack of self-awareness in natural man).[11] The two share a certain openness and boldness—a "force and vigor of the soul" that constitutes their virtue and makes them admirable. Granted, in soldiers this quality is in the service of habit and convention: still, it leads to a simple, unaffected life. Eventually, the *First Discourse* reveals a third version of the force and vigor of the soul in addition to rustic innocence and martial virtue—the virtue of those like Rousseau who are single-mindedly dedicated to a life of learning.[12] Toward the end of the Ninth Walk, when Rousseau recounts his experiences passing by the veterans gathered in front of the *Hôtel des Invalides* (IX.21–23), it is this hidden similarity between him and them that explains his regard for them. At first they treat him as they would anyone else; he wants no more. Gradually they come to know who he is, and their attitude toward him alters. Still, he prefers honest contempt from disabled veterans to the concealed hatred of ordinary men. The honesty of the young is a version of rustic innocence; it shows itself in their open affection for Rousseau. The honesty of the old soldiers shows itself as open hatred.[13] This is simply another version of the problem of the way of life Rousseau has chosen. Although his life and theirs may have a common root, his sense of what makes them good irrevocably separates him from them. Their unwitting similarity to him must inevitably lead to their contempt for him, for their innocent and open attachments are deeply conventional. They are dependent for what they are on the ordinary men who do not share their virtue.

Rousseau returns at the end of the Ninth Walk to the issues present at its beginning. Crossing the Seine to go for a walk on the Isle of Swans, Rousseau shares a boat with an old disabled veteran who does not yet know whom he is with. Rousseau takes the chance to converse with the man and once again finds "how much the rarity of the common pleasures is capable of augmenting their value [*prix*]" (IX.23). Grateful for the conversation and moved, Rousseau hesitantly offers to pay the man's fare. He is worried lest he insult the soldier's pride, and happy that he does not.

> On the contrary, he seemed sensitive to my attention, and especially to what I next did, since he was older than I—helping him out of the boat. Who would believe that I was child enough to cry with relief? (IX.23)

Rousseau is tempted to give him more money but does not dare, and then he justifies his reluctance by saying that

> I would have so to speak acted against my own principles by mixing with honorable things a prize [*prix*] of money which degrades their nobility and soils their disinterestedness. (IX.23)

Rousseau's principles tell him not to pay, but throughout the Ninth Walk he repeatedly pays a *prix*. His natural passions get expressed in conventional coin. The irony is that precisely where one might expect the love of one's fellows to make *amour de moi-même* possible, it does not. Rousseau is critical of the tendency to express all worth in monetary terms.

> We ought to be eager to succor those who have need of it, but in the ordinary commerce of life, let us let natural benevolence and urbanity each to do its work without anything venal or mercantile ever daring to approach a source so pure in order to corrupt or alter it. (IX.23)

He goes on to cite Holland as an example of a place where people expect payment when they tell you what time it is or give you directions. Rousseau calls such people "contemptible." And yet Holland is a republic, a place where "well being, brotherhood and concord dispose hearts there to expand" (IX.17). In Asia, the home of despots (IX.6), hospitality is not sold—"you are lodged for free" (IX.24).

The tension between Europe and Asia has to do with whether everything is to be understood in terms of exchange; the tension between republics and monarchies has to do with the ability to take pleasure in the pleasure of others out of a sense of their freedom. But the freedom characteristic of Holland has led to setting a price on everything. The problem signified by Holland is that the attempt to institutionalize contentment, understood as the pleasure one takes in the pleasure of others, destroys that pleasure and replaces it with conventional signs. This is the underlying theme of the Ninth Walk. The goal is to be able to say to oneself, "I am man and received among human beings; it is pure humanity that gives me shelter" (IX.24). This is the problem of Rousseau's beneficence in the Ninth Walk; the very attempt to keep it pure leads to its failure. His generosity is an expression of his longing really to know men and to be known by them. In fact, Rousseau's relation to the veterans is his relation to others generally: "I noticed that I was no longer an unknown to them, or rather that I was for them even more of one" (IX.22). The more men know him, the less they know him. This is what it means that happiness eludes us here below.

NOTES

1. See, for example II.10, V.17, and VII.5.

2. The first paragraph seems to have been added to the walk after its completion. It appears on a left-hand page just before the numeral 9 that begins the Ninth Walk. See Charles Butterworth, *The Reveries of the Solitary Walker* (New York: Harper & Row, 1979), 135, and *Oeuvres complètes*, vol. 1, 537.

3. See *Emile*, book 2, paragraphs 14–17, *Oeuvres complètes*, vol. 3, 55–56.

4. *Oeuvres complètes*, vol. 3, 56.

5. Compare this with Rousseau's account of natural sympathy in the *Second Discourse* (*Oeuvres complètes*, vol. 2, 223–25).

6. See Butterworth, *The Reveries*, 135, note 3.

7. See Butterworth, *The Reveries*, 135, note 4.

8. Compare this with Aristotle, *Nicomachean Ethics*, 1095b14 ff.

9. The full title of the former is *Julie, ou la nouvelle Héloïse*.

10. A wafer is an *oublie*; forgetfulness or oblivion is *l'oubli*.

11. See *Oeuvres complètes*, vol. 2, 54, 57–58, 63, and 68 as well as Leo Strauss, "On the Intention of Rousseau" in *Hobbes and Rousseau*, Maurice Cranston and Richard Peters, eds. (New York: Doubleday, 1972), 263–69.

12. See Strauss, "On the Intention of Rousseau," 276–87.

13. In his praise of the veterans, Rousseau quotes the beginning of a Spartan song, a line sung by the old and to which the young and then the very young respond. He thus alludes to the temporal character of political life as well as to the structure of the Ninth Walk itself.

14

THE SOUL

1. LOVE

T he Ninth Walk is about the pleasure one takes in the pleasure of others. Rousseau thinks through the consequences of the fact that we can literally sense the contentment of others. Still, while the contentment is visible in the eyes, in the gait and so forth, its cause remains unavailable to us. And despite the fact that "innocent joy is the only [joy] of which the signs gratify [his] heart" (IX.18), it is never altogether clear when joy is innocent. This is the reason for the preponderance of children in the anecdotes of the Ninth Walk; they are more transparent than adults.

We nevertheless wonder how we are to square the claims of the Ninth Walk that the greatest pleasure is to see others pleased (IX.1) and of the Sixth Walk that "to do good is the truest happiness that the human heart can taste" (VI.3) with Rousseau's view in the *Reveries* as a whole that solitude is the most desirable state. The general problem might be put in the following way: what Rousseau longs for is to be able to be what he his when he is alone when he is with others. The conflicting accounts of republics—Geneva versus Holland—in the Ninth Walk imply that no institution can guarantee what he longs for, and in fact any institution will tend to undermine it. Accordingly, the anecdotes of the Ninth Walk are a potpourri of unrepeatable events. Rousseau's happiest moments seem to be necessarily accidental; he happens to be happy.

That one longs to be for others what one is for oneself might well be a formula for *amour de moi-même*. On its face, it seems impossible; it is undermined by the structure of human solitude, which is at the same time the structure of the human soul. And yet the accidental events of

263

the Ninth Walk seem to vouch for the possibility of breaking through this solitude. Granted that Rousseau's attempts to recapture them seem foolish even to him, once having experienced them, he cannot not wish to maximize the chances for repeating this experience. He longs not just for occasional relief but for a way of life, a plan to accomplish this end. In the Ninth Walk, two compromise possibilities begin to emerge. The first is love or friendship—not being with others in general but with a specific other. The second is writing books—being with others without really being with them. These are the dual concern of the Tenth Walk.

Having come to the end of the *Reveries*, one needs to reflect on whether it is really the end. The tenth is by far the shortest of the walks; it is only one paragraph long. This has led Charles Butterworth, the most distinguished commentator on the *Reveries*, to conclude that "as is evident from the most cursory glance, the Tenth Walk is not completed."[1] And yet in his description of the manuscript of the *Reveries*, Butterworth says that "it is quite apparent that it represents a first draft of the Eighth, Ninth and Tenth Walks, whereas the first notebook represents a nearly final copy of the first seven Walks."[2] Since Rousseau had already completed a final version of two-thirds of the book and had heavily revised the last third, it seems plausible to assume that he had finished a version of the whole. And, since the Tenth Walk does not feel particularly unfinished, only its brevity might testify to its incompleteness. But there is no *prima facie* reason why all the walks should be of the same length, and, if any were to differ radically from the others, it might well be the last. Accordingly, it seems reasonable to assume that the book we have is more or less the whole of the book that Rousseau intended us to have. The Tenth Walk is meant to be the conclusion of the *Reveries*. Rousseau begins with a powerful memory.

> Today, Palm Sunday, it is precisely fifty years since my first acquaintance [*connaissance*] with Mme de Warens. She was twenty-eight then, having been born [*étant née*] with the century. I was not yet seventeen, and my budding [*naissant*] temperament, although I was yet ignorant of it, gave a new heat to a heart naturally full of life. (X.1)

Rousseau provides a longer account of this meeting on Palm Sunday in the second book of the *Confessions*. There it becomes clear that he meets Mme de Warens on the way to church and immediately falls in love, a love later confirmed by the fact that she had a "heedlessness alike enough" to his, "a mouth in size" like his and "she had, like [him], lost her mother at birth." [3] Mme de Warens is for Rousseau his soul mate. Palm Sunday is, of course, the day Christ rides into Jerusalem already knowing his fate—namely, that he will be betrayed and so sacrifice himself for mankind. This has some relevance given the end of the Tenth Walk.

> I thought that a provision of talents was the surest resource against misery, and I resolved to use my leisure to put myself into a position [*état*], if it was possible, one day to give back to the best of women the assistance that I had received from her. (X.1)

Rousseau wishes to do what Mme de Warens did for him. Now, clearly he cannot literally give back to her what she gave to him. Is it possible that what Mme de Warens did for him is to be understood on the model of the sacrifice of Christ and that Rousseau's reproduction of her deed is the writing the *Reveries*?

But what exactly did Mme de Warens do for him?

> If it was not astonishing that she could conceive a feeling of good will for an ardent [*vif*] but sweet and modest young man with an agreeable enough face, it was yet less so that a charming woman full of spirit and grace inspired me with the recognition [*reconnaissance*] of more tender sentiments that I did not discern. But what is less ordinary is that this first moment was decisive for me for my whole life and by an inevitable chain fashioned the destiny of the rest of my days. (X.1)

Rousseau's *connaissance*—his acquaintance—with Mme de Warens leads to his *reconnaissance*—his recognition—of certain things within himself. Prior to meeting her he had no self to love. Here it is crucial to examine the language he uses.

> My soul, of which my organs had not developed the most precious faculties, as yet had no determinate form. It/she [*elle*] awaited with a sort of impatience the moment which must give it/her [*la*] to it/her [*lui*], and this moment, accelerated by this encounter, did not, however, come so soon, and, in the simplicity of manners [*moeurs*] that education had given me, I saw this delectable but fleeting state where

love and innocence inhabit the same heart prolonged in me for a long time. She/it [*elle*] alienated me. Everything called me back to her/it [*elle*]; it was necessary to return. This return fixed my destiny, and for a long time still before possessing her/it [*la*] I no longer lived for anything other than in and for her/it [*elle*]. Ah, if I had sufficed for her/its [*son*] heart as she/it [*elle*] sufficed for mine! (X.1)

The passage is systematically equivocal with respect to the meaning of the words *elle*, *lui*, and *la*, so that we cannot be sure at any moment whether Rousseau is speaking of Mme de Warens or of his soul. By intentionally blurring the distinction between Mme de Warens and his soul, he suggests that in some way she is his soul. Since the overarching goal of the *Reveries* has been from the beginning to display Rousseau's soul, the description of Mme de Warens is the true end of the book.

Still, what could this identification mean? Rousseau describes his life with Mme de Warens as a "delectable but fleeting state where love and innocence inhabit the same heart." It is a combination of *connaissance* and *reconnaissance*—of innocence and self-awareness. It was thus a long time before Rousseau possessed "her" even though he always lived in and for "her." "She" alienated him, and he returned to "her." This return settled his fate. Now, all of this is certainly true about Rousseau's affair with Mme de Warens and is the central theme of books 3 through 6 of the *Confessions*. More important here, perhaps, is that Rousseau's love of Mme de Warens is the story of his *reconnaissance* of sentiments in him more tender than he had ever known, sentiments that led first to his separation of himself from himself and then to his return to himself. Rousseau thus traces a movement, by now familiar to us, from *amour de soi-même* to *amour-propre* to *amour de moi-même*. This is what it means to fall in love with *maman*—with mother; it is the nearest that one can get to self-love. This identification of Mme de Warens with Rousseau's soul is confirmed by the sequel: "The taste for solitude and for contemplation was born in my heart with these expansive and tender feelings made to be its/her nourishment" (X.1). If Mme de Warens does not in some way represent Rousseau's soul, how can it be that love of a woman leads to a taste for solitude?

There is nevertheless a difficulty with this identification. The phrase "if I had sufficed for her/its heart as she/it sufficed for mine" on the most obvious level means that Mme de Warens was simultaneously the mistress of two men. Less obviously, it means that Rousseau would gladly contemplate his soul, but the being of this soul is to expand beyond itself. He would love to contemplate the goodness of his soul, but the contemplation would bring with it constriction while the goodness requires others and the expansion typical of reverie.

The young Rousseau has not yet loved, and so has no form to his soul. Mme de Warens gives it form.

> What peaceful and delectable days we would have stolen together! We did pass some of them, although they were short and fleeting and what a destiny followed them! There is not a day when I do not recall with joy and tenderness this unique and brief time of my life when I was fully myself, without mixture and without obstacle and when I may truly claim to have lived. Almost like that praetorian prefect who, disgraced under Vespasian, took himself away to end his days peacefully in the country, I may say "I have passed seventy years on the earth, and I have lived seven of them." Without this short but precious interval, I would have perhaps remained uncertain of myself, for, weak and without resistance all the rest of my life, I have been so agitated, tossed about, plagued by the passions of others, that, almost passive in so stormy a life, I would be at pains to unravel what there is of mine in my own conduct, so much did hard necessity not cease to weigh on me. But during this small number of years, loved by a woman full of a desire to please and of sweetness, I did what I wanted to do, I was what I wanted to be, and by the use that I made of my leisure, aided by her/its lessons and her/its example, I was able to give to my still simple and new soul the form which suited it/her best and which it/she has always kept. (X.1)

Had Rousseau never loved unself-consciously he would never have developed a sense of himself. He discovers what is his own by loving another and reflecting on that love. The young Rousseau loves Mme de Warens. In this activity of loving, Rousseau reveals to himself the truth of his self—the heart that loves in a genuine, natural, and socially unconditioned way.

To elucidate his own case, Rousseau cites the example of a prefect under the emperor Vespasian, but he inverts it. The prefect spends all but a few years living a life governed by strict convention in which he is expected to be willing to die if his duty requires it; only at the end does he return to nature. Rousseau, on the other hand, is so overwhelmed by his love of Mme de Warens that he develops a sense of what is important to him very early. During that period he was thus free.

> The taste for solitude and for contemplation was born in my heart with these expansive and tender feelings made to be its/her nourishment. Tumult and noise constrict them and stifle them; calm and peace reanimate them and exalt them. I persuaded Mama to live in the country. An isolated house on the slope of a valley was our refuge [*asile*], and it was there that in the space of four or five years, I enjoyed a century of life and of a pure and full happiness, which covers with its charm everything frightful in my present fate. I needed a friend in accord with my heart; I possessed her/it. I had desired the country; I had obtained it. I could not endure subjugation; I was perfectly free, and better than free, for, subjected only by my attachments, I did only what I wished to do. (X.1)

The beginnings must thus be innocent and unreflective. Mme de Warens forms his soul by giving his love an object strong enough to make his dominant passions visible to himself. She is his *maman* because she is the means for bringing his *tempérament naissant* to term. By bringing forth his desires, Mme de Warens makes Rousseau's soul what it is. The Tenth Walk depends on the connection between three verbal nouns: *naissance*, *connaissance*, and *reconnaissance*. Rousseau is born when he gains the acquaintance of Mme de Warens, and in recognizing that acquaintance for what it is he is truly born. The refuge he gains with "a friend in accord with [his] heart" is the equivalent of *amour de moi-même*—the simultaneous constriction and the expansion of his soul.

Why, then, does the *Reveries* end with the memory of Mme de Warens? Rousseau acknowledges that only through her did he develop a self discernibly different from other selves. She made him lose his innocence and grow up. He therefore owes to her the very possibility of feeling that sentiment of existence that makes us most happy, not to mention the entire project of *The Reveries of the Solitary Walker*—the description of "the state of [his] soul in the strangest position in which a mortal could ever find himself" (II.1). Now, if Mme de Warens's gift to Rousseau is to make it possible for him to have a self to discover, how does he repay her?

Alone for the rest of my life, since I find only in myself consolation, hope and peace, I neither ought nor want any longer to occupy myself other than with myself. . . . I consecrate my last days for myself to study myself, and to prepare in advance the account I will not delay to give of myself. *Let us give ourselves up entirely to the sweetness of conversing with my soul*, since it alone is what men cannot take away from me [my emphasis]. (I.12)

The *Reveries* as a whole is Rousseau's attempt to do for us what Mme de Warens did for him. His soul is meant to become the vehicle for the realization of our souls; this is what it means for Rousseau to be a parent.

2. PHILOSOPHY

A book like the *Reveries* resists summary, for the way to its conclusions is the most serious of those conclusions. Still, a few things can be said about the structure of the book as a whole. The first seven walks are all in some way concerned with the issue of reverie as a way to human happiness—the solution to the problem of the deep division in the human soul. To be a soul or a self or an intentional being means necessarily to be cut off from others. To intend means to differentiate oneself from everything else—what is other. To be a soul is to be alone and to want to overcome that aloneness. At the same time, to be a soul—an intentional being—means that one's intentions are never transparent. This was the consequence of Rousseau's theory of authorship and of the connection between morality and meaning in the Third and Fourth Walks. Intentions must be hidden intentions. To be happy, of course, means to be happy as an intentional being—one with purposes and desires. Yet there is a tension between our will to be happy and the content of our happiness. In the Third Walk, will in its purity is identified with a will to be happy without any particular content to the will; the soul in its purity experiences itself only as willing. But according to the Second and Fifth Walks the content of happiness is discovered in reverie, a condition in which we have a sentiment of ourselves as not at odds with or set apart from the world at all. The two states seem to differ as "no content" differs from "any content whatsoever." The soul's experience of itself in its purity seems to be at odds with the soul's happiness. The question is how to combine the two. How is it possible to have a self-aware *amour de soi-même,* or *amour de moi-même?*

The first seven walks point to reverie as an experience that overcomes this split in the soul and makes *amour de moi-même* possible. This seems to justify the book's title and point to its intention, and yet what are we to make of the queer fact that reverie disappears from the last three walks, where there is not a single mention of it? The key to this puzzle is the Fifth Walk, where in so many ways reverie turned out to be too perfect—the basin of Lake Bienne was too round. Reverie in the Fifth Walk is a metaphor for a perfect solution. Presented as a complete suspension of action, it completes the version of reverie described in the Second Walk, where walking turns out to be at odds with dreaming. Thus, in both the Fifth and the Seventh Walks purposive action brings an end to reverie. If this is the case, however, reverie can at best be only an intermittent solution to the problem of alienation, and really not even that. As an activity in its own right, it proves impossible. While reverie is supposed to be the selfish pleasure that comes with the complete immersion of the self in the world, such an immersion is at best unconsciousness (Second Walk) and at worst death—the destruction of the self altogether (First Walk). Reverie seems to be the sort of happiness not meant for men here below.

Rousseau presents us with the problem of solitude, followed by what appears the perfect solution to this problem but is really an account of the necessary problematic character of this perfect solution. What, then, is possible according to the *Reveries?* There are hints in the first seven walks—Rousseau's unconsciousness during the moment of reverie and his reconstruction of it in the Second Walk, the way reverie turns into an account of reverie in the Fifth Walk, and the way botany gives way to the study of men in the Seventh Walk. But Rousseau does not openly deal with the issue until the Eighth Walk, the crucial point of which is the necessity of adversity—not, as had been the case in the First Walk, just for Rousseau himself but the necessity of adversity for all happiness.

The first seven walks are thus meant to show that the price paid for experiencing anything is the experience of ourselves as alienated. That we see or experience this fact is meant to reproduce in us the general sense of adversity described by Rousseau in the Eighth Walk. This is Rousseau's reflection on the double sense of the verb *to suffer.* We are thus meant to give ourselves up to the sweetness of conversing with Rousseau's soul for the sake of discovering what it means to be a soul. In this way he reproduces in us, not in a specific but in a general way, the gift of Mme de Warens to him. But with what result?

Rousseau means to alter our particular experiences in the day to day world. Reverie does not come to us as a single experience—a magical solution to the problem of alienation. Rather, we are to experience love affairs, picnics, parties, and botany differently because of Rousseau's book. From the outside, these experiences will no doubt continue to look altogether ordinary and conventional. But Rousseau's teaching about reverie will nevertheless have prepared us to experience them in their strangeness. The *Reveries* is designed to make us feel our solitude, and thereby force us to look at ordinary things differently, in an almost detached way. Yet this detachment is grounded in a sense of what it would mean to be truly attached. This is why Rousseau must seem a monster and a criminal from the perspective of conventional morality, the goal of which is to attach us to each other without ultimately being aware of what attaches us to each other.

Rousseau sees that the ordinary must be experienced as strange and alien to be experienced truly and that only then is it possible to have a genuine sentiment of our own existence. We are only truly ourselves and for ourselves when we grasp ourselves grasping the strangeness of the world. But an awareness of being estranged is an awareness of being alone. In this way Rousseau recovers something of an older view of the grounding of philosophy in wonder. Philosophy requires the suspension of the natures of things as ordinary; like natural man, one must be struck by things as though seeing them for the first time. Unlike natural man, one must also be struck by being so struck if, in turn, one is to be struck by wonder at the soul itself.

None of this means the advocacy of a life that is in any obvious way eccentric, for such a life would not be a more authentic experience of the ordinary but merely a different sort of convention. Rousseau presents his life as the strangest life ever to befall a mortal in the first seven walks and points to floating in a boat as *the* end of life in the Fifth Walk only for the sake of making visible to us the genuinely eccentric character of his life—its openness to the strangeness of the ordinary. He then reverses his ground in the last three walks to show that true eccentricity—the philosophical life—is necessarily invisible.

NOTES

1. Charles Butterworth, *The Reveries of the Solitary Walker* (New York: Harper & Row, 1979), 226.

2. Butterworth, *The Reveries*, 243–44.

3. See *Oeuvres complètes*, vol. 1, 138.

INDEX

ABOUT THE AUTHOR

MICHAEL DAVIS has taught philosophy at Sarah Lawrence College since 1977 and teaches political philosophy in the graduate program of the Political Science Department at Fordham University. He is the author of *The Politics of Philosophy: A Commentary on Aristotle's* Politics, *Aristotle's Poetics: The Poetry of Philosophy*, and *Ancient Tragedy and the Origins of Modern Science*, as well as numerous essays on Plato, Aristotle, Shakespeare, Sophocles, and Euripides.

Made in the USA
San Bernardino, CA
21 November 2014